The **HACCP** Food Safety Manager Manual

For food service and retail establishments

Based off of the 2017 FDA Food Code

Tara DeLotto Cammarata, CP-FS, FMP
Melissa Vaccaro, BS Ed., MS, CP-FS, FMP

This manual is a guide for preparing a systematic approach to training anyone who works in food service and retail establishments to identify, prevent, eliminate, and/or reduce potential safety hazards. This manual is not intended to be a substitute for the user's judgment and common sense. Instruis Publishing Company assumes no liability for the adherence or lack of adherence to the methods prescribed herein. Its contents have been compiled from sources believed to be reliable and represent the best information available. Any errors are unintentional.

Published by Instruis Publishing Company, Gilbertsville, Pennsylvania. Published simultaneously in Canada.

Instruis Publishing Company does or may publish its books in a variety of electronic formats. Some content that appears in print may not be available in electronic books. For more information about Instruis Publishing Company products, including its SURE™ line of books, visit our web site at www.instruis.com. SURE™ is a trademark of Instruis Publishing Company. ISBN- 978-0-9916319-6-4 (paper)

Instruis Publishing Company
Perfection through education.

Table of Contents

Introduction

Our Mission

Our Mission is to provide the best possible training material and support to all those who serve and sell products in the food industry. By fulfilling the mission of a HACCP program, the food industry will minimize the risk of contamination of the food served or sold, minimize the risk of foodborne illnesses, and reduce the risk of allergic reactions to food. In studying HACCP, you now are a part of the mission and have an important responsibility in continuing the mission at your food service or retail establishment.

SURE HACCP Food Safety Series

In an effort to serve the industry and the public, Instruis Publishing Company is proud to introduce The HACCP Food Safety Series. This series forms another link in the Instruis Publishing Company's **SURE** line, which provides the food industry with the finest training material and support. Instruis' **SURE** line provides trainers, managers, and employees **S**afe, **U**seful, **R**esponsible **E**ducation to support the food industry. You can be **SURE** that by using Instruis' comprehensive manuals and support material you are training your employees with the finest and most interactive material available. The **SURE** HACCP Food Safety Series manuals and support aids have been written and prepared by trainers and food industry leaders who understand the most effective way to train your employees in order to provide the safest food to your customers.

Instruis Publishing Company's HACCP Food Safety series applies the HACCP principles to food service and retail establishments that serve and/or sell food to improve the industry by providing the material to train **SURE** Employees, **SURE** Managers, and **SURE** Trainers. There are three training manuals in the comprehensive **SURE** Food Safety HACCP program:

- *The **HACCP** Food Safety Employee Manual*
- *The **HACCP** Food Safety Manager Manual*
- *The **HACCP** Food Safety Trainer Manual*

At the conclusion of each course, the **SURE** HACCP Food Safety Program provides a demonstration of knowledge examination which is graded by the publisher to confirm the integrity of the process. Each successful participant receives a certificate and wallet card demonstrating his or her proficiency. This is valid for four years. Employing **SURE** trained individuals allows managers to know that their employees have the core knowledge needed to properly handle food in order to prevent, eliminate, and reduce foodborne illness. Regulators can be confident that the **SURE** trained staff is committed to food safety and HACCP as well as up to date on the latest regulatory requirements.

The best way for an employer to be **SURE** that the establishment is fully prepared to meet or exceed the latest regulatory requirements and have the best trained and safest staff is to have every person trained either as a **SURE** Employee, a **SURE** Manager, or a **SURE** Trainer.

How to Use This Book

*The **HACCP** Food Safety Manager Manual* is the advanced book for food handlers and management. This manual builds on the foundation of what was taught in *The **HACCP** Food Safety Employee Manual* for food service and retail establishments. In this manual, you will learn how to complete a HACCP system that includes prerequisite programs, standard operating procedures, and the 7 HACCP principles. You will learn that using these 7 HACCP principles, along with prerequisite programs and standard operating procedures, will prevent, eliminate, and reduce hazards to serve and/or sell safe food.

This book is divided into five sections. Each represents one of the five points of the HACCP star. Each Star Point includes the following elements:

- Myth or Fact exercise
- Star Point Goals
- Food for Thought exercise
- Star Point explanation
- Examples
- Star Knowledge exercise
- Pop Quiz
- Check for Understanding exercise
- Conclusion

You are a very important part of the food service and retail industry. We have developed the "HACCP STAR" as a training aid to assist in making you the best, most qualified trained person you can be.

HACCP: Star Points to Food Safety

Consumers have every right to demand, and the food industry has a duty, to provide safe food. Just as the millions of stars in the night sky are unique, each food service or retail operation is unique, whether it be a convenience store, casino, restaurant, armed forces, supermarket, senior care facility, airport, cruise ship, commissary kitchen, contract food service, hotel, hospital, college, university, school or another institution, independently owned or part of a franchise. That is why every operation serving or selling food needs to have a food safety system in place that is uniquely designed to guarantee that the food being sold is safe to eat. This food safety system is called **HACCP** (pronounced "has-sip"), or **H**azard **A**nalysis and **C**ritical **C**ontrol **P**oint. HACCP is a system composed of seven principles that are applied to a written food safety program focusing on the food in your operation.

We have developed the HACCP Star to help train the food service and retail industries to provide an environment that fulfills the establishment's duty to the consumer. Creating a HACCP food safety management program proves your commitment to serve and sell safe food. Your HACCP plan is critical to prevent, eliminate, and reduce food safety problems. Our goal for you is to be able to create an effective HACCP plan unique to your establishment. This manual will guide you through the process. Successful completion of this training program will enable you to earn your HACCP certification valid for four years, and assure that you are creating a culture that will provide the safest environment for customers in your establishment.

The HACCP management system is very important because it can and will save lives! It is estimated, by the Centers for Disease Control and Prevention (CDC) that every year 48 million people get sick and 3,000 people die from eating unsafe food. That is 1 in 6 Americans getting sick annually. The World Health Organization (WHO) is challenged with the task of estimating the global burden of foodborne disease. The latest worldwide statistics from WHO reported an estimated 1.8 million people die each year from diarrheal diseases. These diseases are attributed to food and drinking water contamination.

The HACCP program requires not only the manager, but every person in the food service and retail industries to be responsible and ensure that the food prepared, served, and sold to customers is not hazardous to their health. The HACCP management system requires the management team to provide solid commitment, strong leadership, and adequate resources to create and implement a HACCP program to prevent these tragedies. Management must promote a culture that encourages every team member in the food service and retail establishment to do their part.

The HACCP Star has 5 points. Each point is as important as the next in promoting the culture of food safety and providing the safest environment to consumers. **Prerequisite programs** are basic operational and foundational requirements needed for an effective HACCP plan. In Star Point 1, you will be introduced to a variety of food safety prerequisite programs that are building blocks for creating an effective HACCP plan. In Star Point 2, having a strong Food Defense prerequisite program will be reviewed. If any members of the food service or retail operation do not follow these standard operating procedures (SOPs), even the most well thought out HACCP plan will fail. To ensure the development of an effective HACCP plan for your establishment, the basics of food safety and food defense standard operating procedures must be reviewed.

Once the basics of food safety and food defense standard operating procedures are reviewed, the book will then cover how a HACCP plan is created and how to use an effective HACCP plan for your food service or retail establishment. This book utilizes the United States Food and Drug Administration's (FDA) **Model Food Code**, herein noted as **Food Code**. The Food Code establishes practical, science-based guidance for preventing risk factors that cause foodborne illness. The Food Code is reviewed, amended, and published every four years by the FDA in conjunction with the Centers for Disease Control and Prevention (CDC) and the U.S. Department of Agriculture (USDA). Every two years, a supplement of information and changes to the next Food Code is published. This is a model code for state, city, county, and tribal agencies to uniformly regulate restaurants, retail food stores, vending operations, and various food service operations. **This book utilizes the 2017 FDA Model Food Code.**

The Centers for Disease Control and Prevention (CDC) identified the top five reasons why food becomes unsafe, known as **foodborne illness risk factors**. By knowing the foodborne illness risk factors, management can focus on specific proactive food safety goals for each food service and retail establishment, ultimately achieving active managerial control. The Food Code defines active managerial control as the "purposeful incorporation of specific actions or procedures by industry management into the operation of their business to attain control over foodborne illness risk factors. It embodies a preventive rather than reactive approach to food safety through a continuous system of monitoring and verification." The top five CDC foodborne illness risk factors identified are as follows:

Food From Unsafe Sources

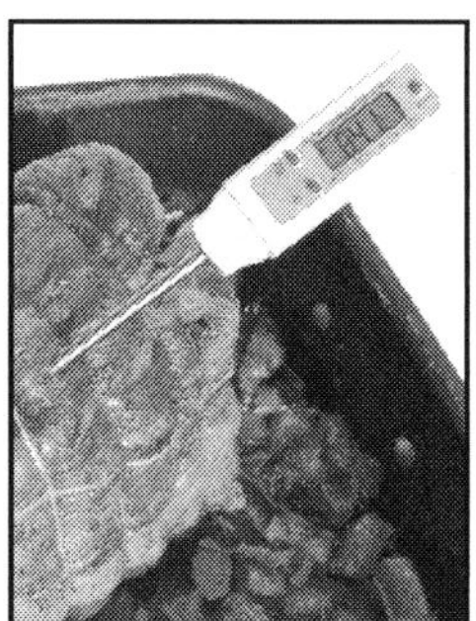

Inadequate Cooking

Improper Holding Temperatures

Contaminated Equipment

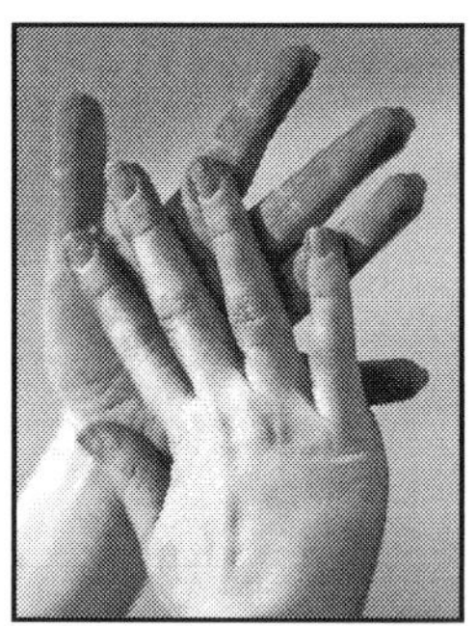

Poor Personal Hygiene

The 5 Star Points to food safety taught in this book specifically address these top five risk factors and how to prevent them. **Active Managerial Control** and prevention of risk factors are achieved by creating food safety management systems that include **prerequisite programs** with an emphasis on developing and implementing **standard operating procedures (SOPs)** and applying the seven HACCP principles. The expectation is that management will use the sample SOPs, charts, and record keeping forms in this book and customize them for their food service or retail operation and work to achieve active managerial control. Using the SOPs, as a checklist, enables you to compare the recommendations in this book with your existing operation. This comparison or evaluation of your current SOPs with the recommendations in this manual will result in the identification of certain needs in your operation called a **needs assessment**. The needs assessment identifies actions that need to be taken in your food service or retail operation to ensure the safe preparation, service, and sale of food. The key words here are **achieve, active, and action**. As you can see, it takes energy to improve your business!

This book is intended to motivate you to **improve your business**. If the quality of your food and the skills of employees improve, then it will enhance the operation's reputation, and your business will increase. The HACCP plan, including establishing prerequisite programs and achieving active managerial control, will help do this. When businesses and schools use HACCP properly, food safety improves, and fewer people become sick or worse, die. Almost every one of the deaths that occur from eating unsafe food could have been prevented. We know how to make food safe, and it is through the use of HACCP and by achieving active managerial control!

In addition to the moral obligation, revenue will increase if you use HACCP. You will make more money because your employees are better trained and more efficient. Focusing on the safety of food products naturally creates a more consistent food product that leads to an added bonus of exceptional food quality. With a HACCP system, every ingredient is important, and every process is documented, which results in an increase in product quality, tighter controls, improved food cost, and a reduction in product loss. Better control of food cost increases profit because you are managing your business ingredient by ingredient.

Schools, retail businesses, grocery stores, restaurants, convenience stores, casinos, senior care facilities, airports, cruise ships, commissary kitchens, contract food services, hotels, hospitals, colleges, universities, mobile units, and institutional, independent and franchise operators face challenges in the operation of their food service or retail establishment. Implementing prerequisite programs and the 7 HACCP principles may be viewed as only adding to the challenges. This book would be remiss if these challenges were not recognized. The safe service and sale of food and the prevention of foodborne illness is not only a moral obligation but one mistake could cause the loss of business. As an operator, manager, or leader, view these challenges as speed bumps. One must slow down and move carefully over the bump. The same is true for dealing with the challenges that face your food service or retail operation; at times, the process can be slow. To manage the operation, you need a carefully thought out plan which includes the HACCP principles. The key to creating a successful plan is to make it unique to your operation, keep moving forward, and work the plan. Some of the common challenges or speed bumps that food service or retail operators face include the following:

- Limited financial resources—capital needed to properly operate;
- Large number of menu items and products;
- Frequently changing menus and procedures;
- Implementation of regulatory requirements/laws;
- Inadequate organizational structure and support;
- Employee turnover;
- Multicultural workforce;
- Varied educational levels; and
- Communication (language barriers).

However big these challenges may appear, none should serve as an excuse for poor execution in the day-to-day operation of your food service or retail facility. Nor should these be reasons why the prerequisite programs and, 7 HACCP principles are not achieved by properly trained operators, managers, leaders, and their team members.

Finally, a properly prepared and executed HACCP plan forces everyone to be involved in the day-to-day activities of your facility and to identify and document areas of needed improvement. It requires everyone to participate, take action, and achieve the goals of HACCP. When food safety, quality, and consistency are improved, your customer transactions should increase, which then increases your sales. By increasing your sales, this gives you more opportunity to increase your profitability.

When the consequences of failure are great, one cannot be too careful!

The HACCP Philosophy

HACCP is internationally accepted. It is important to note that the successful development and implementation of a HACCP plan is not a process conducted by an individual. It involves the effort of an entire team. This is why you are a part of this training session. We are counting on you to do your part in preventing foodborne illnesses in your food service or retail operation. To be successful, a food service or retail facility must have consistent strong leadership; if you are responsible for any part of the operation, then you must demonstrate effective leadership skills. As a leader, ask yourself these questions:

- Can I be a role model for food safety, food defense, and HACCP?
- Can I provide support to the HACCP team?

If you are the top leader/manager in your organization, here are the additional questions that you need to ask yourself:

- Can I provide strong leadership for my HACCP team?
- Have I assembled the best-qualified HACCP team possible?
- Do I encourage and expect my HACCP team to implement the best food safety, food defense, and HACCP plan possible?
- Can I provide the necessary resources for my HACCP team?

Leadership is about making intelligent and informed decisions and establishing a culture that your team will follow. If you are not a proper role model and do not provide solid direction to your team, you risk loss of time and money that you have invested. Worse yet, serious illness or death could occur, resulting in the destruction of your business as well as your brand. Based on your leadership skills, your HACCP plan will fail if food service or retail leaders do not support proper food safety and food defense practices and are not proactive and resourceful in creating and implementing the HACCP plan.

The HACCP philosophy is that biological, chemical, or physical hazards, at certain points in the flow of food, can be:

- **Prevented;**
- **Eliminated; and**
- **Reduced to safe levels.**

From the beginning of time to about the 1850s, all the food a person consumed was produced within 25 miles of that person's home, and for the most part, the food was prepared at home by family members. The eating habits of people around the world have changed entirely. Today, foods are transported all around the world. Produce from South America and seafood from Asia are shipped all over the world for consumption. As a result, there are many more ethnic and exotic products available. This is called the **globalization** of our food supply. The result of globalization is that food products are touched by people from all over the world, sometimes in countries with little or no food safety laws and regulations. People consume more prepackaged and ready-to-eat foods and eat out more often than ever. This leads to the opportunity for contamination, or, even worse, a greater opportunity to spread a foodborne illness. This is why we need HACCP!

Your **SURE** HACCP certification expires in 4 years; therefore, it is critical to keep your certification current. Once you read, understand, and complete this training course, you will be able to:

- Explain the Codex Alimentarius Commission;
- Identify the causes of most foodborne illnesses;
- Understand allergen management;
- Apply FDA and USDA initiatives to your food service or retail operation;
- Explain the 7 HACCP Principles;
- Identify the key points of HACCP;
- Follow standard operating procedures for food safety;
- Use Active Managerial Control;
- Apply standard operating procedures for food defense in your operation;
- Explain how to conduct a hazard analysis;
- Identify three classifications of recipes;
- Determine critical control points;
- Apply correct critical limits;
- Complete monitoring forms;
- Determine effective corrective actions;
- Explain the verification process;
- Apply documentation and record keeping to your operation; and
- Write HACCP plans.

The HACCP Star

The goal of this HACCP training program is to make you a HACCP All-Star! To be a HACCP All-Star, you must understand, implement, and lead in all five points of the HACCP Star. The five Star Points of the HACCP Star define a successful HACCP system.

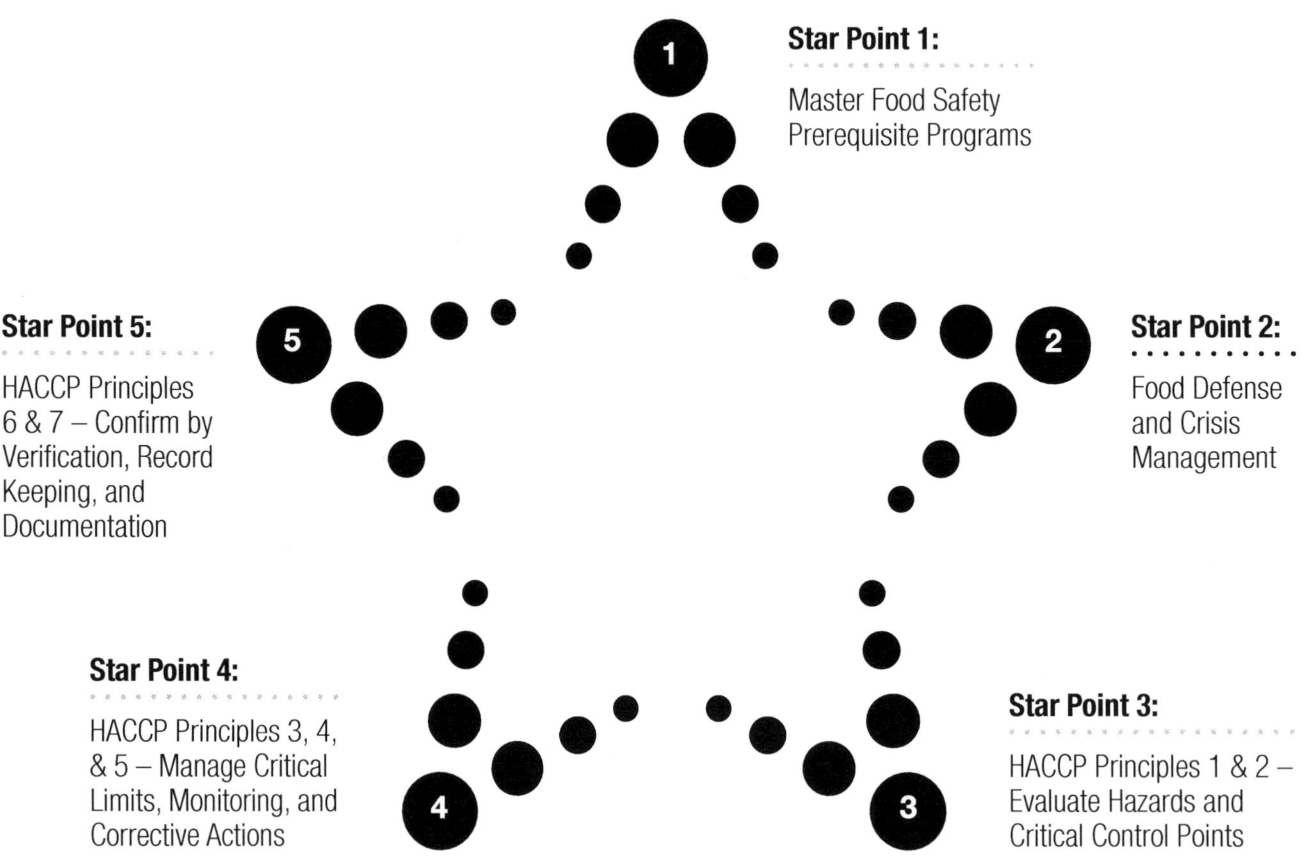

HACCP Star

1. Master Food Safety Prerequisite Programs
2. Apply Food Defense
3. HACCP Principles 1 & 2 – Evaluate Hazards and Critical Control Points
4. HACCP Principles 3, 4, & 5 – Manage Critical Limits, Monitoring, and Corrective Actions
5. HACCP Principles 6 & 7 – Confirm by Verification, Record Keeping, and Documentation

HACCP Pre-Test (Circle one.)

Now, you will take a HACCP Pre-Test to measure your current food safety, food defense, and HACCP knowledge. This HACCP Pre-Test allows the trainer to measure your success as you work toward becoming a HACCP All-Star. Let's get started.

1. **The Codex Alimentarius Commission was created by the ____________________.**
   a. U.S. Food and Drug Administration and the U.S. Department of Agriculture
   b. World Health Organization and the Food and Agriculture Organization of the United Nations
   c. National Advisory Committee on Microbiological Criteria for Foods
   d. Department of Homeland Security

2. **Conducting a hazard analysis includes answering ____________________.**
   a. "What is active managerial control?" and "What are the hazards of operating procedures?"
   b. "What is the risk if the hazard does occur?" and "What are the rational means of ensuring critical control points and verification occur?"
   c. "What is the likelihood of a hazard to occur?" and "What are the standard operating procedures?"
   d. "What is the likelihood of a hazard to occur?" and "What is the severity of the risk if the hazard does occur?"

3. **Verification is ____________________.**
   a. HACCP Principle 4
   b. HACCP Principle 5
   c. HACCP Principle 6
   d. HACCP Principle 7

4. **What are the three spore-forming bacteria that cause illness?**
   a. Bacillus cereus, Clostridium botulinum, and Clostridium perfringens
   b. Norovirus, Salmonella, and Shigellosis
   c. Staph aureas, Clostridium bacteria, and Listeria
   d. Cyclospora, Cryptosporidiosis, and Toxoplasmosis

5. **A critical control point (CCP) is ____________________.**
   a. any step in the product-handling process where controls can be applied and a food safety hazard can be prevented, eliminated, or reduced to acceptable levels
   b. preventing problems in the corrective action, verification, and record-keeping processes
   c. an essential step in the product-handling process where controls can be applied and a food safety hazard can be prevented, eliminated, or reduced to acceptable levels
   d. the common goal of operators and regulators of food service and retail establishments to produce safe, quality food for consumers

6. **Record keeping includes ____________________.**
   a. identifying and documenting biological, chemical, and physical hazards
   b. documenting the product temperature of food received
   c. conducting employee training classes
   d. developing a cooking temperature log

7. Prerequisite programs are ____.

a. food security procedures for your facility

b. cooking food to its proper temperature for a specific amount of time

c. basic operational and foundational requirements that are needed for an effective food service or retail HACCP plan

d. the inspection reports of the local regulatory agency

8. Conducting a hazard analysis is ____.

a. HACCP Principle 1

b. HACCP Principle 2

c. HACCP Principle 3

d. HACCP Principle 4

9. Critical limits are ____.

a. the amount of time spent cleaning food contact surfaces

b. established minimum and maximum specific measurements

c. the maximum amount of time an employee can handle dangerous chemicals

d. the amount of mold that is safe to eat

10. If cooling is the CCP, then the critical limit is ____.

a. 135ºF to 41ºF (57.2ºC to 5ºC) in more than 4 hours

b. 135ºF to 70ºF (57.2ºC to 21.1ºC) within 3 hours and 70ºF to 41ºF (21.1ºC to 5ºC), with an additional 2 hours

c. 135ºF to 70ºF (57.2ºC to 21.1ºC) within 4 hours and 70ºF to 41ºF (21.1ºC to 5ºC), with an additional 4 hours

d. 135ºF to 70ºF (57.2ºC to 21.1ºC) within 2 hours and 70ºF to 41ºF (21.1ºC to 5ºC), with an additional 4 hours

11. What are the three classifications a menu is divided into during a hazard analysis?

a. Ready-To-Eat/Convenience, Full-Service, and Quick Serve

b. Simple/No-Cook, Complex, and Modified Atmosphere Packaging

c. Simple/No-Cook, Same-Day, and Complex

d. Ready-To-Eat, Hot Food, and Complex

12. Corrective action is ____.

a. HACCP Principle 4

b. HACCP Principle 5

c. HACCP Principle 6

d. HACCP Principle 7

13. Monitoring procedures involve ____.

a. ensuring that critical limits for the critical control points are met

b. training employees in preventing cross contamination

c. analyzing how disposed food affects the profit/loss statement

d. installing security cameras outside the establishment

14. A food defense procedure would be developed for ______________________________.

a. cooking food to the proper temperature to defend against pathogens

b. allowing customers to enter the food service facility.

c. a new federal office program under the Department of Homeland Security

d. preventing the deliberate contamination of food

15. An example of a corrective action is ______________________________.

a. issuing a written warning to a food worker mishandling food

b. showing a coworker how to work more efficiently while preparing food

c. rejecting a product that does not meet purchasing or receiving specifications

d. obtaining a medical note to allow a formerly ill employee to return to work

16. To establish a critical limit is ______________________________.

a. HACCP Principle 1

b. HACCP Principle 2

c. HACCP Principle 3

d. HACCP Principle 4

17. Which is not a form of verification for a HACCP plan?

a. Checking equipment temperatures

b. Making sure employees wear clean uniforms

c. Checking critical control point records

d. Point system for cleaning defects

18. What are the characteristics of Time/Temperature Controlled for Safety Foods (TCS)?

a. Moist, neutral acidity, protein

b. Moist, low acidity, vegetable based

c. Moist, sugary, low fat

d. Moist, vegetable based, protein

19. What is food security?

a. This is a newly appointed government office for food protection.

b. An employee assigned to observe customers in self-service areas.

c. Employees keeping food properly wrapped in storage.

d. This is the ability to ensure a 2-year food supply for a particular country.

20. What is TCS?

a. Time control sequence

b. Temperature control sensitivity

c. Time/temperature control for safety

d. Time/temperature conduct for safety

How many points did you earn? ______________

If you scored 18–20 points — Congratulations! You are very knowledgeable already about HACCP!

If you scored 14–17 points — Good job! You have a basic understanding of HACCP and all of its components.

If you scored 11–13 points — There is no time like the present to learn about HACCP! This book will give you a great opportunity to fine-tune your HACCP skills.

If you scored 0–10 points — Everyone needs to start somewhere! It is important to track your progress as you complete each point of the star to earn your HACCP All-Star certification!

HACCP Star Point 1: Master Food Safety Prerequisite Programs

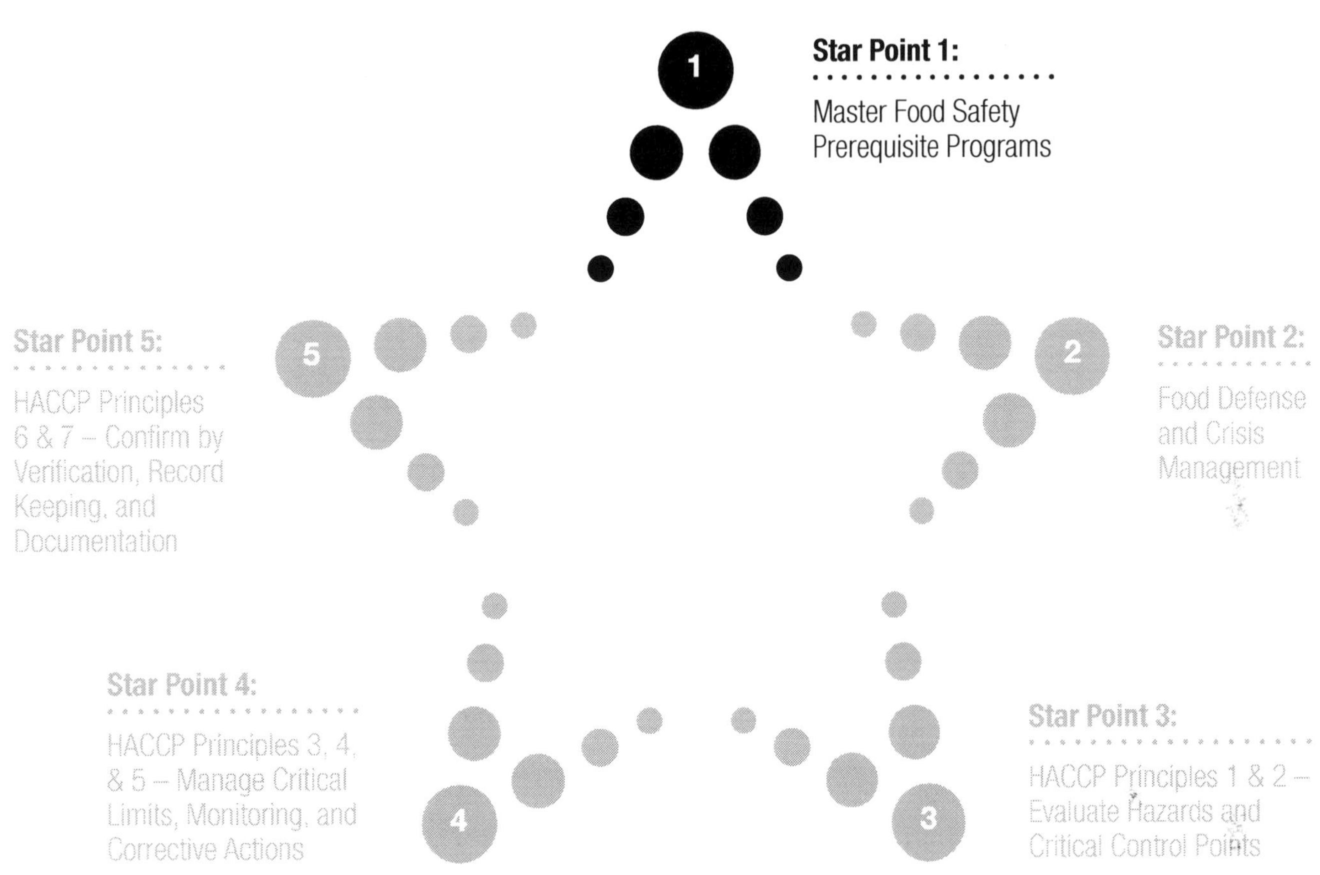

Star Point 1 Myth or Fact (Check one.)

1. Pre-cut or prewashed produce in a bag should be washed before use.
___**Myth** ___**Fact**

2. HACCP is a reactive approach to problems with the flow of food.
___**Myth** ___**Fact**

3. Sanitation is making sure anything that comes in contact with food at any stage of handling does not contaminate the food.
___**Myth** ___**Fact**

4. Hand sanitizers are a good substitute for hand washing for food employees.
___**Myth** ___**Fact**

5. 1 in 3 people do not wash their hands after using the bathroom.
___**Myth** ___**Fact**

Star Point 1 Goals: You will learn to

- Define HACCP and its goals.
- Identify the causes for foodborne illness.
- Understand how HACCP prevents foodborne illness outbreaks.
- Be prepared to assist customers with food allergies.
- Recognize and understand the importance of Standard Operating Procedures.
- Identify the International Food Safety Icons.
- Apply time and temperature controls to ensure food safety.
- Prevent contamination of food.
- Assist customers who have food allergies.
- Identify Food Allergen Icons.
- Explain the personal responsibilities of each HACCP team member with regard to food safety.
- Explain the difference between cleaning and sanitizing.

The focus of Star Point 1 is on having operational awareness of the root causes of unsafe food and the rules and procedures that should be in place to prevent unsafe food in your facility. We will discuss prerequisite programs and food safety standard operating procedures (SOPS) using the International Food Safety Icons. Prerequisite programs are founded on basic food safety and sanitation knowledge and principles and should be incorporated into all HACCP Plans. The food safety materials in the Appendix 1 and 2 will provide reference material for this information.

Active Managerial Control

One of the best ways to avoid foodborne illnesses is to achieve active managerial control of foodborne illness risk factors. **Active managerial control** means "the purposeful incorporation of specific actions or procedures by industry management into the operation of their business to obtain control over foodborne illness risk factors. It embodies a preventative rather than reactive approach to food safety through a continuous system of monitoring and verification." The top five CDC foodborne illness risk factors known to cause 80 percent of foodborne illness outbreaks are:

Food From Unsafe Sources

Inadequate Cooking

Improper Holding Temperatures

Contaminated Equipment

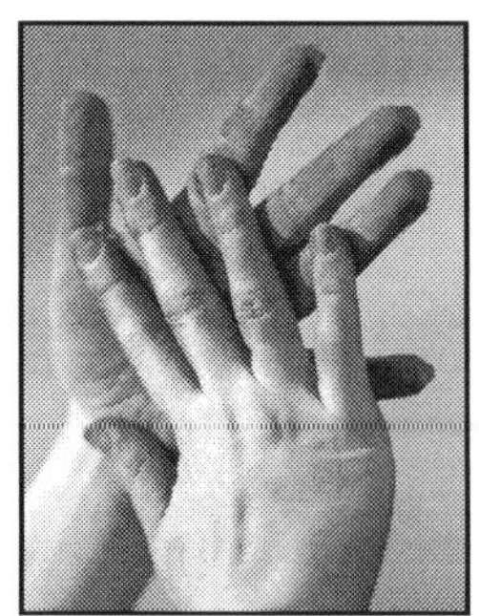

Poor Personal Hygiene

HACCP (Hazard Analysis and Critical Control Point) is a food safety management system that will help you focus on potentially hazardous foods requiring time/temperature control for safety and active managerial control.

Creating a HACCP plan for your operation will compliment and support:

- Conducting self-inspections;
- Implementing TQM (total quality management) strategies;
- Using flow charts to identify food handling steps;
- Identifying where or if there is a critical failure point in the process;
- Developing procedures to lower risks; and
- Preparing for risk-based HACCP inspections.

In order for a successful HACCP program to be implemented, management must be committed to HACCP. A commitment by management indicates an awareness of the benefits and costs of HACCP, which includes education and training of employees. Benefits, in addition to food safety, are a better use of resources and timely response to problems. The result is safer food handling and, consequently, safer food.

Pop Quiz:

Active Managerial Control

Assess whether your food safety management system is up-to-date. Answer yes or no to the questions regarding implementing the following items in your food service or retail establishment.

		Yes	No
1.	Do you have an enforced policy and procedure to ensure proper hand washing?		
2.	Do you have an enforced policy to determine when employees are sick or have flu-like symptoms?		
3.	Do you use FDA forms 1-A, 1-B, 1-C, or do you have a documented infectious disease policy for your food service or retail operation?		
4.	Do you pay attention to food temperatures in your facility?		
5.	Do you have an ample supply of thermometers accessible to all employees throughout your operation?		
6.	Do you calibrate thermometers every shift?		
7.	Do you monitor the process, take corrective actions, verify, and maintain record keeping proving the food is cooled properly?		
8.	Do you monitor the process, take corrective actions, verify, and maintain record keeping proving the food is reheated properly?		
9.	Do you inspect your suppliers?		
10.	Do you know if your suppliers have prerequisite programs with food safety and food defense standard operating procedures, a HACCP plan, and documentation that proves their food is safe?		
11.	Do you have chemicals and food delivered on separate trucks or pallets?		
12.	Do you know without a doubt that a chemical contamination has not occurred?		
13.	Do you know what the correct minimum cooking temperatures are according to the Food Code?		
14.	Do you cook food to the correct minimum temperatures?		

	Yes	No
15. Do you monitor the cooking process, take corrective actions, verify, and maintain record keeping proving the food is cooked properly?		
16. Do you store food correctly?		
17. Do you monitor hot and cold holding of food on a continuous basis, take corrective actions, verify, and maintain record keeping proving the food is held properly?		
18. Do you know at which critical control points (steps) in your food preparation system you are at the highest risk for cross contamination?		
19. Do you have procedures in place to prevent cross contamination of equipment and utensils?		
20. Do you clean and sanitize all food contact surfaces a minimum of every 4 hours?		
21. Do you have a system to test your sanitizer solution, verifying the concentration each time you fill a three-compartment sink, fill a bucket, or make a spray solution?		
22. Do you have a system to verify that the sanitizer is being properly used?		
23. Do you create an environment that prevents the deliberate contamination of food?		
24. Do you have food defense standard operating procedures for employees, customers, vendors, and facility awareness?		
25. Do you train your employees on food defense standard operating procedures for employees, customers, vendors, and facility awareness?		
Tally the total number of "Yes" or "No" responses If you answered "No" to any of the preceding assessment questions, it is highly recommended that you update your current food safety management system and apply active managerial control. If you answered "Yes" to all of the preceding questions, this is validation that your food service or retail operation is focused on achieving active managerial control.		

Understanding and Implementing Prerequisite Programs and Standard Operating Procedures

Prerequisite Programs

Prerequisite programs collectively are **standard operating procedures (SOPs)** and policies that address basic operational and foundational requirements within a food service or retail facility. They need to be developed and implemented for a HACCP plan to be effective. An effective HACCP plan will help an operation meet the food safety requirements established by the Food and Drug Administration in its Food Code.

Prerequisite programs and SOPs give food employees the basic knowledge of food safety, food facility operations, and the importance of each in preventing foodborne illness. Keep in mind that the categories outlined and generalized in this book are prerequisite programs that represent the most common designations. These prerequisite programs must be in place before any food enters a food service or retail establishment. They need to be established as well as explained, demonstrated, and clearly understood by all employees. Following and mastering the directives in the SOPs, can ensure the safe flow of food through your facility. Based on your operation, these prerequisite programs will need to be reviewed before you start to implement an effective HACCP plan:

1. **Personal Hygiene / Employee Health-** Do you have written procedures for hand washing, glove use, apron storage, head covering, dress code, and personal hygiene? Do employees follow the dress code? Do employees know the procedures for reporting an illness or not working when ill?

2. **Food Safety-** Are procedures written and established for proper monitoring of food temperatures, cooling food, and reheating food?

3. **Vomiting and Diarrheal Clean up procedures-** Do you have written procedures in place the instructs your employees how to clean up should an unfortunate event occur in the facility? Do you have an accessible clean-up kit? Have employees be trained on how to use the kit properly?

4. **Product Instructions (receipt and process)-** Do you have clear menu instructions for preparing your foods? Does the recipe identify specific equipment that is required to be used to prepare this menu item? Does the recipe specify minimum internal product temperatures that must be met to ensure the food is safe?

5. **Supplier Selection and Control-** Do suppliers have an effective HACCP plan? Do suppliers have effective food safety programs in place? Do suppliers apply food defense to their operation?

6. **Chemical and Pest Control-** Do you have a secure, locked location for chemicals? Are employees trained in the use of chemicals? Do you have an integrated pest management program with pesticides applied by a licensed pest control operator? Are Safety Data Sheets (SDS) current and readily available to all employees?

7. **Standard Operating Procedures (SOPs)-** Do you have written procedures for purchasing, receiving, storing, preparing, cooking, holding, cooling, reheating, and selling/serving food in your operation? Do you have written procedures for food products and equipment when opening, closing, and changing day parts?

8. **Product Specifications-** Are specifications written for all ingredients, products, and supplies?

9. **Major Food Allergen Management-** Are employees aware of the primary food allergens? Do they know how to respond to customers' concerns regarding allergy questions?

10. **Food Defense-** Do you have food defense standard operating procedures? Has your organization integrated food defense into its organizational chart, job descriptions, orientation process, and team member training?
11. **Food Recall Procedures-** Do you have food recall procedures? Does your management team and employees know how to handle a food recall? Does your organization conduct mock food recalls? Do your suppliers conduct mock food recalls?
12. **Crisis Management-** Do you have a crisis management team? Do you have a crisis management plan with specific responsibilities per crisis team member? Do you have public relations, marketing, and legal support on retainer? Do you have a designated spokesperson?
13. **Equipment-** Does your equipment meet or exceed regulation requirements for design and sanitation?
14. **Facilities Design-** Does your equipment placement help prevent cross contamination?
15. **Sanitation-** Do you have a master cleaning schedule? Does your current cleaning schedule identify the equipment and surfaces that need to be cleaned in the facility? Do you have proper chemicals and procedures established for the equipment and surfaces? Are team members trained on sanitation expectations?
16. **Training-** Do your employees understand basic food safety? Have your employees been trained on all SOPs within their job descriptions? Do your employees know and understand your HACCP plan? Are employees receiving training in prerequisite programs, especially those related to their job duties such as personal hygiene, cleaning, sanitizing, and food safety?

Training

The emphasis in training team members in your organization should establish the understanding that what your team does or does not do is significant to public health and, more specifically, to your customers. Your training in food safety could actually save lives and help raise the quality of food at your food service or retail establishment. An effective HACCP plan includes training as a prerequisite program and is an essential component to your HACCP plan. Employees who are empowered with knowledge will be motivated, more efficient, and more conscientious in their day-to-day work. They need to know that every employee within the facility plays an important role in protecting public health. Effective and ongoing training will reinforce this goal.

As a leader and coach, you need to perform the following actions in your food service or retail operation:

- Check your local regulatory agency for certification requirements for person-in-charge/manager accreditation.
- Develop an organizational chart and job descriptions showing assigned responsibilities for prerequisite programs and HACCP.
- Set food safety and food defense goals that are challenging, measurable, and achievable.
- Establish accountability for meeting food safety and food defense responsibilities.
- Reinforce and recognize success with incentives and awards.

- Demonstrate management's commitment through correct food safety and food defense behaviors and be a positive role model by always setting the example.
- Implement ongoing self-inspection and third-party inspection programs.
- Encourage all team members to alert the person-in-charge to any food safety and food defense concerns immediately.

The basic training components of an effective HACCP plan should:

- Explain the training system and the process used to achieve effective and satisfactory job performance.
- Assess training needs of all team members and every level in your organization.
- Provide training, knowledge, and technical skills instruction prior to all new job assignments.
- Utilize outside/third-party training companies as needed to reinforce management's commitment to food safety and food defense behaviors.

Post-training components should include:

- Update training materials/procedures at least once a year.
- Regularly conduct ongoing 20-minute training sessions using demonstrations and hands-on activities to reinforce acquired skills.
- Encourage all team members to give feedback as to how to improve the training.
- Maintain training records or charts to include the topic, materials, date, length of time, who attended, and the trainer's name.

You can make a difference by following **prerequisite programs**, known as **standard operating procedures (SOPs)**, and by making sound decisions that will help keep your customers safe. The general flow that food follows is: purchase, receive, store, prepare, cook, hold, cool, reheat, and serve. Everyone must know the **flow of food** within the facility. These standards of operation must be understood and practiced for successful control of each step in the flow of food. Approved HACCP plans require that each employee follows prerequisite programs and SOPs at each step in the flow of food; therefore, job descriptions should make it clear that all employees must follow these SOPs.

Sample Job Description

The following is a sample job description of a kitchen manager provided by The Food Experience™.

The Food Experience™ JOB DESCRIPTION

Date: April 2017

Status: Full-Time

Job Title: Kitchen Manager

Reports to: Owner/General Manager

Bonus: Eligible—see bonus program for details

Location: Collegeville, PA

Job Purpose

The Kitchen Manager (KM) functions as the person who will be leading the day-to-day operations of The Food Experience™. The primary role is development, implementation, and communication of company product and service in accordance with the company's mission statement, corporate philosophy, values, and food safety standards. Focus is on meeting and exceeding consumer expectations while ensuring consumer retention via superior service, menu, and operations management.

Job Responsibilities

This is a list of the major responsibilities and duties required of the Kitchen Manager position.

1. Manage consumer relations, vendor relations, shipments/deliveries, and all ordering.
2. Collaborate with company's business owners to ensure successful operations and customer satisfaction.
3. Communicate with consumers and build The Food Experience™ brand name and approach when necessary.
4. Attend Food Safety and Sanitation Program to become a certified food manager, and remain certified throughout your employment.
5. Understand, communicate, and implement prerequisite programs and standard operating procedures, and follow the HACCP plan.
6. Determine product components including menu items, ingredients, execution, and hard costs.
7. Manage daily operations of the kitchen facility, including:
   - Employees (hiring, management, schedules, communication, and work);
   - Receiving;
   - Inventory management;
   - Prepping food;
   - Prepping meal ingredients;
   - Session prep and setup;
   - Meal station assembly;
   - Meal station breakdown;
   - Customer interactions (sessions, calls, inquiries, tours, and special requests);
   - Restocking inventory; and
   - Washing and washroom duties.

8. Implement, enforce, and communicate food safety guidelines, and standard operating procedures.
9. Train and support franchisees when applicable.
10. Prepare ingredients, workstations, and retail outlet for sessions/meal development.
11. Perform project management duties including maintaining good vendor relationships, food ordering/tracing, and internal and external reporting.
12. Maintain food areas and operations in accordance with Health Department Regulations and FDA food safety guidelines.
13. Other related duties as assigned.

Required Qualifications

- Must have 2 to 4 years of management experience
- Must have 4 or more years of food service experience
- Must be a creative self-starter
- Must have strong organization, negotiation, and problem-solving skills
- Must have excellent communication skills, both written and verbal
- Must be able to present effectively to small and medium sized groups
- Must be able to effectively handle multiple tasks and projects simultaneously
- Must be a team player with great people skills
- Must have proven work experience and references
- Must be reliable, honest, trustworthy, hardworking
- Must have experience with Back-of-House and Front-of-House operations
- Must have basic computer skills (ability to utilize Internet, company intranet, and various software)

Physical Demands

In an average workday, associate would perform the following:

Activity	Never (0% of shift)	Occasionally (up to 33% of time)	Frequently (33-66% of time)	Continuously (66-100% of shift)
Sit		X		
Stand			X	X
Walk			X	
Bend and/or stoop			X	X
Crawl and/or climb		X		
Kneel		X		
Push			X	
Pull		X		
Work on unprotected heights	X			
Be exposed to marked changes in temperature and humidity		X	X	

Every job description should be detailed and specify all duties and responsibilities. Job descriptions should not be vague or obtuse. Note that the job description not only meets but also exceeds the food safety and sanitation requirements. The accountability of accepting their role in the organization, their responsibilities, and physical demands essential to the success of the food service or retail operation should be clear to all perspective candidates.

Activity	Never (0% of shift)	Occasionally (up to 33% of time)	Frequently (33-66% of time)	Continuously (66-100% of shift)
Be exposed to harmful fumes and/or other pollutants	X			
Use feet and/or legs for repetitive motion:				
• Left			X	
• Right			X	
Use hands for repetitive motion:				
• Simple grasping				X
• Firm grasping (pushing/pulling arm controls)				X
• Fine manipulation				X
Lifting and/or carrying:				
• Up to 10 lbs.				X
• 11-20 lbs.				X
• 21-50 lbs.			X	
• 51-74 lbs.		X		
• 75-100 lbs.		X		

Food Safety vs. Sanitation

Every day food service and retail managers are at war with an enemy (pathogens) that often cannot be seen, tasted, or smelled. Scientists constantly battle against the threat of emerging pathogens. Because of these new strains of pathogens and the newly developed technologies to combat the threat, management of food safety must constantly change to keep pace. **Food safety involves keeping food safe to eat at every stage of handling as it passes through the flow of food from "farm to table"** (purchase, receive, store, prepare, cook, hold, cool, reheat, and serve). **Sanitation is making sure anything that comes in contact with food at any stage of handling does not contaminate the food.** Sanitation also involves pest control, equipment maintenance, proper cleaning, and sanitizing techniques. Sanitation is a prerequisite to food safety. A well-run establishment and well-developed HACCP plan must include both Food Safety and Sanitation; you cannot have one without the other. Simply keeping things clean does not necessarily lead to food safety.

Traditional sanitation systems relied on observing dirt and then removing it. That is not good enough! As we know, many pathogens are deadly and cannot be seen. Food safety goes beyond what can be seen. A properly managed facility must have a proactive food safety management system that achieves "active managerial control." This system must address the food safety and sanitation requirements for each food product, and it begins with the detailed instructions and accurate recipes.

Product Instructions/Recipes

Product instructions or recipes are just one prerequisite program required for HACCP in your food service or retail operation that will incorporate various critical food safety information and control measures. In HACCP, documented instructions/recipes are needed and applied to all the food products you will offer. An example of this is in the recipe and instructions that follow for Mixed-Fruit Crisp.

Mixed-Fruit Crisp

1 15-ounce can (443.6 ml) mixed fruit

1⁄2 cup (118.29 ml) quick-rolled oats

1⁄2 cup (118.29 ml) brown sugar

1⁄2 cup (118.29 ml) all-purpose flour

1⁄4 teaspoon (1.24 ml) baking powder

1⁄2 teaspoon (2.45 ml) ground cinnamon

1⁄4 cup (59.15 ml) butter or margarine

(Recommendation: Prepare a day in advance.)

1. Preheat oven to 350ºF (176.6ºC).
2. Drain mixed-fruit and set aside.
3. Lightly grease an 8- or 9-inch (20.32- or 22.86-cm) baking pan. Place the mixed-fruit on the bottom of the pan.
4. In a smaller bowl, combine all of the dry ingredients. Cut in the butter or margarine with a pastry blender. Sprinkle mixture over mixed-fruit filling.
5. Bake for 30 to 35 minutes in conventional oven to a minimum internal temperature of 135ºF (57.2ºC) for 15 seconds.
6. Cool properly. Cool hot food from 135°F to 70°F (57.2°C to 21.1°C) within 2 hours; you then have an additional 4 hours to go from 70°F to 41°F (21.1°C to 5°C) or lower for a maximum total cool time of 6-hours.
7. Store in refrigeration at 41°F (5°C) or lower.
8. Using a 350°F oven, Reheat to 165°F (73.9°C) for 15 seconds within 2 hours.
9. Serve warm. Use the process of hot holding without temperature control. After reheating, mark pan with a label of the time and a discard time of 4 hours.
10. Serving size ½ cups. Makes 6 servings.

As you can see in this example, the recipe is detailed with ingredients, required measurements, smallwares, and equipment. Notice in the recipe the time and temperature parameters. Food service and retail establishments must know the recipes to ensure proper facility design and the right equipment can meet the operational demands.

Facility Design and Equipment Overview

Prior to evaluating equipment needs & facility design, the concept for the food service or retail establishment must be established or reassessed, with special focus on menu development, food preparation processes & specific recipes. Before a facility even opens its doors, prerequisite programs must be developed and used to evaluate the facility design and equipment to ensure the safe flow of food. These are core items that will lay the foundation for your HACCP plan and ultimately food safety.

Equipment within your operation must meet production and service needs. Prerequisite programs focus on equipment requirements, sanitary use, and maintenance. To determine the equipment needed, you must first decide on your concept and menu and then the recipes and processes you will use. With the concept and menu in mind and knowing what equipment you will need to produce your food, the facility design can then be laid out in a manner to ensure the safe flow of food. The design of your facility and the layout of your equipment is an important concept in food safety. You cannot just put your equipment anywhere it will fit. A poorly designed facility could lead to unsafe food through cross contamination or time & temperature abuse, not to mention diminished employee productivity. Food needs to flow in a logical pattern from receiving to serving.

With a concept, menu, and well-designed kitchen, you have the ability to safely produce food in the operation. Regulatory officials require a **plan review** before construction begins in a new food service or retail facility. A plan review verifies that you have completely considered and reviewed your concept and food safety before the first nail is hammered.

Equipment

The prerequisite program for commercial equipment is based on product instructions. In the example of the Mixed-Fruit Crisp, the major equipment needed is an oven, pastry blender, refrigerator, and hot holding equipment. The smallwares equipment needed is a baking pan, mixing bowls, spoons, can opener, timer, thermometer, and measuring tools. Using the proper equipment is the foundation for a safe product.

The benefits of using the right equipment are food safety and efficiency, plus better quality of food that increases sales and productivity, thereby saving labor cost. Dirty equipment, no preventive care, or waiting to make repairs is not only unsafe, but also will increase costs because the equipment is not working efficiently, potentially causing more damage and in some cases completely destroying the piece of equipment. Additionally, these oversights could put employees in harm's way, injuring them or worse. No matter the food service or retail operation, when injury occurs, it has a direct impact. It lowers the team's morale and decreases productivity, resulting in a substantial financial loss.

The efficiency of your food service or retail establishment is based on purchasing and using the correct equipment. While not mandatory, the industry standard is that all equipment meets design and construction criteria and has the ANSI (American National Standards Institute), NSF (National Sanitation Foundation) International, and UL (Underwriters Laboratories) seals of approval. Here is a basic list of minimum standards that helps provide for safe and sanitary equipment:

- Equipment should come with written specifications. Normally, equipment specifications are required by regulatory officials for your plan reviews. These specifications also provide instructions on how to install, utility (electrical/gas) requirements, information on performance tests (including maximum performance capability), and recommendations on equipment maintenance.
- Equipment construction requires food contact surfaces to be smooth, nonporous, corrosion resistant, and nontoxic. All corners and edges must be rounded off. If coating materials are used, they must be USDA or FDA approved to resist chipping, be nontoxic and cleanable. Additional sanitary design factors to prevent bacteria buildup must be considered, such as overlapping parts, drainage, exposed threads, and crevices.
- All equipment must be simple to disassemble and easy to clean and maintain. The key is to have all parts of equipment readily accessible for cleaning, sanitizing, maintenance, and inspection without the use of tools. Follow preventive maintenance programs and equipment calibration schedules. Always keep an inspection and equipment maintenance log to track the preventive maintenance care of your equipment.

The final equipment prerequisite program is to set guidelines for inspecting, maintaining, repairing, or replacing equipment and smallwares that fall below standard. These guidelines are based on the manufacturer's recommendations. Another resource you can use is a regular preventative maintenance inspections and/or audits by an independent company to help in the safety evaluation and evaluate the condition of your equipment. Most food service and retail operators use employee feedback, complaints, and the tallying of maintenance bills to help in the decision process of, "Do I replace or do I repair the equipment?"

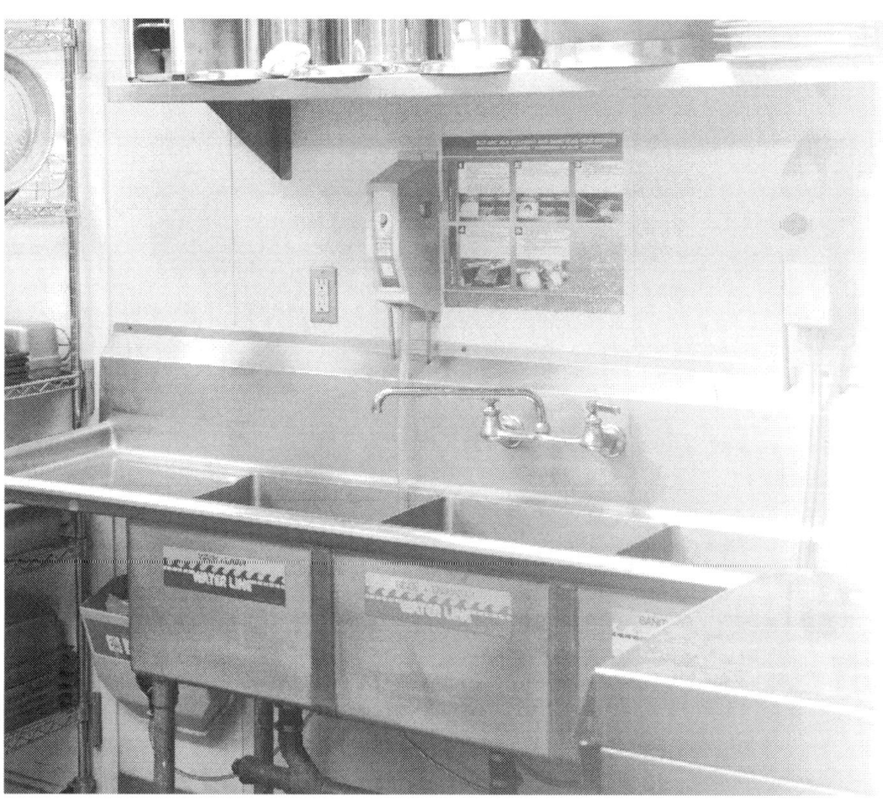

Facility Design

Sanitary facility design is the step that will keep food safe as it travels through the operation. It is safer and more cost effective to do it right the first time. If you have the luxury of preplanning and designing your facility and equipment placement from a "blank slate," take advantage of the situation and plan it right from the start. Doing so avoids having to go back and re-design any flaws due to poor or no planning or cutting corners. In an existing facility, you have to work with what you possess; however, you may be required to add, move, or modify the facility and the equipment to meet food safety standards. Regulatory agencies mandate and have specific laws pertaining to a sanitary facility. In the Food code it is a person-in-charge (PIC) responsibility to always operate a safe and sanitary food service or retail facility.

Whether you are planning a food service or retail facility from scratch or working with an existing footprint, the goal is to prevent the contamination of food, starting with the geographic location of the facility. In business, a crucial factor for success is location, location, location! The location is usually considered first for real-estate value, traffic studies, and marketing potential, but that is not enough. The area surrounding your chosen location needs to be a factor in controlling sanitary facility design.

What contamination can occur from the surrounding area? Are there any airborne contaminants or odors that could affect your business? Would it be safe to build a facility next to a chemical plant? If it is a multi-tenant building (strip mall), are the structures infested with rodents, cockroaches, or other living creatures? Is the proposed site prone to flooding (near a body of water)? Is there a pond/river with ducks and geese? Could your employees step in the duck and geese waste products and potentially transport harmful microorganisms into your facility?

The above examples of environmental contamination sources must be considered by management for their impact on the facility. Controls must then be implemented for these areas such as window/door placement, ventilation systems, pest control systems, waterproofing, drainage systems, shoe/boot cleaning systems, and food delivery methods. Additional environmental concerns may arise based on physical geography, climate, weather conditions, building architecture, and neighbors as other examples.

In addition to selecting a good location, you must be sure the facility itself is correctly constructed with a proper sanitary facility design. Unlike single unit facilities, corporate chain stores and franchise organizations duplicate successful facility design over and over again by using similar sanitary designs. Chains do this because they know their menu, equipment, and how food flows through their facilities so cross contamination will not occur. Also, there is a huge savings of money on labor, creative design, architecture fees, and engineering costs associated with electrical and mechanical systems and plumbing.

Sanitary facility design is a prerequisite program because it is a proactive approach to manage cross contamination and prevent microbial growth. The facility design needs to take into consideration the flow of the products through the operation to the customer. The design begins outside the facility, and then considers the ingredients coming in, the proper storage of these products, complete preparation and processes used, as well as proper disposal of waste. Here is a list of facility considerations:

- Interior materials (walls, floors, ceiling)
- Equipment locations (flow)
- Spacing of shelving and equipment 6 inches (15.23 cm) off of the floor and away from walls
- Easy to clean and sanitize equipment and surfaces
- Adequate lighting
- Proper ventilation
- Appropriate temperature: 50°F to 70°F (9.9°C to 21.1°C)
- Correct humidity: 50%–60%

- Potable water source
- Water control (floor drains, self-draining equipment)
- Effective plumbing (back-flow prevention devices, air gaps, vacuum breakers)

Whether new construction or modification of an existing structure, once the equipment is in place, the best practice going forward is to use a master cleaning schedule. The master cleaning schedule identifies who is responsible as well as, what, where, when, why, and the how of cleaning and sanitizing hoods, filters, grease traps, ceilings, walls, floors, and food contact surfaces. This prerequisite is usually audited by visual inspections of the person-in-charge, who performs a "manager's walk" or uses a detailed checklist of your equipment and facility. A sample master cleaning schedule follows to assist you in creating your own schedule. You should include on your master cleaning schedule any equipment to be cleaned on a scheduled time interval, including hoods, grills, ranges, ovens, fryers, etc...

Sample Master Cleaning Schedule

Master Cleaning List and Equipment Maintenance	Remarks and X marked items have specific SOP Instructions	Cut Sheets	Cleaning Frequency	Every 4 hrs.	Daily	1st	2nd	3rd	Weekly
Exterior Maintenance									
Sweep parking lot/detail around curbs						X			
Empty and clean ashtrays							X		
Outside Trash: empty and clean lids						X	X	X	
Outside Trash: clean containers									X
Clean dumpster and corral areas									X
Clean front doors and all glass						X	X	X	
Clean front doors, cooler doors, all glass								X	
Window/ledges, inside and outside									X
Store Interior Maintenance									
Clean counter walls								X	
Clean behind counter						X			X
Sweep behind counter							X		
Sweep and mop entire store								X	
Sweep carpets						X	X	X	
Clean kick plates on all doors							X		
Clean all walls at: coffee, fountain, kiosk, counter areas						X	X	X	
Clean wall and ceiling fixtures									X

Standard Operating Procedures (SOPs)

Standard Operating Procedures (SOPs) are required for all HACCP plans. It is critical for you to understand that SOPs are an important part of your HACCP plan and serve as the foundation for the safe service of food at your facility. They provide acceptable practices and procedures that everyone in your food service or retail organization is required to follow to keep your operation consistent and your customers safe. SOPs are only effective if they are followed. We recommend that you take advantage of the information provided in Star Point 1 by developing and then applying these food safety standard operating procedures to your food service or retail operation.

The U.S. Department of Agriculture (USDA, www.usda.gov) has prepared and organized sample SOPs in a simple, consistent, and easy to follow format. This format includes a description of the purpose, scope, key words, instructions, monitoring, corrective action, verification, and record keeping. This format also indicates dates for implementation, review, revision, and requires a signature verifying each action has taken place. A variety of sample SOPs from USDA can be found in the Appendix 2 of this book and have been modified for this publication. A properly trained staff following the SOPS will lead to an efficient, safer facility serving the safest food possible, diminishing the possibility of an outbreak of foodborne illness.

Example of Food Safety Standard Operating Procedures (SOPs)

Here is a list of common SOPs used in food service facilities. Examples of some standard SOPs can be found in Appendix 2. In the next few pages we will explore Purchasing and Storage SOPs.

- Purchasing
- Receiving Deliveries
- Storage - Storing Food Properly
- Washing Hands
- Personal Hygiene
- Using Suitable Utensils When Handling Foods
- Washing Fruits and Vegetables
- Time-/Date-Marking Food
- Cooking TCS Foods
- Hot and Cold Holding of PHF/TCS Foods
- Cooling
- Reheating
- Cleaning and Sanitizing
- Serving Food
- Food Safety for Self-Service Areas

You can't just leave food on the loading dock! Food delivered during non-operating hours must be: from approved sources, placed in appropriate storage locations, maintained at the required temperatures, and also packaged in such a way to prevent cross contamination.

Sample Purchasing SOP

Purpose: To prevent contamination of food, foodborne illness, and to ensure safe foods are served to customers by purchasing food products from approved suppliers.

Scope: This procedure applies to food service and retail managers who purchase foods from approved suppliers.

Key Words: Approved suppliers, regulatory services

Warning: Suppliers must be approved by appropriate regulatory services.

Instructions:

Contact regulatory services to ensure you are purchasing foods from approved suppliers. To find out if a supplier is approved, call:

- CDC—404-639-2213 or visit www.cdc.gov
- EPA—202-272-0167 or visit www.epa.gov
- FSIS—888-674-6854 or visit www.fsis.usda.gov
- FDA—888-463-6332 or visit www.cfsan.fda.gov

1. Domestic / imported food (including produce, bottled water, and other foods) but not meat and poultry	• Evidence of regulatory oversight: copy of suppliers' local enforcement agency permit, state or federal registration or license, or a copy of the last inspection report • Third-party audit results [many vendors now provide third-party guarantees, including NSF International or American Institute of Baking (AIB)] • Microbiological or chemical analysis/testing results. • Person-in-the-plant verification (i.e., chain food facilities may have their own inspector monitor food they buy) • Self-certification (guarantee) by a wholesale processor based on HACCP • For raw agricultural commodities such as produce, certification of Good Agricultural Practices or membership in a trade association such as the United Fresh Fruit and Vegetable Association • A copy of a wholesale distributor or processor's agreement with its suppliers of food safety compliance
2. Domestic / imported meat, poultry, and related products such as meat- or poultry-containing stews, frozen foods, and pizzas	• USDA mark on meat or poultry products • Registration of importers with USDA
3. Fish and Fish Products	• Evidence of regulatory oversight: copy of suppliers' local enforcement agency permit, state or federal registration or license, or a copy of the last inspection report • Third-party audit results • Person-in-the-plant verification

3. Fish and Fish Products	• Self-certification (guarantee) by a wholesale processor based on HACCP • A copy of a wholesale distributor or processor's agreement with its suppliers of HACCP compliance. • U.S. Department of Commerce (USDC) approved list of fish establishments and products located at seafood.nmfs.noaa.gov
4. Shellfish	• Shellfish tags • Listing in current Interstate *Certified Shellfish Shippers publication* • Gulf oyster treatment process verification if sold between April 1 and October 31 (November 1 to March 31 certification may be used in lieu of warning signs) • USDC-approved list of fish establishments and products located at seafood.nmfs.noaa.gov
5. Drinking water (non-bottled water)	• A recent certified laboratory report demonstrating compliance with drinking water standards • A copy of the latest inspection report
6. Alcoholic beverages	• Third-party audit results • Self-certification (guarantee) by a wholesale processor based on HACCP • Person-in-the-plant verification • Evidence of regulatory oversight: copy of suppliers' local enforcement agency permit, state or federal registration or license, or a copy of the last inspection report • A copy of a wholesale distributor or processor's agreement with its suppliers of food safety compliance

Monitoring:

1. Inspect invoices or other documents to determine approval by a regulatory agency.
2. Food service and retail managers are encouraged to make frequent inspections of the suppliers' on-site facilities, manufacturing facilities, and processing plants/farms. Inspections determine cleanliness standards and ensure that HACCP plans are in place and followed.

Corrective Action:

Food service and retail purchasing managers must find a new supplier if the supplier is not approved by the above regulatory services.

Verification and Record Keeping:

The food service and retail purchasing manager must maintain all documentation from food suppliers. Documentation must be maintained for three years plus the current year.

Date Implemented: ____________________ By: ______________________________

Date Reviewed: ______________________ By: ______________________________

Date Revised: _______________________ By: ______________________________

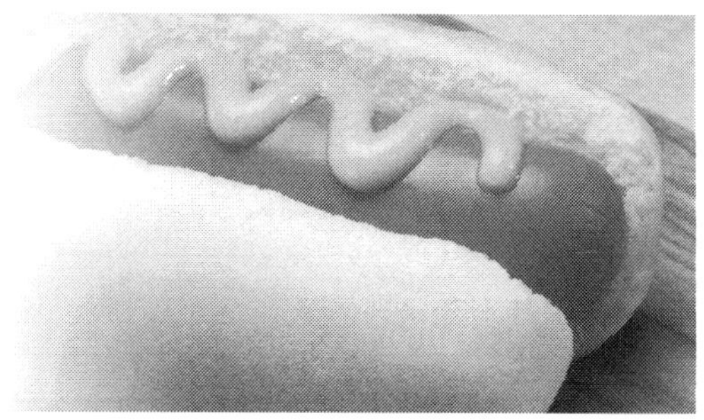

Star Knowledge Exercise:

Storing Food Properly

In the space provided, using your general knowledge of proper storage practices and effective food safety, list the directions for storage instructions, monitoring, corrective action, verification, and record keeping. Food items to consider should be generic frozen foods, generic refrigerated foods, and generic dry goods.

Storage SOP - Storing Food Properly

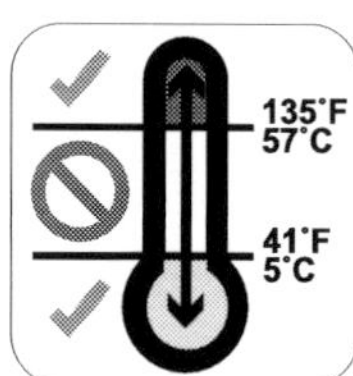

Purpose: To ensure that food is stored safely and put away as quickly as possible after it enters the food service and retail operation.

Scope: This procedure applies to food service and retail employees who store, handle, prepare, or serve food.

Key Words: Cross contamination, temperatures, storing, dry storage, refrigeration, freezer

Instructions:

1. ______
2. ______
3. ______
4. ______
5. ______
6. ______
7. ______
8. ______
9. ______
10. ______

Monitoring:

______

______

______

______

Corrective Action:

____

____

____

____

____

Verification and Record Keeping:

____

____

____

____

____

____

Date Implemented: ____________________ By: ______________________________

Date Reviewed: ______________________ By: ______________________________

Date Revised: _______________________ By: ______________________________

Understanding Hazards in Food

Standard operating procedures are put in place to control hazards. There are potential hazards in all areas of food service or retail establishments from production through consumption. Hazards fall into three basic categories:

Biological Hazards (microorganisms) - bacteria, viruses, parasites, and fungi. Biological Hazards are the greatest threat to food safety and human health. These hazards also receives the greatest attention in HACCP plans.

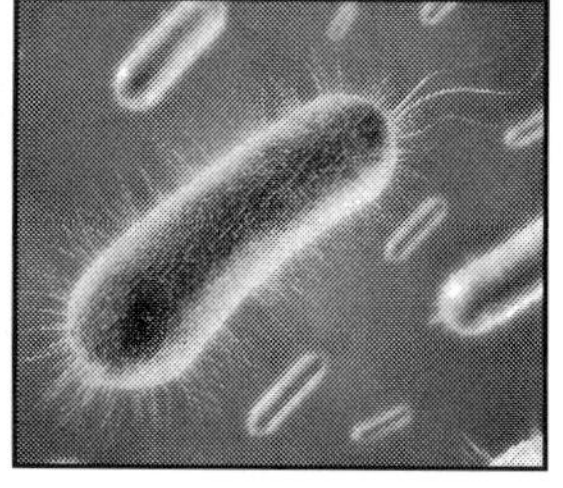

Bacteria

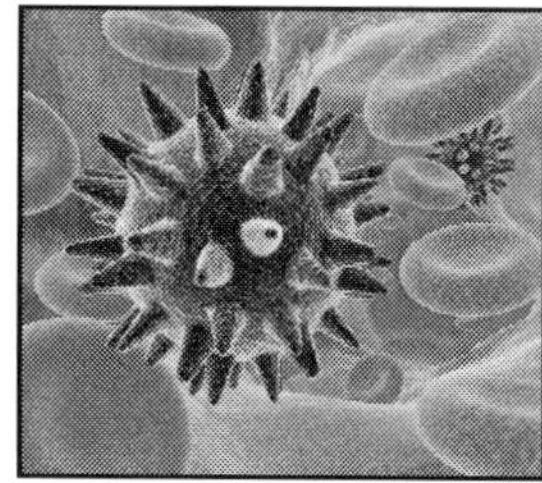

Viruses

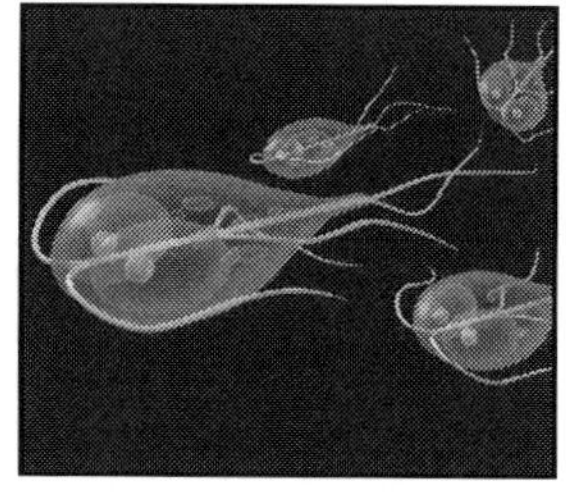

Parasites

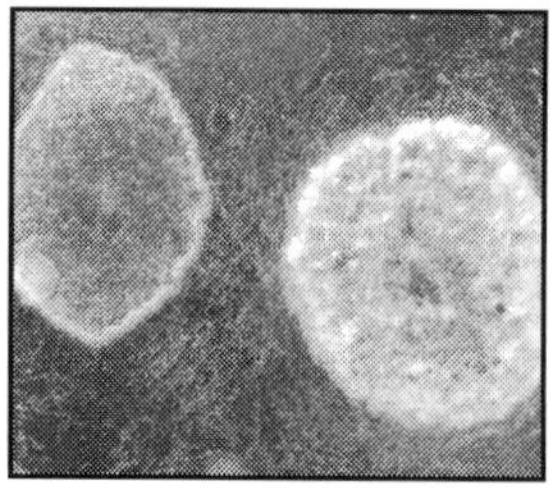

Fungi

Chemical Hazards - pesticides, unapproved additives or food colors, toxic metals, natural poisons, cleaning chemicals, food allergens, personal care items, medicine, first aid items, and similar.

Physical Hazards - foreign objects that do not belong in food. Some common examples are hair, dirt, fake fingernails, plastic wrap, band aids, cherry pits, and fish bones.

When SOPs are properly written, staff are well trained, and SOPs are followed, hazards are controlled. Control hazards… and you prevent illness, injury, or even death. As Star Point 1 moves through various SOPs, keep these three hazards in mind.

Basic Microbiology

As mentioned, biological hazards are of great concern as they are most often associated with illness. To understand how to control illness caused by biological hazards, you need to have a basic understanding of how microorganisms live and grow.

Microorganisms are living organisms. All living organisms have basic needs to live, grow, multiply, or reproduce. Just as humans, microorganisms need **f**ood, controlled **a**cidity, **t**ime, **t**emperature, **o**xygen (or lack thereof), and **m**oisture to survive. This is easy to remember if you can remember **FATTOM**.

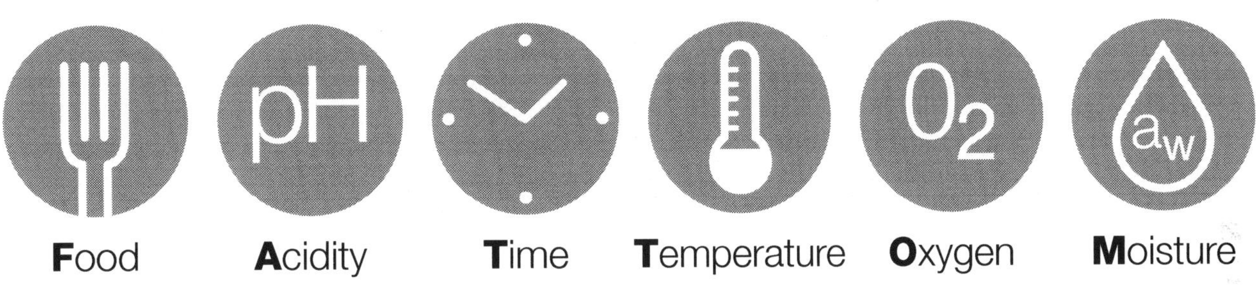

The goal is to increase or decrease these FATTOM elements to levels that inhibit the growth of pathogens. A considerable increase or decrease of these elements will likely cause the organisms to die.

- **F—Food** - All organisms need food to live. Nutrients such as protein must be available for bacteria to grow.
- **A—Acidity** - pH is the measurement used for acidity. On a measurement scale of 0 – 14, 0 is acidic, 7 is neutral and 14 is basic (alkaline). All bacteria have an ideal environmental pH needed to grow. Outside those ideal limits they will not survive.
- **T—Time** - Bacteria do not grow instantaneously when they get into food. They need time to adjust to their environment and begin to grow.
- **T—Temperature** - Most bacteria will not grow if their environment is too warm or too cold. The temperature danger zone for food pathogens is 41°F to 135°F (5°C to 57.2°C). If in this zone, bacteria will grow.
- **O—Oxygen** - All living organisms have ideal oxygen levels that they will grow best in and survive.
- **M— Moisture** - Organisms need moisture in order to survive. Moisture (available water), must be available for bacteria to grow.

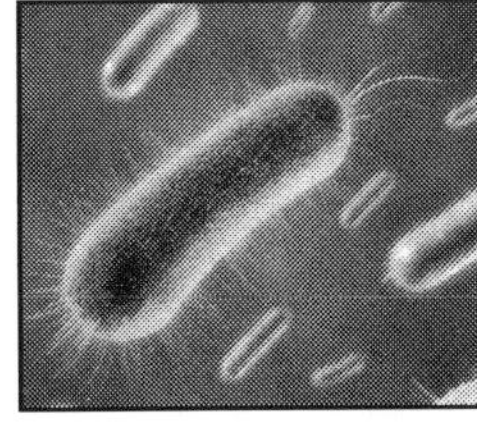

Generally **bacteria** thrive in warm, moist, protein-rich, not too acid or not too basic environments (close to neutral). Sound familiar? ...it should. This describes a lot of the food we eat. If you want to control the growth of germs, you have to take away or control the things that make them live and grow. Not all bacteria are similar, just like humans. Some like salty environments, while some thrive in a low oxygen environment. Some like starchy foods and some like high protein foods. If you control **FATTOM**, you control growth, and in turn control illness. You need to put barriers in place so that you deny conditions that support the possible growth of bacteria.

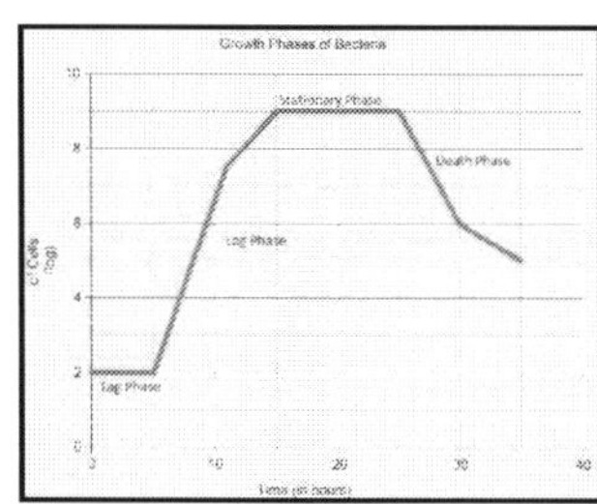

Bacteria follow a predictable pattern of growth with four phases:

Lag phase: very little to no bacterial growth.

Log phase: the number of bacterial cells doubles at a constant, exponential rate.

Stationary phase: population growth levels off as the rate of cell death equals the rate of cell division.

Death phase: a steady decline in numbers.

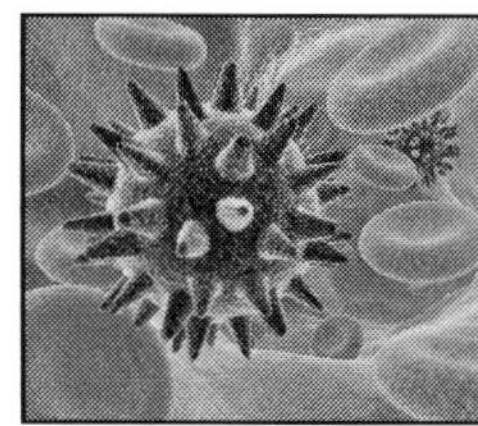

Viruses are the smallest and simplest form of life. They are little bundles of genetic material that can cause big problems. Viruses are the leading cause of foodborne illness in the US. Viruses will not multiply in food; they need a living host. Humans make great hosts. Viruses will live and survive in food and can then be transferred to a human (you or your customer) who in turn becomes sick. The best way to control illness, due to a virus, is not allowing it to get into food in the first place. The best defense is good personal hygiene.

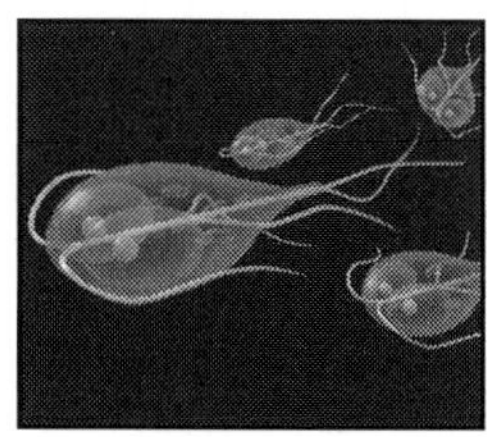

Parasites are microscopic creatures, like viruses, that need a host to survive. They can travel in food and waste. Parasitic hosts can be humans, rats, pigs, bears, fish, or wild game. Once in a human host, they can cause some very unpleasant illnesses. Not using contaminated water and properly cooking or freezing foods will destroy most parasites.

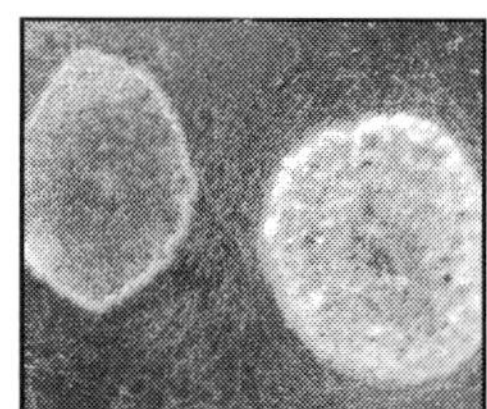

Fungi, usually in the form of mold or yeast, are controlled by purchasing from a reputable supplier, conducting a visual inspection, and carefully monitoring time, temperature, and moisture in the environment.

Prerequisite programs and SOPs are put into place to control harmful disease-causing microorganisms from getting into food in the first place, others to control the growth of or destroy those that may have accidentally gotten into food. Again, SOPs control hazards (biological, chemical, or physical) and prevent illness or injury. Star Point 1 explores many of these controls.

Foodborne Illness

Understanding Foodborne Illness

If prerequisite programs and SOPs aren't followed, the risk that you and your customers may contract a foodborne illness increases dramatically. Illnesses that travel to you through food are called **foodborne illnesses**. A foodborne illness is caused by eating food that has been contaminated with a chemical or biological agent that makes you ill. **Contamination is the unintended, accidental, or deliberate presence of substances or disease-causing microorganisms in food.**

A foodborne illness, caused by dangerous germs or disease causing microorganisms called **pathogens**, occurs when these pathogens get into your body and make you sick. There are three general categories of foodborne illness.

Foodborne infections - This occurs when the pathogen itself makes you sick. A foodborne infection is caused by ingesting pathogens or disease causing microorganisms. Once consumed, these pathogens multiply to the point that the person shows symptoms of a foodborne infection. Symptoms for a foodborne infection take longer to occur than foodborne intoxication because the disease-causing microorganisms need time to multiply. Some examples of foodborne infections are salmonella, with the onset of symptoms, occurring 8 to 72 hours, following consumption, and listeriosis, which takes 3 to 21 days to affect someone after the unsafe food is consumed.

Toxin-mediated infection - Occurs when you consume food containing pathogens in it. Unlike a case of foodborne infection, a toxin–mediated infection has pathogens that produce toxins made by the pathogen after you consume it. It is the toxin that makes you sick. A toxin-mediated infection can be very severe because it is a combination of pathogens and toxins. The person ingests the pathogens, and then the infection produces toxins that begin to affect and/or damage organs in the body. An example of a toxin-mediated infection is hemorrhagic colitis, known as E. coli 0157:H7. The onset of this disease occurs 12 to 72 hours after food consumption, with symptoms of bloody diarrhea, severe abdominal cramping, and kidney failure. Toxins like verotoxin and shiga-like toxins cause severe damage to the lining of the intestines.

Foodborne intoxication - The pathogen produces a toxin (poison) in the food before you eat it. Once a toxin is produced or contaminates a product, there is no getting rid of it. All the cooking in the world will not get rid of a toxin. You are eating food with a chemical in it. Foodborne intoxication can also occur when chemicals accidentally get into food. When someone ingests a toxin, the symptoms that occur very quickly are nausea and vomiting. These symptoms occur because the body is trying to eliminate the poison from the body as quickly as possible. This is actual "food poisoning." *Staphylococcus aureus*, foodborne intoxication, has a short incubation period of 1 to 6 hours with the duration of 24 to 48 hours. Besides nausea and vomiting, diarrhea and dehydration are common symptoms of *Staphylococcus aureus*.

Foodborne intoxication is similar to alcohol intoxication. Alcohol is a poison. When a person consumes large quantities of alcohol, it affects the person immediately. If a large amount of alcohol is consumed, then vomiting typically occurs, similar to foodborne intoxication. As a quick review, foodborne intoxication is caused by ingesting a toxin or a poison in food, the symptoms appear very quickly, and usually vomiting is one of the first symptoms to occur.

We tend to use food poisoning as a generic term to describe any foodborne illness. This is because most people assume that if they are sick, the most recent food they ingested caused it. In fact, most foodborne illnesses are foodborne infections, which generally have incubation ranges of 6 hours to 21 days.

A **foodborne illness outbreak** occurs when two or more people eat the same food and get the same illness. Following a HACCP program helps prevent foodborne illness outbreaks because HACCP is a proactive approach to control every step in the flow of food. Here are some questions to ask yourself in order to determine if you have ever suffered from a foodborne illness.

- Have you ever eaten food that made you sick?
- Did you vomit?
- Did you have stomach cramps?
- Did you have diarrhea?
- Did you cough up worms?

Experiencing vomiting, diarrhea, stomach cramps, and flu-like symptoms are the most common symptoms associated with foodborne illnesses. Becoming sick from contaminated food could be the result of not following prerequisite programs and SOPs as required by the food service or retail establishment. This chapter should help you to understand food safety so that you can protect yourself, your family, your friends, your neighbors, your fellow employees, and your customers. Remember, it is not just the food you serve at the facility that must be safe but what you eat at home, at your neighbor's house, and when you go out.

Healthy people have immune system antibodies that fight off many of the pathogens that we ingest daily. But, when there are too many germs consumed, or the germs multiply in the system, the germs win the fight, and we get sick. There are some people who simply cannot fight off illness as well as healthy people. That is why two people can eat the same food yet only one gets sick. Different people have different immune capabilities. In the food industry, those persons who are more likely to become ill are considered part of the **Highly Susceptible Population (HSP)**. If you work in a hospital nursing home, senior center, daycare, medical treatment or similar, you are serving a HSP. Your facility's SOPs will be much more stringent in these facilities. When the consequences of failure are great, one cannot be too careful. It takes a much lower dose of pathogens to make these people sick.

The people at the most risk for a foodborne illness are:

Children

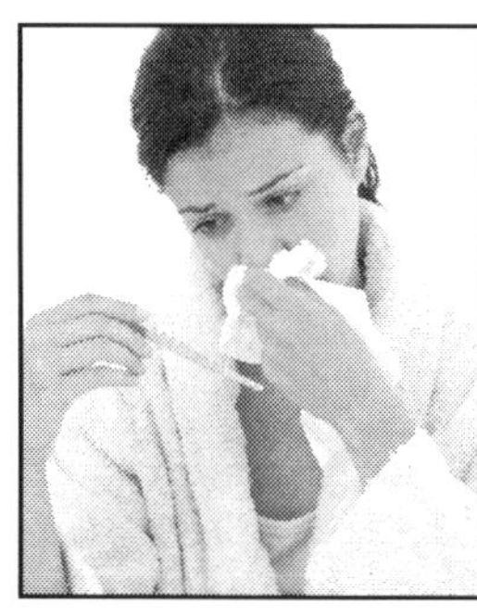

People already sick

People taking medication

Elderly people

Immune compromised persons

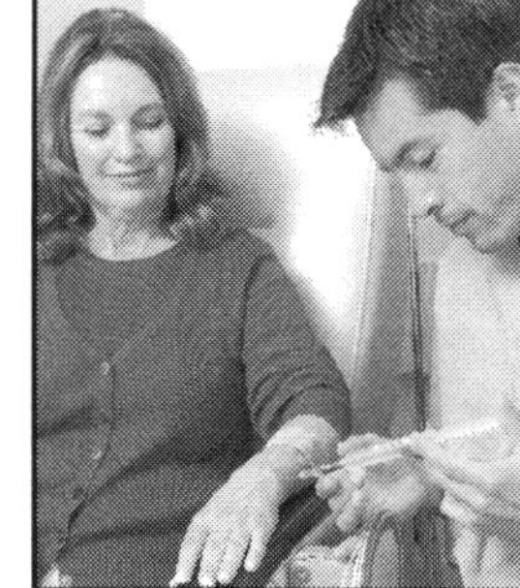

Persons with certain diseases

Did You Know...

Infected employees are the source of contamination of 1 in 5 foodborne illness disease outbreaks reported in the U.S. Most of these are fecal-oral contamination.

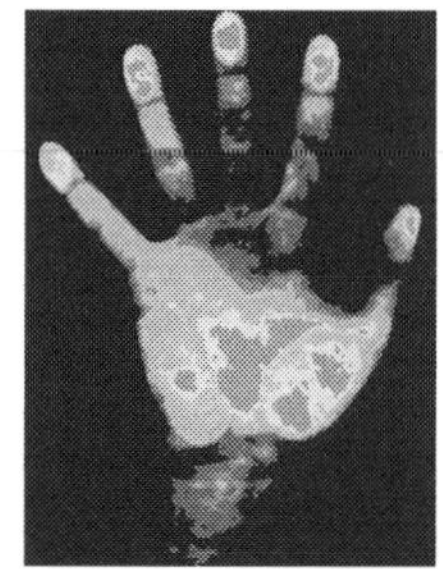

The skin on your hands is very thick and pathogens cannot easily penetrate the skin. A food handler may not get sick from this kind of contact with a pathogen, but the consumer may become violently ill.

Common Foodborne Illnesses

These illnesses are the most alarming because they are highly contagious and very serious. These illnesses are easily transmitted to others when food handlers do not wash their hands properly after using the restroom and then touch ready-to-eat (RTE) foods with bare hands. Spreading disease in this way is called the **fecal-(hand)-oral route**. Keep in mind that these are fecal-(hand)-oral route employee diseases that are spread from person to person. The five highly contagious foodborne illnesses (known as the **"BIG 6"**) you need to know are:

Hepatitis A (virus)

E. coli – scientifically known Hemorrhagic colitis (bacteria)

Norovirus Infection (virus)

Salmonella typhi , i.e. Typhoid Fever (bacteria)

Salmonella nontyphoidal (bacteria)

Shigellosis (bacteria)

A good way to remember the Big 6 is simply remember H.E.N.S.S.S. These illnesses are especially crucial to know and recognize because they are highly contagious and very serious, sometimes fatal.

Disease	Common Causes
Hepatitis A Virus Infection	Not washing hands properly; infected employee; receiving shellfish from unapproved sources; handling RTE foods, water, and ice with contaminated hands; Highly contagious—**must report** to person-in-charge.
***E**. coli* (Hemorrhagic colitis)	Undercooked ground beef; unpasteurized juice/cider and dairy products; contact with infected animals; and contaminated produce; Highly contagious—**must report** to person-in-charge.
Norovirus Infection	Poor personal hygiene, receiving shellfish from unapproved sources and using unsanitary/non-chlorinated water; Easily passed among people in close quarters for long periods of time (dormitories, offices, and cruise ships); Highly contagious—**must report** to person-in-charge.
Salmonella typhi, i.e. Typhoid fever (Salmonella spp.)	Poor personal hygeine. Consumption of food or water contaminated with human feces. Human to human transmission—**must report** to person-in-charge.
Salmonellosis nontyphoidal (SNT, Salmonella spp.)	Improper handling and cooking of eggs, poultry, and meat, contaminated raw fruits and vegetables; Highly contagious—**must report** to person-in-charge.
Shigellosis (Bacillary Dysentery), Shigella spp.	Flies, water, and foods contaminated with fecal matter; Highly contagious—**must report** to person-in-charge.

There are countless other bacteria that can cause foodborne illness. The focus on the Big 6 is not meant to downplay any other foodborne illness pathogen, such as Listeria, Staphylococcus and many more. But the H.E.N.S.S.S. the most commonly found in the food industry and are highly contagious, very serious illnesses. Many of these other pathogens are described in the tables to follow.

Did You Know...

In most cases, you do not get ill immediately from consuming food contaminated by any of the Big 6 or similar pathogens. It can take 30 minutes or up to 30 days for you to begin showing signs of illness depending on the pathogen. The average time where symptoms are displayed is 2 – 24 hours after the food is eaten. This is called the incubation period. Food with toxins will make you sicker much sooner, within seconds in some cases.

Listed in the following tables are the most common foodborne illnesses and the sources associated with each illness. The Big 6 are noted with this symbol:

You need to be aware of the potential biological hazards related to the foods that you produce, serve, or eat. In addition, this information will be useful in HACCP Principle 1, "Conducting a Hazard Analysis."

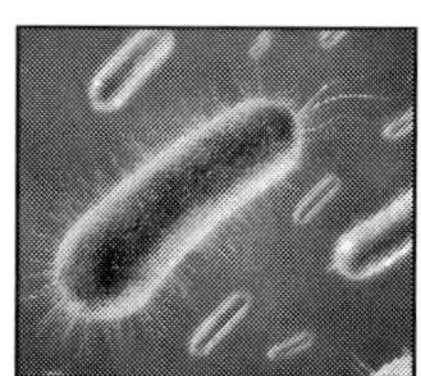

Bacteria

Disease: Bacteria	Common Causes
Typhoid Fever *Salmonella typhi*	Ingesting contaminated water or eating raw fruits and vegetables that have been washed or irrigated with contaminated water with human feces. Highly contagious—**must report** to person-in-charge.
Salmonellosis *Salmonella* nontyphoidal (SNT)	Ingesting of food, such as egg, meat, and poultry or water that has been contaminated with animal feces. Highly contagious—**must report** to person-in-charge.
Shigellosis (Bacillary Dysentery) Shigella spp.	Flies, water, and foods contaminated with fecal matter Improperly handling RTE foods and time/temperature abuse Found in the intestine of humans. Wash your hands! Highly contagious—**must report** to person-in-charge.
Hemorrhagic colitis (*E. coli*)	Undercooked ground beef, unpasteurized juice/cider and dairy products, contact with infected animals, and cross contamination Highly contagious—**must report** to person-in-charge.
Gastroenteritis *Bacillus cereus*	Improper holding, cooling, and reheating of rice products, potatoes, and starchy foods
Botulism *Chlostridium botulinum*	Time and temperature abuse, garlic-and-oil mixtures, improperly sautéing and holding sautéed onions, serving home-canned products and improperly cooling leftovers, improper processing and storing of canned goods
Campylobacteriosis *Campylobacter jejuni*	Not cooking food, especially chicken, to proper internal temperatures, cross contamination and using unpasteurized milk and untreated water

Disease: Bacteria (Continued)	**Common Causes**
Gastroenteritis *Clostridium perfringens*	Improper temperature control, reheating, cooling, and holding cooked food like meat, poultry, beans, and gravy Found in the intestinal tract of humans
Listeriosis *Listeria monocytogenes*	Not cooking food to the required minimum internal temperature, not washing raw vegetables, and not cleaning/sanitizing food preparation surfaces Associated with hot dogs, processed lunch meats, soft cheeses, unpasteurized milk/dairy products, and cross contamination during packaging and processing
Staphylococcal Gastroenteritis *Staphylococcus aureus*	Unwashed bare hands, having a skin infection while handling and preparing food; found on skin, hair, nose, mouth, and throat Improperly refrigerating or cooling prepared food
Vibrio Vulnificus Vibrio Parahaemolyticus Vibrio Cholerae	Eating raw or partially cooked crabs, clams, shrimp, and oysters, receiving seafood from an unapproved supplier
Yersiniosis *Yersinia* spp.	Using unsanitary/non-chlorinated water and cross contamination, unpasteurized milk and not thoroughly cooking food to the required minimum internal temperature

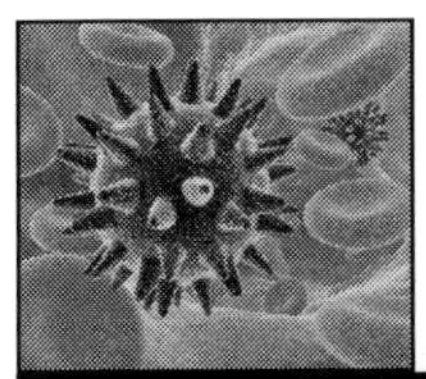

Viruses

Disease: Virus	**Common Causes**
Hepatitis A Virus Infection THE BIG 6	Not washing hands properly; infected employee coming to work; receiving shellfish from unapproved sources; handling RTE foods, water, and ice with contaminated hands Highly contagious—**must report** to person-in-charge.
Norovirus Infection THE BIG 6	Poor personal hygiene; receiving shellfish from unapproved sources; and using unsanitary/non-chlorinated water Very common with people in close quarters for long periods of time (dormitories, offices, and cruise ships) Highly contagious—**must report** to person-in-charge.
Rotavirus Gastroenteritis	Not cooking foods to the required minimum internal temperature; not maintaining time/temperature control Poor personal hygiene Not cleaning and sanitizing properly

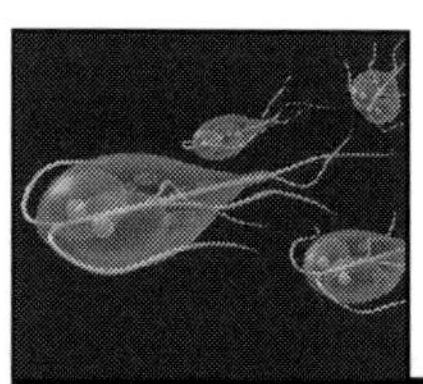

Parasites

Disease: Parasites	Common Causes
Anisakiasis	Receiving seafood from unapproved sources, and serving undercooked or raw seafood
Cyclosporiasis	Drinking or using unsanitary water supplies
Giardiasis	Drinking or using unsanitary water supplies
Cryptosporidiosis	Drinking or using unsanitary water supplies
Trichinosis	Improperly cooking pork and game meat, improperly cleaning and sanitizing equipment and utensils used to process pork and other meats, receiving meats from an unapproved supplier
Toxoplasmosis	Not properly washing hands after touching raw vegetables, cat feces, soil, or raw/undercooked meats (particularly poultry, lamb or wild game); and not cooking meats to the required minimum internal temperature

Major Food Allergens

A food allergy is caused by a naturally occurring protein in a food or a food ingredient, which is referred to as an allergen. Simply stated, some people are allergic to certain types of food while others are not. Some people have food allergies from birth and are aware of their allergies and know not to eat certain foods. However, in some instances, a person can develop a food allergy. They may have eaten a food their entire life and without warning suddenly have an allergic reaction. Someone in this case, will not know they have developed a food allergy until the reaction occurs. Some of the symptoms associated with a foodborne illness are the same symptoms associated with an allergic reaction. Some people may have minor discomfort from eating foods that they are not supposed to eat, while others may suffer serious allergic reactions which may result in death. When it comes to food safety, allergies are just as dangerous as foodborne illnesses. The Food Code reports that recent studies indicate over 11 million Americans suffer from one or more food allergies.

Is your customer having an allergic reaction to food? Let's find out...

- Is your customer's throat getting tight?
- Does your customer have shortness of breath?
- Does your customer have itching around the mouth?
- Does your customer have hives?

Sometimes people do not know they have a food allergy until they have a reaction to a food that causes some or all of the symptoms listed. In severe cases, anaphylactic shock and death may result. We have included food allergies in the food safety standard operating procedures point of the HACCP Star because they are a growing concern in the effort to serve safe food.

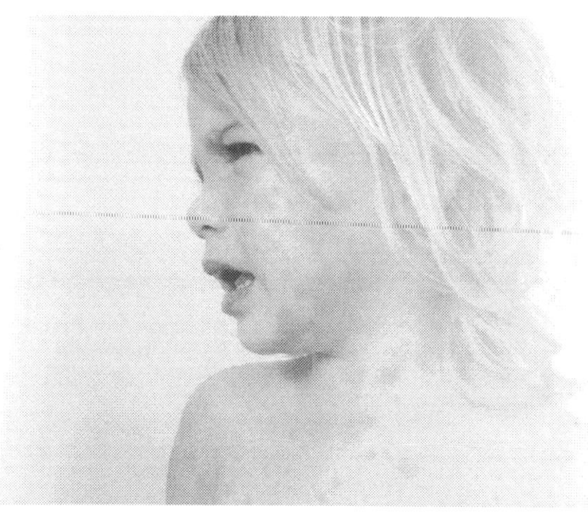

If you are someone who has had an allergic reaction to food or know someone who has a food allergy, you can understand how important it is to know the ingredients in the foods you, your family, friends, neighbors, fellow team members, and customers are consuming. The first step in understanding food allergies is to be aware of the most common allergens. Although there are others, the most common are known as major food allergens or the "**Big 8**". These foods account for 90 percent or more of all food allergies. They are as follows:

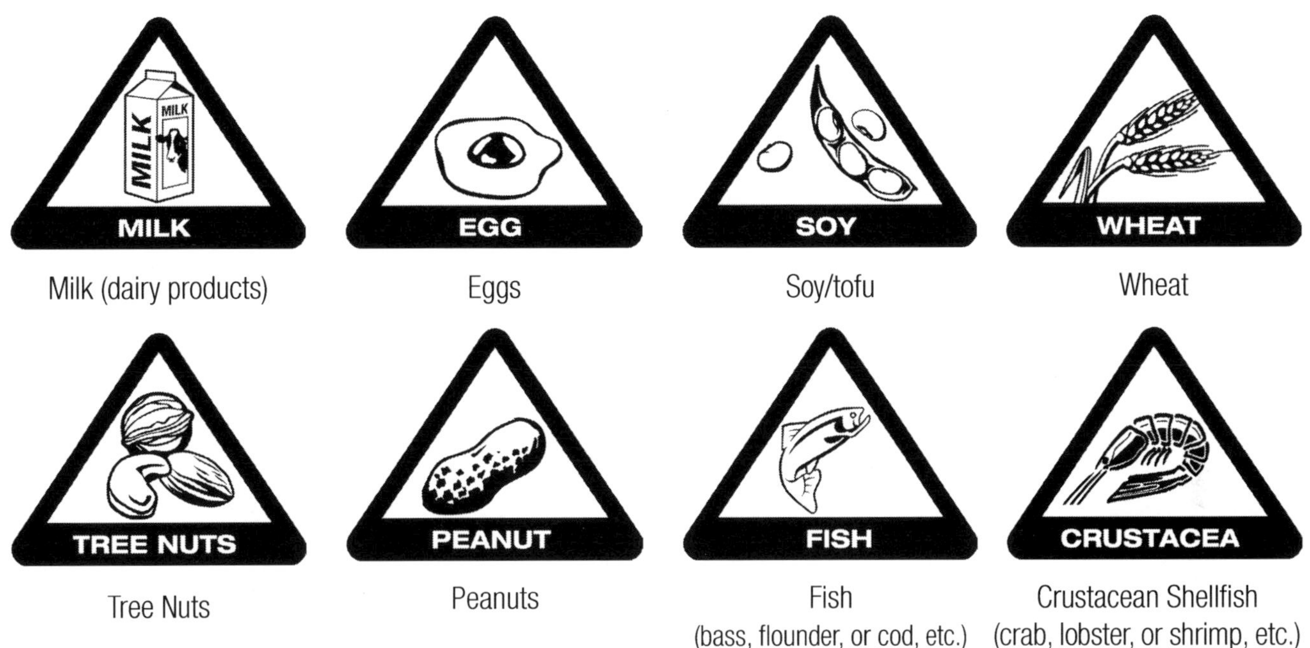

Milk (dairy products)

Eggs

Soy/tofu

Wheat

Tree Nuts

Peanuts

Fish
(bass, flounder, or cod, etc.)

Crustacean Shellfish
(crab, lobster, or shrimp, etc.)

What are Tree Nuts?

- Almond
- Brazil Nut
- Cashew
- Chestnut
- Hazelnut
- Hickory Nut
- Macadamia Nut
- Pecan
- Pine Nut
- Pistachio
- Walnut

In August 2004, the Food Allergen Labeling and Consumer Protection Act was enacted, which defines the term "major food allergen." As of January 1, 2006, the new law required food manufacturers to identify in plain language on the food label any major food allergen used as an ingredient. Also, the FDA is required to conduct inspections to ensure food facilities comply with practices to reduce or eliminate **cross contact** of a food with any major food allergens that are not intentional ingredients of the food. This new law helps food service or retail operators assist their customers by identifying allergens quicker and faster because the label will be easier to read.

Be aware that some allergy symptoms are a result of intolerance to certain foods. For example, milk has a type of sugar in it called lactose. Lactose inhibits digestion in some people, referred to as lactose intolerance. A lactose intolerant person consuming any dairy product may result in experiencing symptoms like nausea, diarrhea, abdominal bloating, excessive gas, and cramping.

It is the duty of the person-in-charge (PIC) to know and understand potential allergens contained in the food they serve. They must provide training to employees on understanding allergens. The Food Code requires, "The person-in-charge to demonstrate knowledge by describing foods identified as major food allergens and the symptoms that a major allergen could cause in a sensitive individual who has an allergic reaction." The PIC must also assure "employees are properly trained in food safety, including food allergy awareness, as it relates to their assigned duties."

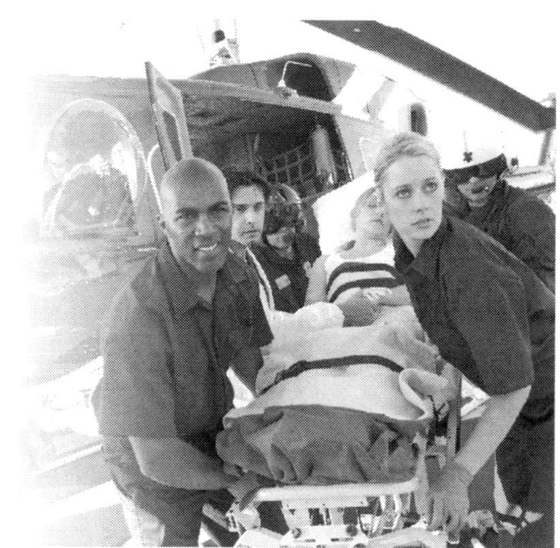

Considering some allergens can cause reactions that may be mild or may be severe enough to cause death, you should take the following steps to ensure your customers avoid eating foods to which they are allergic. If a customer has an allergic reaction at your food service or retail establishment, then seek immediate medical treatment. Every second counts!

Although all customers are special, an allergic customer will have a limited amount of food service or retail establishments that he or she will be able to frequent. If you earn the trust of an allergic customer, you also earn their repeat business. Think about how you would like to be treated if you were the customer with a food allergy, and then consider the following steps:

1. **Ask the customer** if he or she has any food allergies.
2. **Know your company's SOP.** What should you do if your customer indicates he or she has a food allergy?
3. **Know your menu.** Describe **all** ingredients and the preparation of foods you are serving to anyone who asks, even if it is a "secret recipe."
4. **Be honest.** Teach your employees that it is OK to say, "I don't know." Instruct them to immediately notify a member of management so they can be assisted.
5. **Be careful.** Make sure your customer is not allergic to anything in the food you are serving. You should also make certain that he or she is not allergic to anything the food has come in contact with at your facility. Refer to the Prevent Cross Contamination SOP.
6. **Be thoughtful and concerned**, but never tell a customer you are sorry he or she has an allergy to certain foods, because no one is at fault for someone having an allergy.
7. **Manage allergens by limiting the contact** of food for any allergic customer. It is best if **only 1 person** handles the customer's entire food preparation and service. Even utensils and plates can cause cross contamination of allergens to several surfaces.

Life Threatening Allergies and Refusing the Sale

In these challenging economic times, believe it or not, the best solution may be to refuse the sale to the customer with a life threatening allergy. It is important to understand that some companies are instructing their managers and employees to kindly explain to their guest with an allergy that they need to refuse the sale. This is a sample script managers can use with their customer if the corporate directive is to refuse the sale.

> *"I am concerned about your safety. Here at Company XYZ we take allergies very seriously. Our concern is for you and the potential cross contact in our food preparation area. I sincerely want your business; however, I cannot guarantee the product is allergen free. I would rather turn you away as my customer than see you have an allergic reaction or worse, potentially die. The food that you are allergic to is in use throughout our entire kitchen and I do not feel comfortable selling you food. I am sorry for any inconvenience this may cause you."*

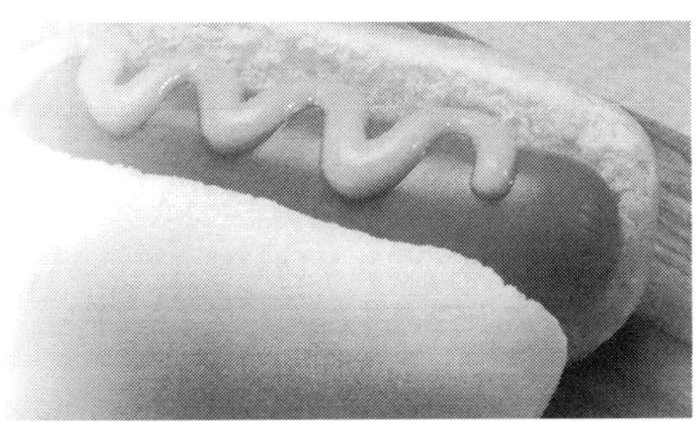

Star Knowledge Exercise:

Foodborne Illness and Allergens

How well do you understand foodborne illnesses and food allergens? Answer the following questions:

1. If you have been diagnosed with or come in contact with someone who has hepatitis A, what should you do?

2. Name the Big 6 foodborne illnesses. How do these diseases typically occur?

3. What is your corporate directive concerning allergies? How would you handle a customer who tells you he is allergic to walnuts but wants to order the chicken salad, which has toasted walnuts in it?

International Food Safety Icons

We all know what the blue handicapped parking sign means when we see one in a parking lot. Signs with simple pictures tell us when it is safe to cross the street, when to check the oil in our cars, or how to get to the airport. With the same purpose in mind, International Food Safety Icons help make food safety easier for everyone to understand and helps you remember basic food safety rules and procedures for food preparation. The leadership team at any food service or retail operation has the responsibility to establish policies, procedures, and recipes that must be followed. The International Food Safety Icons make it easy for everyone working at the establishment to understand, remember, and reinforce these procedures.

In this section, you will see the various International Food Safety Icons, which will help you succeed in HACCP Star Point 1. The International Food Safety Icons provide a visual definition and reminder of the standard operating procedures for the food service or retail industry.

Pop Quiz:

International Food Safety Icons Match Game

Complete the following exercise by matching the letter from the International Food Safety Icons with the phrase that best describes the icon.

1. ________ Do Not Work If Ill

2. ________ Cold Holding—Hold cold foods 41°F (5°C) or below

3. ________ No Bare-Hand Contact—Do not handle food with bare hands

4. ________ Hot Holding—Hold hot foods 135°F (57.2°C) or above

5. ________ Temperature Danger Zone (TDZ)—41°F to 135°F (5°C to 57.2°C)

6. ________ Time/Temperature Control for Safety Food (TCS)

7. ________ Cook All Foods Thoroughly

8. ________ Wash Your Hands

9. ________ Do Not Cross Contaminate—between raw to RTE or cooked foods

10. ________ Wash, Rinse, Sanitize

11. ________ Cooling Food

a. **b.** **c.** **d.** **e.** **f.**

g. **h.** **i.** **j.** **k.**

How many points did you earn? ________________

If you scored 10–11 points — Congratulations! You are a Food Safety All-Star!

If you scored 8–9 points — Good job! You have a basic understanding of food safety.

If you scored 5–7 points — The time for review is now! What a great opportunity to fine-tune your food safety skills.

If you scored 0–4 points — Everyone needs to start somewhere!

How can you use the International Food Safety Icons in your food service or retail operation?

____

____

____

Responsibilities Related to Food Safety

As a HACCP team member, your personal responsibilities related to providing safe food include staying home when sick, washing your hands, using gloves properly, and following a food-safe dress code. As a manager, it is your responsibility to assure your employees are adhering to these policies. As challenging as it is to be an employee short for a few days because of illness, it would be far greater to contend with the illness of multiple employees or food becoming contaminated and dealing with a foodborne illness outbreak.

We are confident that if you follow the prerequisite programs, and the standard operating procedures in this manual, you will better understand why the basics of food safety must be mastered. The HACCP team must master food safety basics as the first step toward creating an effective HACCP plan. You, and those responsible, must know the proper ways to cook and prepare food before you can identify any mistakes in the preparation of food at your facility. Then you need to take that information and prepare standard operating procedures, unique to your operation, in order to avoid mistakes in handling, preparing, and serving food to ensure food safety going forward.

As we mentioned previously, each of the International Food Safety Icons represents a food safety standard operating procedure to help make food safer and avoid foodborne illness. We will now examine each one.

Do Not Work If Ill

If you have gastrointestinal symptoms like running a fever, vomiting, and diarrhea or you are sneezing and coughing, you should not work around or near food and beverages. If a manager or employee is diagnosed with a foodborne illness, it is critical that he or she stay home until a physician gives him or her permission to work around food again. It is important for employees to notify the PIC/manager of any illnesses they may have, especially if they have **Norovirus, Hepatitis A, E. coli, Typhoid Fever (*Salmonella typhi*), Salmonellosis (*Salmonella* nontyphoidal),** or **Shigellosis (Shigella spp.)**, because these diseases must be reported to the regulatory authority by the PIC. The food employee is personally responsible for reporting this information to the PIC. This communication requirement should be made very clear to all employees prior to employment and reinforced during subsequent training.

An employee **must report** to the PIC if they have any of the following symptoms:

- Vomiting;
- Diarrhea;
- Jaundice (unnatural yellowing of the eyes or skin);
- Sore throat with fever; or
- A lesion containing pus or an infected wound that is open and draining on the arms or hands.

A food employee **must** also report to the PIC:

- If they are currently diagnosed with any of the Big 6;
- Have had an illness in the past 3 months or diagnosed with Typhoid fever *(Salmonella typhi);*
- Have been exposed to or is a suspected source of a confirmed foodborne illness outbreak; and
- Lives with or has been in close contact with someone who has, has been exposed to, or has been potentially exposed to the Big 6.

What do you do about a common cold? Or seasonal allergies? If you are sure that the employee has only a common cold or an allergy, and not experiencing any of the above listed symptoms, they can typically report to work. Employees should always check with their manager to discuss their work for the day. As a PIC, you may decide to assign the employee to a duty that has the least exposure to food. No one wants someone sneezing all over their food! Your company might have a much stricter SOP for any kind of sniffling, sneezing, or cold type symptoms. Though colds (and seasonal flu) do not cause foodborne illness, they are easily transmitted through the air and surfaces to other people. You do not want one sick team member to be the cause of making the entire staff sick. Staying home and resting is always the best choice.

According to the Food Code (www.cfsan.fda.gov), **the following charts summarizes the CDC list and compares the common symptoms of each pathogen**. Symptoms may include diarrhea, fever, vomiting, jaundice, and sore throat with fever. CDC has no evidence that the HIV virus, Hepatitis B virus, or Hepatitis C is transmissible via food. Therefore, a food employee who has one of these illnesses is not of concern unless he or she is suffering from a secondary illness listed in the chart. Lists I and II include pathogens likely to occur in foods.

Key: D = Diarrhea F = Fever V = Vomiting J = Jaundice S = Sore throat with fever

List I. Pathogens often transmitted by food which has been contaminated by infected persons who handled the food.

	D	F	V	J	S
1. Noroviruses	D	F	V		
2. Hepatitis A virus		F		J	
3. *Salmonella typhi* (Typhoid fever)		F			
4. *Shigella* species	D	F	V		
5. *Staphylococcus aureus*	D		V		
6. *Streptococcus pyogenes*		F			S

List II. Pathogens occasionally transmitted by food which has been contaminated by infected persons who handled the food, but usually transmitted by a contaminated source or in food processing or by non-foodborne routes.

	D	F	V	J	S
1. *Campylobacter jejuni*	D	F	V		
2. *Crypotosporidium parvum*	D				
3. Enterohemorrhagic *Escherichia coli*	D				
4. Enterotoxigenic *Escherichia coli*	D		V		
5. *Giardia lamblia*	D				
6. *Salmonella* nontyphoidal	D	F	V		
7. *Vibrio cholerae* 01	D		V		
8. *Yersinia enterocolitica*	D	F	V		

Management's Duty to Report Foodborne Illness Diseases

If you find out you have contracted or have been exposed to any of the illnesses in the virus, bacteria, and parasite tables, notify your supervisor immediately. If you are a supervisor, report it to your managers, general managers, or owner. If your employees are experiencing any of the illnesses or symptoms noted above, they must report it to you or another person-in-charge. The PIC is responsible for making decisions as to whether to exclude or restrict employees from working with or around food. The Food Code has guidance documents to assist PICs with making those decisions. Do not forget to reach out to your regulatory authority for help as well. They would much rather assist you in making sound decisions whether to exclude and restrict employees than to investigate a foodborne illness related to your facility.

The Food Code requires that the PIC contact his or her local regulatory authority and report any of these symptoms or illnesses as noted above. The purpose of calling your regulatory authority is to ask if any additional measures are needed to assist your employee and protect your company. Any food handler with these symptoms should be seen by a physician to determine if the illness is caused by a foodborne pathogen. It is very easy to just sit at home and wait out an illness. The only way to tell if you have a foodborne pathogen is to have stool, vomit, blood, or other bodily fluid examined. Not a fun thing to do, but it is the only way to confirm a foodborne illness.

Some companies have an infectious disease policy and procedure to follow. In the Food Code, there are several forms designed to assist those responsible for reporting foodborne diseases. The Food Code, as a model for regulatory agencies, specifies that the permit holder is responsible for requiring applicants to use these forms to report certain symptoms, diagnoses, past illnesses, high-risk conditions, and foreign travel, as they relate to diseases transmitted through food by infected workers. Keep in mind, your regulatory agency may or may not require the use of these forms. Regardless, they are good tools to incorporate into your Employee Health SOPs.

Here is another opportunity to take action and use these forms to make a difference in your operation. Once an employee is confirmed with one of the Big 6 illnesses, a health practitioner or physician needs to release the food employee to return to work. The Food Code provides a sample form for the health practitioner to use. If the health practitioner denies your employee to return to work, because the employee might still be a carrier, then your employee might want to consult an infectious disease specialist.

Cleaning Up After a Vomit or Fecal Matter Incident

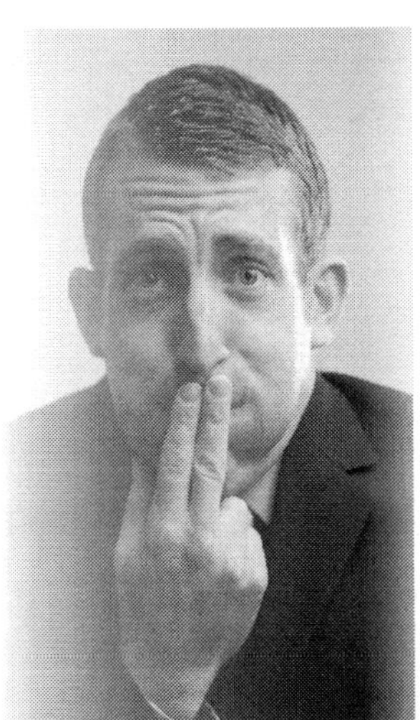

If an employee or a customer becomes ill within a food facility, the PIC and employees must know how to handle and contain the situation and how to properly clean up after the event. Some foodborne illnesses, like Norovirus, are easily spread through aerosolization of the vomitus.

The Food Code requires a food service or retail establishment to have written procedures for employees to follow when responding to vomiting or diarrheal events that involve the discharge of vomitus or fecal matter onto surfaces in the establishment. The procedures must address the specific actions to take in order to minimize the spread of contamination and the exposure to employees, customers, food, and surfaces to vomitus or fecal matter.

Though you hope that this would never happen in your facility, it will. You need to have SOPs in place to deal with situations of this nature that will inevitably arise.

Wash Your Hands

Washing your hands frequently is extremely important in preventing illness.
Wash your hands! Wash your hands! Wash your hands!

Have employees use the following hand washing recipe:

The entire handwashing process should take 20 seconds.

1. If the paper towel dispenser requires you to touch the handle or lever, the first step should be to crank down the paper towel. Let the paper towel hang there. Do not do this if the paper towel touches and cross contaminates with the wall or the waste container.
2. Wet your hands and exposed arms with 100ºF (37.8ºC).
    - Always have your hands in a downward position with your fingers toward the sink drain. This will assure the "germs" you are trying to remove do not contaminate your forearm.
3. Add soap
4. Scrub for 10 - 15 seconds
    - Do not forget your nails, thumbs, and between your fingers!
    - Some regulators require nailbrushes.
5. Rinse
6. Dry with a paper towel
    - Use the paper towel to shut off the faucet and for opening the door handle when exiting the restroom.
    - **Put on gloves** if touching ready-to-eat food.
    - If exiting a restroom, wash your hands again when you reenter the kitchen or food preparation area. This two hand wash method is recommended to reduce any contamination that may have occurred along the way.

When Do You Wash Your Hands and Change Your Gloves?

- After going to the bathroom
- Before and after food preparation
- After touching your hair, face, or any other body parts
- After scratching your scalp
- After rubbing your ear
- After touching a pimple
- After wiping your nose and using a tissue
- After sneezing and coughing into your hand
- After drinking, eating, or smoking
- After touching your apron or uniform
- After touching the phone or door handle
- After touching raw food and before touching ready-to-eat products
- After cleaning and handling all chemicals
- After taking out the trash
- After touching any non-food-contact surfaces
- Every 4 hours during constant use
- After touching a pen
- After handling money
- After receiving deliveries
- Before starting your shift
- Reenter kitchen or food preparation area

Did You Know…

- Hand antiseptics should only be used on clean hands.
- Hand antiseptics are not a substitute for hand washing in a food service or retail industry.
- Use only antiseptics approved by the FDA.

No Bare-Hand Contact

You must not touch Ready-To-Eat (RTE) foods with bare hands. RTE foods are foods that are exactly that: "ready to eat," like bread, pickles, lunchmeats, cherries, lettuce, lemon wedges, cheeses, everything served at a salad bar, and sushi too. These foods should be handled with gloves, deli paper, tongs, or utensils. Why? Even a good thorough handwashing does not get rid of all bad germs on your hands. No bare-hand contact with RTE food is another precaution to avoid foodborne illness. One in three people do not wash their hands after using the bathroom. Do not assume food handlers will follow the hand washing policy. For these reasons, there is **no bare-hand contact with RTE food.** It stops the fecal-(hand)-oral route of contamination.

Some food service or retail operators strongly disagree with the no-bare-hand contact of ready-to-eat food. Some of the reasons they state are as follows:

- "I've been in business for decades and I have never gotten anyone sick."
- "It takes too much time if you have to wash your hands between every customer. People will be waiting forever!"
- "If you are the only one making the food and using the cash register, it's not realistic."
- "I am being forced to spend my hard-earned money on smallwares and gloves. Do you know the cost of gloves, serving utensils, spoons and tongs these days?"
- "The gloves make the employees wash their hands less."
- "The gloves are hard to get on after you wash your hands."
- "The gloves do not fit right and they make my hands hot."
- "I do not want to change."

A regulatory agency may consider a request and allow bare-hand contact with ready-to-eat foods As the PIC, knowing that **one out of three people** do not wash their hands after using the restroom, the choice is this: smallwares, gloves, and additional training. These solutions are considered a minor inconvenience versus possible contamination with fecal matter. Food safety is about leadership, being a role model, and making sound decisions. Although not recommended by the authors, to request a waiver from mandatory glove use.

Your food facility may have an SOP for glove use. Be sure all food employees follow that SOP exactly. Gloves are not worn so your hands do not get messy. Gloves assure that any germs that may be left on your hands, even after a good handwashing, are kept away from foods. Gloves are an extension of your hands. If they get contaminated, they must be changed. Even if not contaminated, they should be changed at least every 4 hours. If glove use is not an SOP for your facility, the Food Code still requires that you not touch RTE foods with your bare hands.

If a RTE food is going to be added as an ingredient to a food item that will be fully cooked to its required minimum cook temperature,, like a topping for a pizza or adding vegetables to a casserole, no bare-hand contact is not required prior to the cook step. Once cooked, hands off! This policy does not apply if the food will only be lightly heated, melted, browned, or otherwise undercooked.

Do you have to wear gloves when washing raw, whole fruits, and vegetable? No. The Food Code does allow for fruit and vegetables to be handled with bare hands **only during the washing** step. However, employees must be sure to properly wash their hands prior to washing the fruit and vegetables.

Pre-cut or prewashed produce in bags should **not** be washed before use. Pre-cut bagged produce items are considered a RTE food and should not be touched with bare hands.

Cross Contamination

Between Raw and RTE or Cooked Foods

Raw food is food that needs to be cooked before it is eaten, like raw meat and eggs. Ready-to-eat food is food that either has been cooked or doesn't need to be cooked and is ready to be eaten, like a sandwich roll or lettuce. Cooked food is food that has been properly cooked by reaching a specific temperature for an appropriate amount of time, like a cooked hamburger that reaches 155°F for 15 seconds. Once food has been properly cooked, it is now considered a ready-to-eat food.

Food-Contact Surfaces

Cross contamination occurs when raw food touches or shares contact with ready-to-eat and/or cooked foods. If you touch the walk-in (refrigerator/cooler) door handle, or a pen, or the telephone, and then make a sandwich, without washing your hands and putting on gloves you have cross contaminated. Using the same knife to cut both chicken and rolls is cross contamination. If raw chicken is stored in the refrigerator above lettuce and the chicken juice drips onto the lettuce, this is cross contamination.

To avoid cross contamination:

- Properly store raw food below ready-to-eat food (chicken below lettuce);
- Never mix food products when restocking;
- Properly clean and sanitize utensils, equipment, and surfaces;

- Clean and sanitize work areas when changing from raw food preparation to RTE food preparation; and
- Never store any food near any chemicals.

Between Tasks

It is critical to change gloves, wash hands, and use clean and sanitized utensils, cutting boards, and work surfaces between tasks to prevent contamination. One system to help prevent cross contamination is to use color coding. Color coding assists management to prevent cross contamination by providing a simple visual cue. For instance, you can use different colored gloves for different jobs. This system makes it easy to differentiate food handling jobs from non-food handling jobs. Does your company have a SOP for gloves? Here are some examples of color coding gloves:

- Use clear gloves for food preparation;
- Use blue gloves for fish;
- Use yellow gloves for poultry;
- Use red gloves for beef; and
- Use purple gloves for cleaning and for non-food-contact surfaces.

A similar practice designates different cloths and containers and color codes them to separate food and non-food contact surfaces:

- Use a white cloth for food contact surfaces;
- Use a blue cloth for non-food contact surfaces;
- Use a green container for cleaning (water and soap);
- Use a red container for sanitizing (water and sanitizer); and
- Use color-code cutting boards, knives, containers, and gloves.

Dress Code

Why dress code? We learned earlier in this section that microorganisms and pathogens can live on clothing and that foreign objects can contaminate food. One way to help avoid this contamination is to have a dress code. A dress code not only gives a uniform appearance to customers, but also allows the supervisors to quickly assess whether the team members are in compliance as part of a HACCP plan. It is equally important for the supervisor to set an example and be a role model by following the dress code. A dress code will include the following:

- Cover all cuts and burns with a bandage and a glove if you have an injury on your hand.
- Wear your hat or proper hair restraint. This includes shift managers and managers who are in exposed food areas.
- For safety, wear clean, closed-toe shoes with rubber soles.
- Take a bath or shower every day.
- Always have clean and neat hair.
- Properly groom fingernails and clean your hands.
- Do not wear nail polish or false nails.

- Do not wear rings, watches, bracelets or any jewelry on hands or arms. According to the Food Code the **only exceptions** are that a plain wedding band may be worn. A medical alert necklace can be tucked under the shirt, or a medical alert ankle bracelet can be used. It is highly recommended that you also not wear other jewelry such as necklaces, dangly or hoop earrings, nose rings, eyebrow rings, or other facial jewelry or any other exposed body jewelry. Check your company policy on body jewelry. Though not in direct contact with food, these items could fall off and be the source of physical contamination. Where did my earrings go? Oops!
- Do not chew gum.
- Only eat, drink, and smoke in designated areas.
- Do not touch your hair, your face, or any other body parts when handling or serving food.
- Remove aprons before leaving the food preparation areas.
- Wear a clean apron, uniform, or outer clothing at all times.
- Never take your apron into the bathroom.

Sampling Foods

Cross contamination can occur when employees sample foods at their workstation. It is your responsibility as the person-in-charge, to train your team on the correct procedure for sampling food. Employees should never eat at their workstations unless they are taste testing food they are preparing.

These are the steps employees should follow when taste testing their food. Use a single-use spoon. Do not double dip! Single-use means exactly that—only one taste per single-use spoon. Or take a small dish; ladle a small portion of the food into the small dish. Put down the ladle. Step away from the pan or pot. Then taste the food. Place items in the dirty dish area of the food service or retail establishment. Always wash hands properly and return to work.

Washing Fruits and Vegetables

Washing fruits and vegetables is critical for food safety. As discussed earlier, employees must wash hands prior to washing the fruit and vegetables; therefore, employees may touch the fruit and vegetables with bare hands only during the washing step. Once fruits and vegetables are cleaned and are considered ready to eat, you must then implement no bare-hand contact with ready-to-eat foods.

Pre-washed or pre-cut, ready-to-eat (RTE) produce, such as bagged salad mixes, that come into a retail food facility should not be re-washed prior to use. Though there have been some instances of foodborne illness from bagged RTE produce, there is a higher probability of contamination by excessive handling or mishandling in food facilities during re-washing than there is with using the RTE produce as is. Additionally, these products are considered ready-to-eat therefore, should not be touched with bare hands.

Time/Temperature Control for Safety of Food (TCS)

A **TCS** is any food capable of allowing pathogens to grow rapidly. TCS foods have a greater potential to cause foodborne illness outbreaks than other food. They are usually moist (like watermelon), have lots of protein (like dairy and meat), and are close to a neutral acidity.

There is no easy way to produce a list of all the foods that are TCS. Regulations are often based on the characteristics of food. Does a food have the characteristic that will support the growth of bacteria? Remember FATTOM? Bacteria have specific needs in order to grow. If you can alter these needs, then you will prohibit or reduce their growth. The utilization of these characteristics will change a food from a TCS to a non-TCS food. For example, adding vinegar to cooked rice will increase the acidity and make the rice non-TCS. "A", acidity in FATTOM, has been altered making the rice a non-TCS food. This is the process used in sushi operation for making cooked rice safe to be stored and used at room temperature.

Barriers That Prohibit Growth of Bacteria

Food manufacturers often alter TCS foods to make them non-TCS foods. When they arrive at the retail food facility, they are already non-TCSs and do not require refrigeration. This is done by use of various barriers that may include processes such as altering salt levels, adding preservatives, adjusting available chlorine, changing the viscosity of food, changing the acid level of the food, reducing the water activity of a food, and other similar methods. These **barriers** alter the environment of the food, making it harder, if not impossible, for bacteria and pathogens to grow. These complex methods are often only seen in food manufacturing facilities as they typically need precise equipment and scientific measurements to accurately verify if the critical limits are met and the food is safe.

More often, and in the interest of maximizing profits, retailers are experimenting with adding barriers to food themselves to make them non-TCS. If a TCS food becomes a non-TCS food, it does not require refrigeration as a control for bacteria growth, and its shelf life will be extended. You must, however, be able to accurately measure and verify your process. Some of these qualities are easy to measure; others will require tools or gauges to measure, such as a pH meter. Measuring these factors and/or the interaction between factors will help us make sure we are correctly identifying potentially hazardous foods. If verification cannot be done at the food service or retail facility, the product may need to be taken to a food laboratory to specifically test the product. You should discuss these procedures with your regulatory authority to verify they are being done accurately. If not correct, you could make people sick.

The following are barriers commonly used in food service or retail facilities to render a food non-potentially hazardous or safe:

- Altering pH, or acid level, of a food, such as acidifying or canning a food.
- Decreasing water activity (a_w), or the amount of water available for use by bacteria. This can be done by drying a food or increasing the salt or sugar concentration within a food, all of which will reduce any free water from being available to bacteria to use and grow.

Any combination of these factors, or **barriers**, can make a food non-TCS.

pH and a_w Interaction Matrix

Although the criteria to identify foods that need TCS (Time/Temperature Control for the Safety) have expanded, it may decrease the amount of foods that actually need time/temperature control for safety. For example, the previous definition of TCSs listed only moisture, protein, and neutral acidity as the combination of factors to classify a food as TCS. But now, using a matrix and tables of refined values, and the interaction of water activity (a_w) and pH values, we can more accurately identify food that need TCS. Let's first review water activity and pH definitions and measured values of food.

Acidity (pH) is the measure of the degree of acidity or alkalinity of a solution based on a scale of 0 to 14.

Water activity (a_w) refers to the availability of water in a food or beverage. It is the amount of water that is available to microorganisms.

Acidity of Foods

The pH and/or acidity of a food are generally used to determine processing requirements and for regulatory purposes. pH is the symbol for a measure of the degree of acidity or alkalinity of a solution based on a scale of 0 to 14. Values between 0 and 7 indicate acidity, and values between 7 and 14 indicate alkalinity. The value for pure distilled water is 7, which is considered neutral. pH values are the relationship between whether something is an acid (acidic) or a base (alkaline). A food ingredient can be acidic (i.e. a lemon) or a base (i.e. cooking oils). Both have a pH value. Electrodes and pH meters are available from various manufacturers to determine pH. To assist readers in determining the pH levels of different food products, Appendix 1 lists the approximate ranges of pH values.

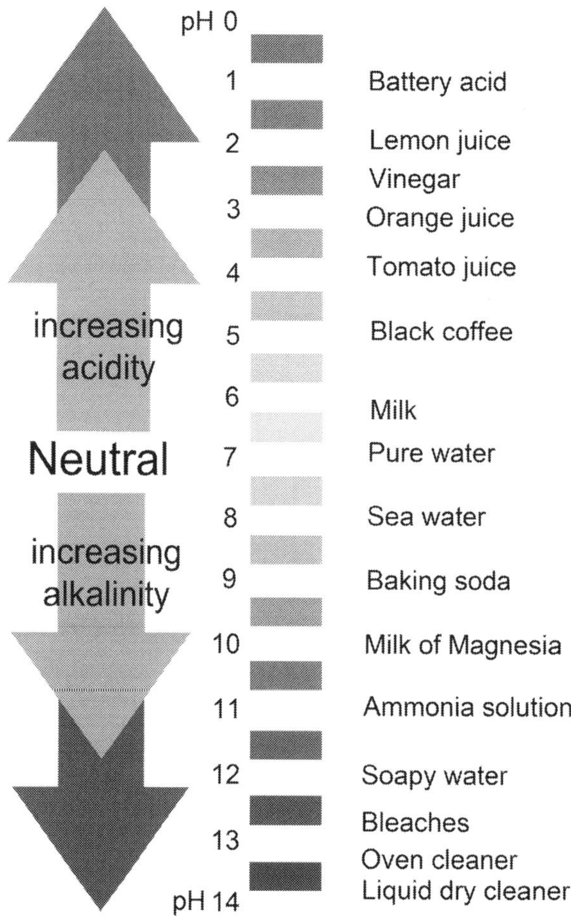

How does this work in real situations? According to the USDA, *Campylobacter* bacteria are the second most frequently reported cause of foodborne illness. The minimum pH for *Campylobacter* spp. to grow is 4.9, meaning below that number the bacteria does not survive. The optimum condition for growth is between 6.5 and 7.5. The maximum pH for growth is 9.0. Science tells us that eighty percent of all poultry have *Campylobacter* spp., and poultry has an approximate water activity of 0.99 to 1.00 and a pH range of 6.2 to 6.4. You must factor the water activity ranges that can support *Campylobacter* spp. The minimum is 0.98, and the optimum is 0.99. The higher the water activity the better the conditions for bacterial growth and this tells us why poultry is a potentially hazardous food. The water activity and acidity level are used to determine if time/temperature control for the safety of foods is required and must be included in the HACCP plan.

Water Activity of Foods

Water activity (a_w) is a critical factor that determines shelf life. While temperature, pH, and several other factors can influence if and how fast organisms will grow in a product, water activity may be the most important factor in controlling spoilage. Water activity refers to the availability of water in a food or beverage and in turn the amount of water that is available to microorganisms. It is not the moisture content of food. Pure water has an activity level of 1.00. Crackers have a water activity of 0.10. Most bacteria, for example, do not grow at water activities below 0.91, and most molds cease to grow at water activities below 0.80. By measuring water activity, you can predict which microorganisms will be potential sources of spoilage and which will not. Various food products are highlighted in the table in Appendix 1. These tables show the a_w of organisms and food.

Hurdle Effect

The **Hurdle Effect** is when two or more independent variables work together to make a non-TCS Examples of hurdles include increasing the acidity, lowering the water activity, high temperature during processing, low temperature during storage, and the presence of preservatives. The matrix in Tables A and B in this section provide a scientific approach for the interaction of water activity and pH values. Acidity and water activity are two barriers to the growth of pathogens that can be used in combination with each other to delineate if a food is or is not a potentially hazardous food. These interaction tables were included with the definition of foods that require time/temperature control for safety to limit pathogen growth or toxin formation. The matrix is easy to use with the supporting tables in Appendix 1 of this book. Simply reference the water activity and the pH of the food product in the tables, and then compare it to Tables A and B. If a food is not in the table, ask your manufacturer to assist you with the water activity and pH levels in the foods you use.

In food service or retail operations, sometimes an operator adds ice to quickly cool food. Sometimes water is added to reconstitute the food or to improve the quality. Remember, each time you alter the product, it impacts the characteristics of the food and could change it from a non-TCS food to a TCS food.

TCS Matrix

Table A. Interaction of pH and a_w for control of spores in food heat-treated to destroy vegetative cells and subsequently packaged			
a_w values	**pH values**		
	4.6 or less	**> 4.6 - 5.6**	**> 5.6**
≤ 0.92	non-TCS food **	non-TCS food	non-TCS food
> 0.92 - .95	non-TCS food	non-TCS food	PA***
> 0.95	non-TCS food	PA	PA

** **TCS** Food means **T**ime/**T**emperature **C**ontrol for **S**afety Food
*** **PA** means **P**roduct **A**ssessment required

Table B. Interaction of pH and a_w for control of vegetative cells and spores in food not heat-treated or heat-treated but not packaged				
a_w values	**pH values**			
	< 4.2	**4.2 - 4.6**	**> 4.6 - 5.0**	**> 5.0**
< 0.88	non-TCS food **	non-TCS food	non-TCS food	non-TCS food
0.88 - 0.90	non-TCS food	non-TCS food	PA***	PA***
> 0.90 - 0.92	non-TCS food	non-TCS food	PA	PA
> 0.92	non-TCS food	PA	PA	PA

** **TCS** Food means **T**ime/**T**emperature **C**ontrol for **S**afety Food
*** **PA** means **P**roduct **A**ssessment required

Time/Temperature Control for Safety

A **time/temperature control for safety of food (TCS)** is any food capable of allowing bacteria to grow or form toxins. These TCSs have the potential to cause foodborne illness outbreaks. Pathogens love TCS foods. They are usually moist (like watermelon), have lots of protein (like dairy and meat), and do not have very high or very low acidity (neutral acidity). Adding lemon juice or vinegar to foods to increase the acidity can slow the growth of the germs. Remember FATTOM? When trying to control a pathogen from growing, one of the things you need to control is **Time and Temperature**. It is the most common and easily achieved control measure in the food service and retail food setting.

TCS food requires strict time and temperature controls to stay safe. Food has been time–temperature abused any time it has been in the **temperature danger zone (TDZ)** (41°F – 135°F/5°C – 57.2°C) for too long (4 hours). Temperatures must be checked often to make sure that potentially hazardous foods stay safe. The caution sign includes a clock and thermometer to stress the importance of monitoring time and temperature. The clock is the reminder to check food at regular time intervals (like every 2 or 4 hours). The thermometer required must be properly calibrated, cleaned, and sanitized after each use.

Here is a list of time/temperature controlled for safety food (TCS):

- Cut tomatoes (sliced/diced)
- Mixtures with cut tomatoes (tossed salad, Gazpacho soup)
- Cut leafy greens (lettuce, spinach, cabbage, kale, escarole, endive, spring mix, arugula, and chard)
- Milk and milk products
- Shell eggs
- Fish
- Poultry
- Shellfish and crustaceans
- Meats: beef, pork, and lamb
- Baked or boiled potatoes
- Cooked rice, beans, and pastas
- Heat-treated plant food (cooked vegetables)
- Garlic-and-oil mixtures
- Sprouts/sprout seeds
- Sliced melons
- Tofu and other soy-protein food
- Synthetic ingredients (i.e., soy in meat alternatives)
- Most moist baked goods

These foods require **time/temperature control for safety of food (TCS)** because of their moisture, protein, and acidity characteristics. Remember FATTOM?

Here is a list of some **Non-TCS** foods:

- A loaf of bread (low moisture)
- Lemon wedges (acidic)
- Pickles (acidic)
- Dry Cereals (low moisture)
- Some, but not all, fruit pies (low moisture and/or acidic)
- Jelly/Jams (high sugar)
- Mustard (acidic)
- Chocolate chip cookies (low moisture)

Notice these are very dry, very sugary, or very acidic. Remember FATTOM? Non-TCS foods all have barriers to keep pathogens from growing.

Pop Quiz:

FATTOM

What does each letter of FATTOM represent as a basic need for living organisms to live, grow, and/or multiply/reproduce?

F = ______________________

A = ______________________

T = ______________________

T = ______________________

O = ______________________

M = ______________________

In summary, it is important to understand and manage water activity and pH in controlling the growth of known pathogens. The tables in Appendix 1 are provided for a simple and clearer understanding of pathogens that threaten the foods you prepare and serve. Identifying time and temperature control for the safety of food helps you avoid putting your operation at risk.

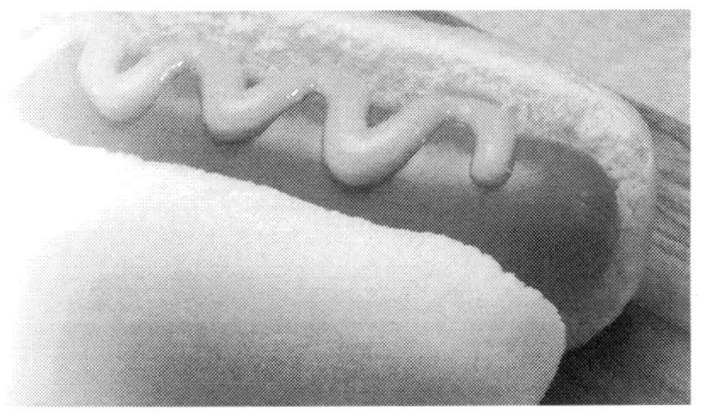

Star Knowledge Exercise:

Product Assessment

In this star knowledge exercise you will use the food product TCS Matrix Table, pH and water activity charts in Appendix 1 of the book to evaluate the potential safety concerns for selected food products.

Use Appendix 1 on page 195, look up the water activity and pH levels for the following food items:

Natural Cheddar Cheese Water Activity (a_w): ____________ pH: ____________

Parmesan Cheese Water Activity (a_w): ____________ pH: ____________

White Bread Water Activity (a_w): ____________ pH: ____________

Whole Raw Shell Egg Water Activity (a_w): ____________ pH: ____________

Condensed Milk Water Activity (a_w): ____________ pH: ____________

Which TCS Matrix Table, A or B found on page 196, would you use to evaluate these food products?

Natural Cheddar Cheese: A ______ B ______

Parmesan Cheese: A ______ B ______

White Bread: A ______ B ______

Whole Raw Shell Egg: A ______ B ______

Condensed Milk: A ______ B ______

Using the TCS Matrix, will you be able to display these products without refrigeration because they are a non-TCS food or will a product assessment (PA) be needed?

Natural Cheddar Cheese: Non-TCS ______ PA ______

Parmesan Cheese: Non-TCS ______ PA ______

White Bread: Non-TCS ______ PA ______

Whole Shell Egg: Non-TCS ______ PA ______

Condensed Milk: Non-TCS ______ PA ______

Temperature Danger Zone (TDZ)

Be Safe — Monitor Time and Temperature

This symbol means no food should stay between **41°F and 135°F** (5°C–57.2°C), as this is the **temperature danger zone (TDZ)**. Germs and bacteria grow and multiply very, very fast in this zone. If a TCS food stays in the temperature danger zone for more than 4 hours, it is time–temperature abused and can make people very sick. It is important to practice temperature control (TC) to make sure foods are not time–temperature abused. The Food Code does allow for TCS foods to purposely be in the danger zone if TIME is controlled. This is called 'Time as a Public Heath Control'. If you use these procedures, you MUST have a written plan in place that has been approved by your regulatory agency. These procedures will be covered later in this Star Point.

If you are not purposefully using 'Time as a Public Health Control', to control hazards, then TCS foods should always be temperature controlled (TC) and never in the danger zone. However, mistakes and accidents do happen in the food service industry. You should also holding units (ovens / refrigerators / freezers / warmers / serving lines) at regular intervals to ensure food safety. For example, if the steam table was accidentally unplugged, it could result in the food temperature dropping to 120°F (48.9°C). Using your knowledge of food safety, you now have to make an assessment of that food. Is it safe to serve? Could it make someone ill? If the last time you took the temperature of the food on the table was less than 4 hours ago, you can reheat the food to 165°F (73.9°C) for 15 seconds within 2 hours and continue to serve the product. But if the last time you took the temperature was more than 4 hours ago, then you MUST discard all the foods that are time–temperature abused. This unsafe food can make anyone who eats it sick.

Something to think about…What is the temperature of a healthy human? If you answered 98.6°F (37°C), you are correct. 98.6°F (37°C) is right in the middle of the temperature danger zone. Our bodies are ideal for germs because we are in the TDZ! Germs love people! Those germs will be transferred to people's food if you are not careful. That is why controlling time and temperature along with maintaining good personal hygiene are keys to the success of food safety.

Checking Food Temperatures with Calibrated Thermometers

What is the point of checking temperatures if you do not know whether the thermometer is working properly? Calibrated thermometers ensure that the temperatures being read reflect the true temperature of the foods. There are many types of thermometers. Here are some types of thermometers commonly used in food service or retail establishments:

- Bimetallic
- Thermistor (digital)
- Thermocouple
- Disposable temperature indicators (t-stick)
- Infrared
- Infrared with Probe

Thermometers must be checked every shift for correct calibration. The simple act of dropping a thermometer on the floor or banging the thermometer against a prep table can knock the thermometer out of calibration. All food must be checked with a properly calibrated, cleaned, and sanitized thermometer.

Ice-Point Method

Step 1: Fill a container with crushed ice and water

Step 2: Submerge sensing area of stem or probe for 30 seconds or until indicator needle stops moving

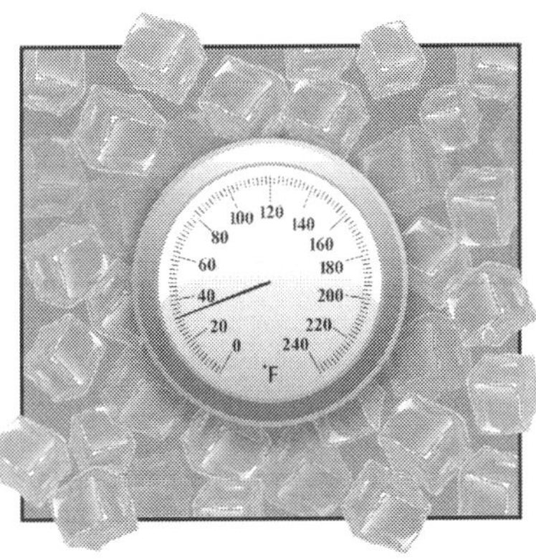

Step 3: Hold calibration nut and rotate thermometer head until it reads 32°F (0°C)

Boiling-Point Method

Step 1: Bring a deep pan of water to a boil

Step 2: Submerge sensing area of stem or probe for 30 seconds or until indicator needle stops moving

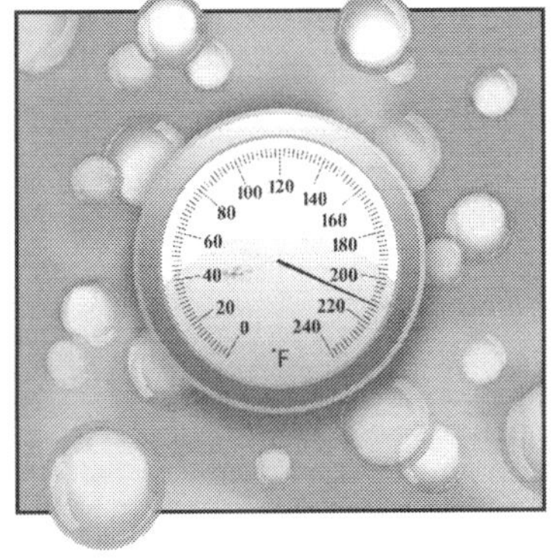

Step 3: Hold calibration nut and rotate thermometer head until it reads 212ºF (100ºC) at sea level

Remember, to avoid cross contamination; clean and sanitize the thermometer before each task change! Always, follow the manufacturer's procedures for calibrating thermometers.

Did You Know...

You cannot thaw foods:

- Using a dishwasher
- In a bath tub
- In an electric blanket
- On a countertop

Properly Thaw Foods

Often we need to thaw food prior to starting the cooking process. How many times have you thought, "We can pull the turkeys from the freezer and let them sit on the work table and thaw?" Setting frozen food on the counter to thaw is not a safe food handling practice. Food should not enter the TDZ and thaw. If it does enter the TDZ, it needs to be done in a safe and controlled way. As a manager, make sure your employees follow these procedures for properly thawing foods.There are four safe and approved methods for thawing food:

Method 1: Thaw in the refrigerator. As foods thaw they may produce extra liquid. Be sure to place TCS in a refrigerator, in a pan or on a tray to avoid cross contamination. You must plan ahead to thaw. Larger and denser food items might take several days to thaw in the refrigerator.

Method 2: Thaw in running water. Foods to be thawed under **running water** must be placed in a sink with running water at 70°F (21.1°C) or cooler. The sink must be open to allow the water to push the microorganisms off the food and flow down the drain. Do not allow the sink to fill with water. Also, **do not allow food to exceed 41°F (5°C) for more than 4 hours total time**.

Method 3: Cooking. Frozen food can be thawed by following the cooking directions for the product. Frozen food may take longer to cook depending on the size and type of product.

Method 4: Microwave. Food can be thawed using the microwave only if it will then be immediately cooked. When thawing food in the microwave, remember that there will be uneven thawing and some of the food may have started to cook, taking some of the food into the TDZ. This is why you must finish the cooking process immediately after microwave thawing.

Cook All Foods Thoroughly

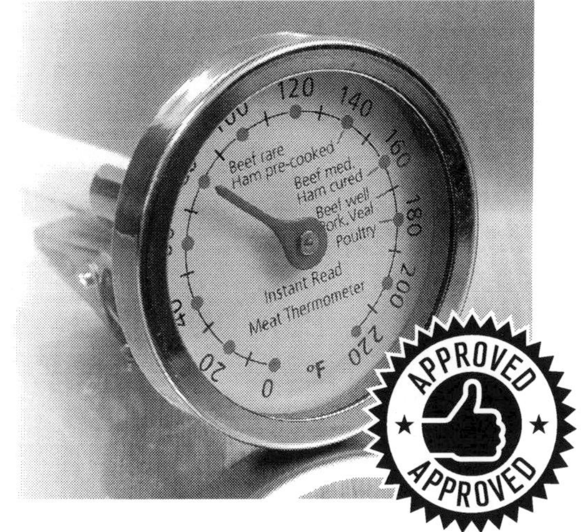

Each TCS food has a minimum internal cooking temperature that must be reached and held for 15 seconds to ensure that it is safe and less likely to make anyone sick. These safe cooking temperatures will assure that most harmful bacteria or viruses are killed or reduced to harmless levels. Foods known to cause serious illness or death such as eggs and ground meats must be monitored routinely for proper cooking temperatures with a properly calibrated, cleaned, and sanitized thermometer.

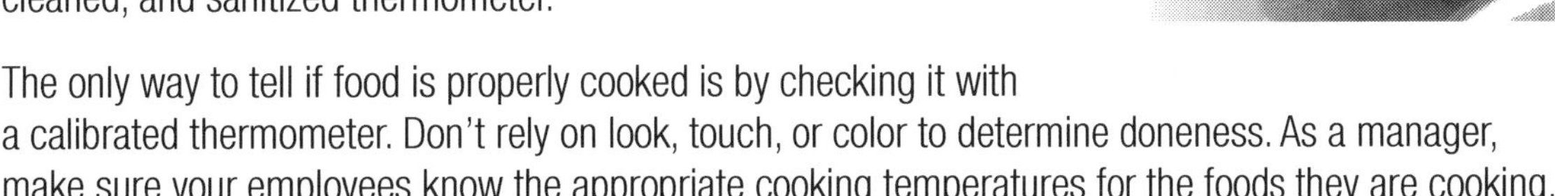

The only way to tell if food is properly cooked is by checking it with a calibrated thermometer. Don't rely on look, touch, or color to determine doneness. As a manager, make sure your employees know the appropriate cooking temperatures for the foods they are cooking.

Minimum Internal Cooking Temperatures

Here are some minimum internal cooking temperatures your employees should follow when preparing food:

165°F (73.9°C) for < 1 Second

- Reheat all leftover TCS food (for 15 seconds holding time).
- Cook all poultry, including, duck, ratites, emu, ostrich and similar.
- Cook all stuffed products, including pasta.
- Foods cooked in a microwave, then let sit for 2 minutes.
- When combining already cooked and raw TCS products (casseroles).
- Cook all wild game animals.
- Stage 2, Par-Cooked raw animal foods.

155°F (68.3°C) for 17 Seconds (Note: Alternate temperatures/holding times are available in the FDA Food Code for this category.)

- Cook all ground animal foods: fish, beef, commercially raised game animals, ratites (emu, ostrich, and rhea), and pork.
- Cook all flavor-injected meats.
- Cook all eggs for hot holding and later service (buffet service).

145°F (62.8°C) for 15 Seconds

- Cook all fish and shellfish.
- Cook all intact meat including, chops/steaks of veal, beef, pork, commercially raised game animals, and lamb.
- Cook fresh eggs and egg products for immediate service. (cooked to order)
- Cook roasts to 145°F for 4 minutes. (Roasting temperatures vary; see Chart I and Chart II on the following page for the proper procedure in your establishment.)

135°F (57.2°C)

- Commercially processed products for hot holding.
- Cooking vegetables and fruits for hot holding.

Chart I: Time/Temperature Ranges for Roast in Seconds

Cook to selected internal temperature and hold for specific time (seconds) at that temperature to destroy organisms.

°F	°C	Time in Seconds
158°F	**70°C**	**0 seconds**
157°F	69.4°C	14 seconds
155°F	68.3°C	22 seconds
153°F	67.2°C	34 seconds
151°F	66.1°C	54 seconds
149°F	65°C	85 seconds
147°F	63.9°C	134 seconds

Chart II: Time/Temperature Ranges for Roast in Minutes

Cook to selected internal temperature and hold for specific time (minutes) at that temperature to destroy organisms.

°F	°C	Time in Minutes
145°F	**62.8°C**	**4 minutes**
144°F	62.2°C	5 minutes
142°F	61.1°C	8 minutes
140°F	60°C	12 minutes
138°F	58.9°C	18 minutes
136°F	57.8°C	28 minutes
135°F	57.2°C	36 minutes
133°F	56.1°C	56 minutes
131°F	55°C	89 minutes
130°F	54.4°C	112 minutes

Note: Alternate roast temperatures from the *FDA Food Code*.

Hot Holding

Here are time and temperature food safety rules for hot holding of foods:

- All foods must be cooked before being placed in hot holding units.
- Store all hot food in hot holding/self-service bars (steam table) at 135°F (57.2°C) or above.
- Check temperatures of the food in hot holding a minimum of every 4 hours with a calibrated, cleaned, and sanitized thermometer.
- Always keep food out of the TDZ.

Cold Holding

Here are time and temperature food safety rules for cold holding of foods:

- In cold holding/self-service bars (refrigeration), store all cold food at 41°F (5°C) or below.
- Check temperatures of the food in cold holding a minimum of every 4 hours with a calibrated, cleaned, and sanitized thermometer.
- Always keep food out of the TDZ.

Time as a Public Health Control

The Food Code does allow for the safety of food to be controlled by time instead of temperature. This is called "time as a public health control". Bacteria will grow if they are in the TDZ for too long. If you cannot control the temperature of the food, you can control the amount of time the food does not have temperature control (TC). **There must be a written and approved procedure in the facility in order to use time as a public health control**. Make sure all employees are aware of these approved procedures.

- **Hot Foods** - If the internal temperature of hot food is 135°F (57.2°C) or higher, once it is removed from TC, hot food can remain out of temperature for up to 4 hours before being consumed or discarded. As a manager, you should have an approved written plan that details how this process is to be controlled and monitored. Remember, it must be eaten before or thrown out after 4 hours.
- **Cold Foods** - If the internal temperature of cold food is 41°F (5°C) or higher, once it is removed from TC, cold food can remain out of temperature for up to 4 hours before being consumed or discarded. As a manager, you should have an approved written plan that details how this process is to be controlled and monitored. Remember, it must be eaten before or thrown out after 4 hours.
- **Cold Foods kept below 70°F (21.1°C)** - If the internal temperature of food is 41°F (5°C) or lower, once it is removed from TC it can remain out of temperature for up to 6 hours as long as the internal temperature does not go above 70°F (21.1°C). **You must have a written procedure in place**. Again, it must be eaten before or thrown out after 6 hours.

Cooling Food

Two-stage cooling allows TCS food to be in the temperature danger zone for more than 4 hours only if these strict guidelines are followed. Cool hot food from:

135°F to 70°F (57.2°C to 21.1°C) within 2 hours; you then have an additional 4 hours to go from 70°F to 41°F (21.1°C to 5°C) or lower for a maximum total cool time of 6 hours.

Have employee's cool food as quickly as possible. Keep in mind, **6 hours is the maximum amount of time, but only if it reaches 70°F (21.1°C) within 2 hours.** This additional 4 hours is because the food moves through the most dangerous section of the TDZ within the first two hours. Less time is better. Your employee's goal when cooling food is to move food as quickly as possible through the TDZ.

If the food does not reach 70°F (21.1°C) within 2 hours, the food must be either discarded or immediately reheated to 165°F (73.9°C) for 15 seconds and begin the cooling process again from that point.

Food cooled from room temperature [ambient, approximately ~70°F (21.1°C)] has a 4 hour cool time. An example is a can of tuna removed from dry storage used to make tuna salad. Once opened, you have 4 hours to bring the tuna/tuna salad down to 41°F (5°C) or below.

Did You Know...

Food must cool from above 135°F (57.2°C) to 70°F (21.1°C) in 2 hours otherwise harmful pathogens might grow.

Proper ways to cool food quickly

- Use a clean and sanitized ice paddle.
- Stir food to release the heat.
- Use an ice bath.
- Add ice as an ingredient.
- Use a quick-chill unit such as a blast chiller.
- Separate food into smaller portions or thinner pieces.

Once food has cooled to 70°F (21.1°C), it should be placed in the refrigerator as follows.

- Place food in shallow stainless steel pans (no more than 4 inches deep).
- Make sure the pan cover is loose to allow the heat to escape.
- Place pans on top shelves in refrigeration units.
- Position pans so air circulates around them. (Be cautious not to overload refrigerator tray racks.)
- Monitor food to ensure cooling to 41°F (5°C) or lower occurs as quickly as possible, so as not to exceed the two-stage cooling process.

The warmest food that can be placed in a refrigerator is 70°F (21.1°C); in a freezer, 41°F (5°C). If hot food is placed in a refrigerator or freezer, it will cause the equipment to work harder to cool the food. Also, the warm food will cause the temperature and any refrigerated or frozen food that is already stored there to rise. When this happens, the temperature of the properly stored food may rise into the temperature danger zone (TDZ). By taking this dangerous action one risks foodborne illness, ruining the food, and may damage the refrigerator or freezer.

Reheating for Hot Holding

The goal of reheating is to move food as quickly as possible through the TDZ. It is critical when reheating food for hot holding to reach a **minimum of 165°F (73.9°C) for 15 seconds within 2 hours**. If food takes longer than 2 hours to reheat (bring to the required internal temperature), it must be discarded or thrown away. Instruct your employees to use steam when possible to reheat food and not dry heat. Also, they should never use hot holding equipment to reheat (or cook) food, because the equipment is not designed to heat food rapidly.

Commercially prepared, hermetically sealed foods and foods in unopened packages from food processing plants that are RTE are considered cooked unless the label has cooking instructions. An example of this would be canned soup or frozen RTE chicken patties. If being reheated for hot holding, these types of food must be reheated to 135°F (57.2°C) or above within 2 hours and hot held at 135°F (57.2°C) or above.

Foods that are being reheated and **not hot held** (reheated to a customer's request) can be reheated (warmed) and served at any temperature. Only foods that will be hot held must be rapidly reheated before they are placed in hot holding units. You can take a cold pizza out of your refrigerator the next morning and eat it cold right away. If you want to warm up the pizza and keep it in the oven until your friends come over at lunchtime, then you need to reheat it to **165°F (73.9°C) for 15 seconds within 2 hours**.

Cleaning and Sanitizing Food Contact Surfaces and Equipment

Wash, Rinse, Sanitize

Clean and Sanitize! "Sparkle!"

Follow Proper Cleaning and Sanitizing Food Safety Rules

In order to have the safest healthiest environment for the preparation and service of food at your facility, it is important for your employees and you to follow proper cleaning and sanitizing food safety rules.

What Is Cleaning?

Cleaning is removing the soil, dirt, and other contaminates from items or surfaces. The expectation is for everything to look clean and to "sparkle!" A sparkling-clean food service or retail operation impresses every customer. To do this, clean all surfaces, equipment, and utensils every **4 hours** or when they become soiled or no longer sparkle. Your employees can use detergents or solvents or scraping to clean.

What Does It Mean to Sanitize?

Sanitizing is reducing any unseen germs or pathogens on a surface to a safe level. As a manager, have all your employees follow these proper procedures for sanitizing. Remember to always have them wash and rinse before they sanitize! They must:

1. Sanitize all things that come in contact with food, including utensils, cutting boards, and prep tables.
2. Clean and sanitize all equipment and utensils in contact with TCS foods at a minimum every **4 hours**.
3. Manually sanitize with water that is at least **171°F (77.2 °C) for 30 seconds** or use a chemical sanitizer.

Warning: Water temperature above 125°F (31.6°C) is a safety hazard that requires proper procedures to ensure worker safety.

4. When a dish machine is used, the sanitizing process will be based upon the manufacturer's specifications whether hot water or chemical sanitizer is used.

Your employees must follow the proper SOP for your food service or retail operation. There are five important points they must remember:

- Always use a **sanitizer test strip** when preparing a chemical sanitizer solution.
- Use **separate cloths** for food surfaces like a prep table and non-food surfaces like a wall or floor. Remember, cross contamination.
- Use a **designated sink system** like the three-compartment sink to clean and sanitize dishes and utensils. Never clean and sanitize dishes in the hand washing sink. Mop water can only be emptied into the utility sink, never in the three-compartment sink.

- Always **keep chemicals and food products separate**. Never receive cleaning products and chemicals on the same pallet as food. Remember, to prevent cross contamination, your employees should always be alert when receiving deliveries. This is a serious concern associated with the potential chemical contamination of deliveries.
- Keep copies of the **Safety Data Sheets** (SDS) for each chemical used on premises.

Manual Cleaning and Sanitizing Using a Three Compartment Sink

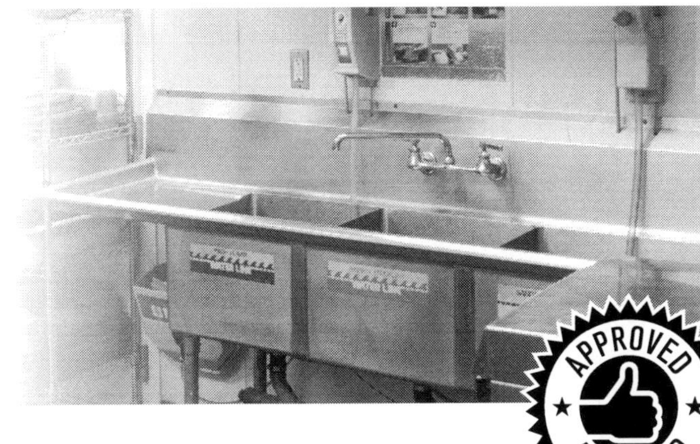

Step 1: Clean and sanitize entire sink and drain boards before starting.

Step 2: Scrape and rinse dirty dishes.

Step 3: Wash at 110°F (43.3°C) with soapy water.

Step 4: Rinse with clear water.

Step 5: Sanitize using your SOP.

Step 6: Air-dry.

Wiping Down Surfaces

Many surfaces throughout a food service or retail operation are wiped down regularly throughout the day. Simply because a surface is wiped down does not mean it is clean or sanitized.

The following practices DO NOT constitute cleaning and sanitizing:

- Using a reusable wet cloth and sanitizer;
- Using a dry cloth or disposable towel only; and
- Using dry disposable towels with a spray bottle of pre-mixed sanitizer solution.

Wiping Cloths

Wiping cloths are often stored improperly when not in use. An in-use wiping cloth, if not dry, must be:

- Stored in sanitizing solution of proper concentration; and
- Have the solution concentration periodically checked with an appropriate chemical test kit.

Chemicals

When working with chemicals (poisonous and toxic), prerequisite programs need to be in place and followed in order to prevent a chemical contamination or misuse. All operations should have a chemical management plan clearly stating that only approved chemicals necessary to the establishment should actually be in the establishment. Your program needs to outline the specific storage procedures of all chemicals in a secure cabinet away from all food and utensils. The prerequisite programs also must illustrate the proper use of the chemicals.

According to the Food Code, medicines necessary for the health of employees may be allowed in a food service or retail establishment. Medicines must be properly labeled and stored to prevent contamination of food and food contact surfaces. All chemicals should bear a legible manufacturer's label. All spray bottles, buckets, and working containers must be clearly labeled with the common name of the chemical. Chemicals must be stored in a separate location away from food and **never** use any bucket, bottle, sponge, or anything used to work with chemicals to prepare food.

Other chemical hazards include:

- **MSG**, or **monosodium glutamate** (used as a food additive/flavor enhancer);
- **Sulfites** or **sulfur dioxide** (used as a vegetable freshener/potato whitening agent); and
- **Latex** (latex residue can be transferred from the latex gloves to foods, such as tomatoes, before they are served).
    - It is recommended that employees not wear latex gloves when touching food.

Make sure chemicals are not being delivered or received on the same truck or pallet as food. Have your supplier verify that food is protected from chemical contamination during shipment. Any food that has been suspected or cross contaminated with chemicals should be rejected or discarded immediately. Discard chemicals used in working containers and mop buckets in an appropriate service sink to prevent contamination of food and food contact surfaces. Managers must make sure your employees are aware of the proper procedures when dealing with chemicals.

Pest Control

The pest control prerequisite program should define the established pest control system and the use of a pest control log. It also addresses the grounds surrounding your facility, blocks pest access into the facility, monitors, and maintains facilities on a regular basis. This prerequisite program must be coordinated with and work in cooperation with your licensed pest control operator (PCO). Your PCO should thoroughly survey and inspect the interior and exterior of your facility. It is necessary to develop a customized program based on detected problems, and to execute an effective treatment plan. Finally, enact preventative measures in place to maintain control over pests that may enter your facility during deliveries.

Let's go into further detail for your pest control prerequisite program:

- **Establish a pest control system.** This system must include routine inspections as well as daily cleaning as described in the master cleaning schedule. The chemicals and pesticides used to control the pests must be locked in a cabinet. Keep a copy of the corresponding Safety Data Sheets (SDS) on the premises. Dispose of empty containers according to local regulations and manufacturer's directions. Under no circumstances should any pest control products be kept in close proximity to food and must be clearly marked as pest control products to avoid accidental contamination.
- **Use a pest control log.** Document the pest control actions taken by your PCO. File the pest control records with the HACCP records.
- **Maintain the grounds in good condition.** Properly landscape the outside of your facility. For example, tall grass provides excellent nesting and hiding places for pests.
- **Block access of pests into facility.** Keep windows and doors closed. Seal all openings into the facility to

prevent future entry of pests, rodents, or unwanted pets. Ensure that any rodents/pests that may have entered the facility are no longer present. Remove dead pests and sanitize any food contact surfaces that have come in contact with pests.

- **Monitor and maintain facilities regularly.** Condition of the physical structure of the establishment should be in compliance with local building and occupancy codes. This should not compromise the safe and sanitary handling of food and equipment, and the safety of employees. Conduct routine inspections of the facility.

Serving Food and Operating Self-Service Bars

Serving Food

Can you answer YES to any of these questions?

- Are dinner plates and/or coffee cups stacked when serving food and drink to customers?
- Are the server's fingers on the top or edge of the plate in the food?
- Are customers served, tables cleared, the phone answered, and payments taken without washing hands?
- Are rolls, unwrapped butter, and uneaten garnishes (pickles) from plates recycled?
- Are utensils, towels, or order pads stored in pockets or waistband?

If you answered YES to any of these questions, the food at your establishment is not being served safely. Do not let food safety end in the kitchen! Everyone in the food service or retail operation has an important role of food safety. Servers should never stack dinner plates and cups on top of one another, or on arms, or carry too many in one hand. This leads to cross contamination of foods.

Today's customer is more educated and more aware of servers who bus tables and then touch plates or glasses as they deliver food without washing their hands between each task. This same customer is also aware of the server who answers the phone, writes down an order, prepares the food, uses the cash register, and collects the money while wearing the same pair of gloves he or she wore when going through the same routine for the three previous customers. Think about the serving practices that need improvement in your food service or retail operation.

Never reuse food that has been served and left at the table when the customer leaves. For example food such as rolls, unwrapped butter, and uneaten pickle garnishes should be removed and discarded. To avoid cross contamination and foodborne illness, the safest rule to follow is that any food that leaves your food service or retail establishment or your control should never be served to another customer.

All utensils must be carried by the handle, carry all glasses by the side, and carry all plates from the bottom. Do not store utensils and cloths in your pockets or in the waistband of your clothes.

There is no place at any food service or retail facility for pets. The only animals permitted in a facility should be approved working guide dogs and then only allowed in the serving area.

Food Safety for Self-Service Areas

As trained servers, managers, supervisors, and owners, we are aware of the dangers of foodborne illness and the proper ways to avoid the dangers and lessen the risk. Customers, on the other hand, do not have the benefit of your training and do not understand the dangers of cross contamination, poor proper hygiene, and foodborne illness. Think of all the potential problems that can occur at salad bars, beverage stations, and condiment areas. Since we cannot "train" a customer on how to properly and safely handle food in these areas, signage is important. For example, "Please use a new plate when returning to the salad bar," is appropriate; as well as, "Please use tongs to pick up food."

It is also very important that employees are vigilant in maintaining all self-service areas.

In order to keep food safe at self-service food bars and buffets:

1. Separate raw meats and fish from cooked and ready-to-eat food. There are very few raw animal foods that can safely be on self-service bars. They might include shellfish raw bars, Mongolian barbecues, and sushi bars. These raw items, though RTE, should be separated from cooked RTE foods.

2. Monitor the customers at the self-service area and eliminate any item that has been contaminated. Monitor customers for unsanitary hygiene practices, such as the following:

    - Tasting items;
    - Handling food like bread with their bare hands;
    - Putting fingers directly into the food; and
    - Reusing plates and utensils; instead, hand out fresh plates to customers.

Note: Act immediately, if you see a food being contaminated by a customer. Discretely remove the product and alert the PIC.

3. Label all food items. Every item must be labeled, so customers will not "taste it" for identification purposes.

4. Ensure every item on a buffet has its own serving utensil. Serving utensil handles should be long enough to not slide down in the food. The handle should always be up and out of the food.

5. Maintain proper temperatures. Monitor and check frequently.

6. Practice First-In First-Out (FIFO) rotation of products. Always use the oldest product first. When refilling, do not mix the old food and new food together.

7. Do not store an in-use utensil in a container of water with or without sanitizer. In-use utensils (like ice cream scoops and rice spoons) must be kept in cold running water. Other alternatives might exist, but check with your regulator for other approved options for in-use utensil storage.

8. Maintain the cleanliness of the area without contaminating any food with cleaner.

9. The Food Code requires that consumer self-service operations such as buffets and salad bars shall be monitored by a food employee who is trained in safe food procedures.

Star Point 1 Conclusion

We now know the dangers associated with serving unsafe or contaminated food. We know that food may become unsafe accidentally because of cross contamination, poor personal hygiene, improper cleaning and sanitizing, and time-temperature abuse. It is important that you keep the food, yourself, other employees, and your customer's safe at all times. We do this by having well thought out and properly written prerequisite programs and standard operating procedures. Now that you have read this chapter, let's see how much you know about food safety.

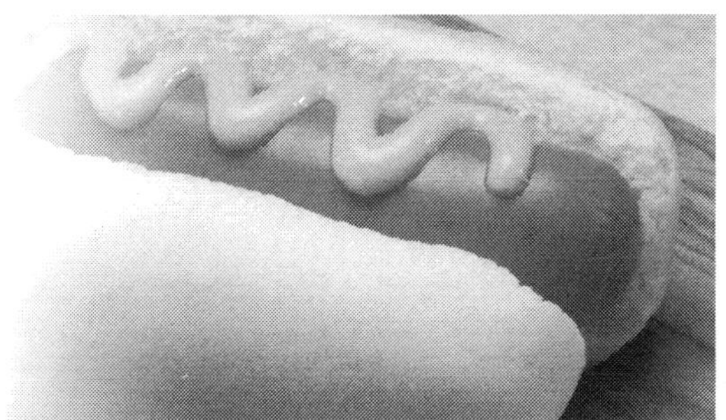

Star Knowledge Exercise:

Food Safety - What Should I Do If

Circle the risk factor(s) that apply to the situation and write in what you would do to correct the problem.

Situation	Risk Factors: **a.** Cross contamination **b.** Poor personal hygiene **c.** Improper cleaning and sanitizing **d.** Time-temperature abuse	What do you do to correct the situation? Make it a "REAL" solution!
1. You are stocking shelves with shredded cheese and notice the expiration date has passed.	**a.** Cross contamination **b.** Poor personal hygiene **c.** Improper cleaning and sanitizing **d.** Time-temperature abuse	
2. A fly lands on the cutting board at the prep table.	**a.** Cross contamination **b.** Poor personal hygiene **c.** Improper cleaning and sanitizing **d.** Time-temperature abuse	
3. An employee's hat looks stained from automotive oil.	**a.** Cross contamination **b.** Poor personal hygiene **c.** Improper cleaning and sanitizing **d.** Time-temperature abuse	
4. At 3 p.m., you find a pan of luncheon meats left on the prep table. Lunch service started at 10:30 a.m.	**a.** Cross contamination **b.** Poor personal hygiene **c.** Improper cleaning and sanitizing **d.** Time-temperature abuse	

Situation	Risk Factors: **a.** Cross contamination **b.** Poor personal hygiene **c.** Improper cleaning and sanitizing **d.** Time-temperature abuse	What do you do to correct the situation? Make it a "REAL" solution!
5. The clean apron supply is stored in the prep area. A fellow manager walks into the prep area tying their apron.	**a.** Cross contamination **b.** Poor personal hygiene **c.** Improper cleaning and sanitizing **d.** Time-temperature abuse	
6. A customer returns a hot roast beef sandwich because it is cold.	**a.** Cross contamination **b.** Poor personal hygiene **c.** Improper cleaning and sanitizing **d.** Time-temperature abuse	
7. The sanitizer solution is supposed to be 200ppm (parts per million). You see a new coworker set up the three-compartment sink and pour the sanitizer into the sink rinse water.	**a.** Cross contamination **b.** Poor personal hygiene **c.** Improper cleaning and sanitizing **d.** Time-temperature abuse	
8. A meatloaf was partially cooked and properly cooled. An employee then cooked the meatloaf to an internal temperature of 135°F (65.3°C) for service.	**a.** Cross contamination **b.** Poor personal hygiene **c.** Improper cleaning and sanitizing **d.** Time-temperature abuse	
9. You have your employee clean the exhaust hood and filters. A customer rushes in and places an order.	**a.** Cross contamination **b.** Poor personal hygiene **c.** Improper cleaning and sanitizing **d.** Time-temperature abuse	
10. An employee is angry with a disgruntled customer and licks the luncheon meat that is being used to make the customer's sandwich.	**a.** Cross contamination **b.** Poor personal hygiene **c.** Improper cleaning and sanitizing **d.** Time-temperature abuse	

Star Point 1 Check for Understanding

(Circle one.)

1. HACCP stands for ______________________.

- **a.** Hazard Analysis, Cooking and Cooling Procedures
- **b.** Hazard Analysis and Critical Control Procedure
- **c.** Help Analyze Chicken Cooking Points
- **d.** Hazard Analysis and Critical Control Point

2. Standard Operating Procedures (SOP) are __________.

- **a.** unacceptable practices and procedures for your operation
- **b.** written document regarding your employment
- **c.** seven steps in the food flow process
- **d.** written methods of controlling a practice in accordance with predetermined specifications to obtain a desired outcome

3. Which of the following is NOT a Big 6 Pathogen?

- **a.** E. Coli
- **b.** Shigella
- **c.** Norovirus
- **d.** Hepatitis B
- **e.** Salmonella Typhi (Typhoid Fever)

4. The Temperature Danger Zone (TDZ) is ____________.

- **a.** 0°F – 212°F (-17.7°C – 100°C)
- **b.** 41°F – 165°F (5°C – 73.8°C)
- **c.** 41°F – 135°F (5°C – 57.2°C)
- **d.** 70°F – 125°F (21.1°C – 51.6°C)

5. Prerequisite programs ______________________.

- **a.** require that all food employees take a national food safety exam
- **b.** require that all food employees have a physical exam before beginning work in a food facility
- **c.** are procedures, including standard operating procedures, that address basic operational and sanitation conditions in an establishment
- **d.** both a and c

6. Which of the following is NOT a TCS food?

- **a.** Chicken patty
- **b.** Hamburger
- **c.** Pickled beets
- **d.** Cut lettuce
- **e.** Cut tomatoes

7. A foodborne illness outbreak occurs when __________.

- **a.** dinner guests eat the same food and get sick after eating it
- **b.** one person eats a food that makes them sick
- **c.** five or more people eat the same food and get the same illness
- **d.** two or more people eat the same food and get the same illness

8. What are the three basic categories of hazards that might be identified in a HACCP Plan?

- **a.** Bacteria, Virus, Fungus
- **b.** Chemical, Physical, Biological
- **c.** Biological, Physical, Viral
- **d.** Virus, Parasite, Bacteria

9. What is the symbol for the measure of acidity or alkalinity based on a scale of 0 to 14?

- **a.** a_w
- **b.** PH
- **c.** pH
- **d.** AW
- **e.** °F

10. What is it called when two or more independent variables work together to make a food non-TCS?

- **a.** Hurdle Effect
- **b.** Acidification
- **c.** FATTOM
- **d.** Available Water

HACCP Star Point 2:
Food Defense and Crisis Management

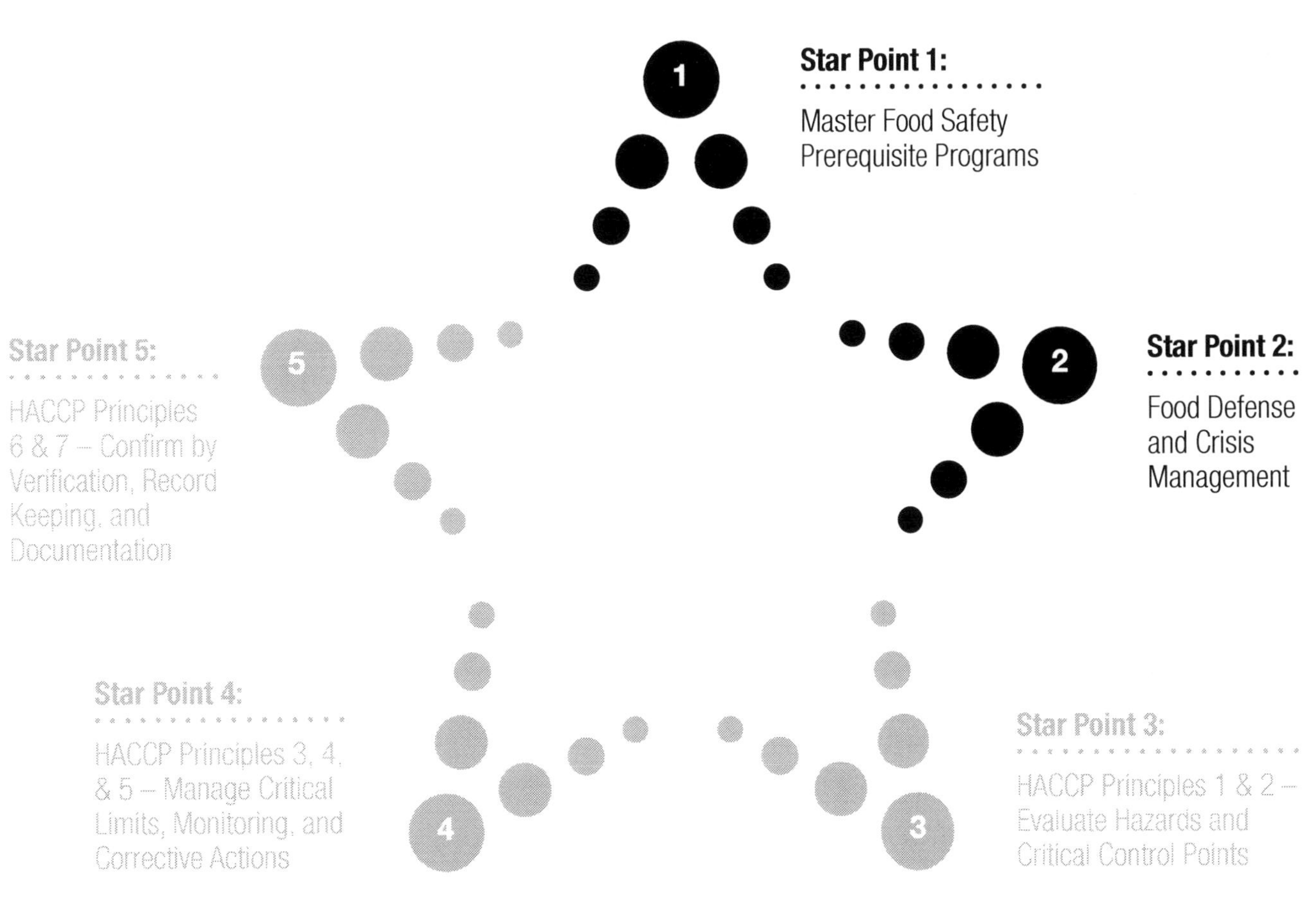

Star Point 2 Myth or Fact (Check one.)

1. Food defense accepts and does not address managers and employees with the belief and attitude "It Won't Happen to Me" in "My Operation".
   ___**Myth** ___**Fact**

2. To decrease vulnerabilities in the operation management should develop a food defense plan as part of their HACCP plan.
   ___**Myth** ___**Fact**

3. Management does not need to be concerned with insider compromise or possible outside threats.
   ___**Myth** ___**Fact**

4. Crisis management is an organized and systematic effort to restrict the possibility of a likely crisis; manage and conclude existing crisis; as well as evaluate and learn from a crisis incident.
   ___**Myth** ___**Fact**

5. The Food Safety Modernization Act's (FSMA) goal is to ensure the U.S. food supply is safe by shifting the concentration of federal regulators from being reactive to proactive.
   ___**Myth** ___**Fact**

Star Point 2 Goals: You will learn to

- Identify sources of potential threats of food contamination in your organization.
- Appreciate the federal action taken by the U.S. government to protect our food.
- Differentiate between food defense, food security, food safety, and alleged contamination or hoaxes.
- Recognize the importance of food defense in all aspects of the food industry—from the farm to the patron's table.
- Reverse the "it won't happen to me" attitude.
- Identify your role in food defense as a responsible leader.
- Determine how to handle different food defense situations.
- Identify appropriate food defense standard operating procedures to teach employees when training them in today's world.
- Investigate food recall procedures and what is needed in your operation.
- Create a crisis management plan in case a food crisis occurs at your establishment.

We in the food industry must be concerned with what the U.S. Department of Homeland Security calls food security and food defense standard operating procedures. As a responsible manager, you must be aware of the safety issues in your food service or retail operation, food industry, and the entire country. We must work as a team. Each of us must do our part, from the farm to our table, to stop any potential deliberate food contamination. In this chapter, we discuss documented acts of food terrorism and how we can, through a well thought out and developed HACCP plan, prevent, eliminate, and reduce the threat of intentional food contamination. It is important for you to recognize that as a food handler, supervisor, manager, director, and leader in the food service or retail industry, it is your responsibility to take action to prevent acts of food terrorism from occurring.

Federal Action Taken to Protect Our Food

The FDA's plan, "Protecting and Advancing America's Health: A Strategic Action Plan for the 21st Century," outlines various steps the agency is taking to respond to the food defense challenges faced in today's world.

Evolution of Food Defense

2002	FDA Bioterrorism Act
	FSIS Security Guidelines for Food Processors
2003	DHS Homeland Security Presidential Directive 7 (HSPD 7) DHS Homeland Security Presidential Directive 8 (HSPD 8) FSIS Safety and Security Guidelines for Transportation and Distribution FDA Guidance for Industry: Retail Food Stores and Food Service Establishments: Food Security Preventive Measures Guidance (December 2003; Revised October 2007)
2004	DHS Homeland Security Presidential Directive 9 (HSPD 9) FDA Administrative Detention FDA Establishment and Maintenance of Records (Final Rule)
2005	FDA Registration of Food Facilities (Final Rule)
2006	FSIS / FDA Guidelines for the Disposal of Intentionally Adulterated Food Products and the Decontamination of Food Processing Facilities
2007	FDA/FSIS CARVER + Shock Vulnerability Assessment Tool
2008	FSIS – Guide to Developing a Food Defense Plan FDA Prior Notice of Imported Food (Final Rule)
2009	FSIS Food Defense Guidelines for Slaughter and Processing
2010	FDA Reportable Food Electronic Portal If You See Something Say Something
2011	Food Safety Modernization Act Food Emergency Response Plan Template (NASDA)

Food Safety Modernization Act (FSMA)

The events of September 11, 2001 reinforced the need for enhanced security in the United States. Congress responded to this security need by passing the Public Health Security and Bioterrorism Preparedness and Response Act of 2002 (the Bioterrorism Act). This landmark legislation provided the FDA with new and significant resources to help protect the nation's food supply from the threat of intentional contamination and other food-related emergencies.

The Food Safety Modernization Act (FSMA) was signed into Law in 2011. Its goals are to ensure the US food supply is safe by shifting the concentration of federal regulators from responding to contamination to preventing it protectively rather than reactively. FSMA encompasses many rules for both animal and human food. These rules include: Registration of Domestic and Foreign Facilities, Preventive Controls for Human and Animal Foods, Produce Safety, Foreign Supplier Verification Program, Accredited 3rd Party Certification, Intentional Adulteration, and Sanitary Transportation of Human and Animal Food. These rules apply to any facility who manufacturers, processes, packs or holds food for consumption.

Are these new enhanced regulations only concerned with foreign terrorists doing harm to the food supply? The answer is no. Long before September 11, 2011 there have been cases of intentional contamination from citizens who mean to do harm to others. As you will see in the next section, one must be vigilant not only to foreign sponsored food terrorism but domestic situations as well. A prime example could be a disgruntled employee.

Food Defense vs. Food Security vs. Food Safety vs. Hoaxes

Food Defense

Food Defense is the **protection** of food products from **intentional** adulteration/contamination.

Why is Food Defense important and why should you be prepared and take action?

Terrorist attacks can occur at any time during the various stages of the food chain from farm to table. It can be foreign or domestic and can take place in the cultivation of crops, the raising of livestock, or in the distributing, processing, retailing, transporting, and storing of the food product. It is crucial to practice food defense during all phases of the farm to table chain to ensure that food is safe.

Why would someone target the food supply?

Some of the reasons are:

- Some people are mentally ill and for no understandable reason mean to do harm;
- Significant public health consequences because everyone eats;
- Instill widespread fear;
- Political;
- Result in a loss of public confidence in the food industry and governments' ability to protect the public; and
- Money, which can lead to devastating economic consequences and disruption in trade, resulting in an increase in food insecurity.

Examples of intentional incidents include:

Year	
2010	A disgruntled restaurant employee contaminated salsa with pesticide. This incident caused a reported 48 people to become ill.
2007	A disgruntled temporary employee contaminated Gyoza better known as "Japanese potstickers" three times with a pesticide. This incident caused a reported 10 people to become ill and the investigation of 586 individuals that had access to the refrigeration room.
2003	A disgruntled supermarket employee contaminated 200 pounds of ground beef with a nicotine-based pesticide. This incident caused a reported 92 people to become il.
1993	A disgruntled former employee contaminated a tray of doughnuts and muffins with *Shigella dysenteriae* Type 2, which caused 12 employees to suffer severe gastrointestinal illness and 4 employees were hospitalized.
1984	Several cult members in Oregon added *salmonella* to several restaurant salad bars in an attempt to affect the outcome of local elections. This incident caused 751 illnesses and hospitalization of 45 people.

Food Security

Food security is defined by the World Health Organization (WHO) as "The implication that all people, at all times, have both physical and economic access to enough food for an active, healthy life." Internationally, food security means a **2-year supply of food** in a particular country.

Unlike the rest of the world, the United States originally referred to food defense as food security. This terminology shifted when the U.S. government realized that food security was not compatible when the term was used in other parts of the world. While food security and food defense may be used interchangeably depending on where you are in the world, the common goal is to prevent the deliberate contamination of food and to make sure the food we serve is safe.

Food Safety

Food Safety is **protection** of food products from **unintentional or accidental** contamination. Note the distinction; food defense is the protection of food products from **intentional** contamination.

Examples of unintentional incidents include:

Year	
2009	*Salmonella typhimurium* caused more than 714 confirmed illnesses and 9 deaths in 46 states. All the victims consumed either peanut butter or peanut paste.
2008	Milk powder contaminated with the chemical melamine caused more than 300,000 confirmed illnesses and 6 infant deaths in China. All the victims consumed tainted milk.

Year	
2003	Hepatitis A caused more than 650 confirmed illnesses and 4 deaths in seven states. All the victims consumed raw or undercooked onions.
1994	*Salmonella enteritidis* caused 150 confirmed illnesses when the pasteurized ice cream mix produced at one facility became cross contaminated.
1985	*Salmonella typhimurium* caused more than 16,000 confirmed illnesses and 17 deaths in six states. All the victims consumed re-contaminated pasteurized milk from milk produced at one dairy plant.

Hoaxes

Hoaxes are **false accusations** or **fraudulent reports** of deliberate contamination of food. Although hoaxes do not cause any physical harm (make people sick), they can damage or destroy the reputation of a facility, create panic in the community, and instill fear.

By way of a real life example, Company XYZ was victimized by a hoax when a customer announced on social media that they had found a horrifying foreign object in the food. This caused widespread panic and a large portion of the population stopped using the product. The person that instigated the hoax then made a personal injury claim against the company demanding a large cash settlement. Although caught and confronted, this hoax damaged the employees (the business shut down temporarily), the company, and the brand (people stopped eating the food product as a result of negative press). The food service and retail industries can be damaged if people lose confidence in the food supply. When hoaxes happen the damages are far reaching and affect everyone!

According to the United States General Accounting Office Resources, Community, and Economic Development Division: "Threats of contamination with a biological agent occur infrequently: from October 1995 through March 1999, federal agencies reported receiving three such threats—two of these were hoaxes, and the other is still an open investigation." More common are incidents using physical objects to contaminate food.

The Center for Disease Control and Prevention, and the National Center for Infectious Diseases, reported that an e-mail rumor circulating about Costa Rican bananas causing the disease necrotizing fasciitis, also known as flesh-eating bacteria, was false. Again, hoaxes are costly to the industry and/or the establishment related to the allegation, the employees in the industry, and the government agency that investigates the false claim.

When handling reported incidents, you must train your employees to act responsibly. They should be trained to report all incidents or suspected incidents, regardless of how farfetched they may appear. In all cases, they must notify the person-in-charge.

Importance of Food Defense

Why is Food Defense Important?

Consider the following scenarios that occur daily in food service or retail facilities that may lead to potential threats and are hazardous. Do any of these occur in your facility?

- Someone leaves the kitchen door open for a long period of time.
- A customer or a coworker exhibits strange behavior around the food.
- You do not recognize a person who is in your kitchen.
- You do not check to make sure your deliveries are safe and intact.
- There is no designated employee who monitors salad bars and food displays.
- Chemicals are stored near the food in your operation.
- Chemicals are not properly labeled.

As the manager of a facility, you have an obligation to put into practice food defense SOPs to ensure food defense. You must avoid and prohibit practices, like those listed above, to ensure that the food being served is safe. If a well thought out and implemented food defense program is not included in the HACCP plan, the risk that people may become ill or die from consuming contaminated food from your food service or retail operation increases.

Some other consequences of food contamination include:

- Financial devastation of the establishment;
- Lack of consumer and governmental trust; and
- Potentially, the destruction of an entire global industry.

Practicing food defense is very simple. If you know how a food defense system works, are alert, and pay attention to your surroundings, fellow employees, and customers, you can help to ensure these disasters do not occur.

Having an "It Won't Happen to Me" Attitude Can Be Very Dangerous!

The, "it won't happen to me attitude," of managers and employees in a food service or retail establishment can create vulnerability when it comes to food safety. It is natural to become complacent and think that nothing bad will happen to you or your establishment. However, this attitude can lead to disaster. Food terrorism can potentially occur when there is:

- **Lack of awareness.**
  If managers and employees are not concerned about the condition of their workplace, they likely will not concern themselves with food defense either. The employee who thinks it is not his or her job to worry about food defense and the management team that does not have sufficient food defense procedures in place together makes the food supply of the operation extremely vulnerable.
- **Limited budget for food defense measures.**
  Because many facilities have limited capital, they may not have budgeted for food defense. Since it is new to food service and retail industries, its importance is not fully understood. This has a direct impact on the food service and retail establishment's profit-and-loss statement, and additional sales must be made to recoup the difference.
- **Lack of training.**
  Management's lack of knowledge about food defense may limit employees abilities to provide appropriate food defense because the team does not know or understand why it is important. It is critical to educate your employees about the key principles of food defense and overall awareness of your customers, fellow employees, and your surroundings. It's important to let employees know that the typical aggressor, the one wanting to contaminate the food in your establishment, relies on employees who are distracted and careless.

Your Responsibilities as a Manager

Be alert and aware. Managers should make efforts to inform and involve staff in all aspects of food defense. This means you should talk about food defense awareness with all team members on a regular basis. An informed and alert team is more likely to detect weaknesses in a food defense system, and properly detect signs of intentional or unintentional contamination. Employees should be encouraged to report suspicious activity, possible product tampering, or suspected security system weaknesses to management. Provided in Appendix 3 of this book is a Food Defense Self-Inspection Checklist. Use this tool to evaluate your facility.

Keys to a successful defense program include the following:

- **Encourage communication.**
  Communication among all employees will help identify and correct food defense issues, raise awareness, and decrease vulnerabilities in the food defense plan. Communication also helps employees understand how important their job responsibilities are to the success of the overall operation. This realization will also help improve their food defense behaviors and attitudes.

- **Decrease vulnerabilities.**
  To decrease vulnerabilities, management should develop a food defense plan as part of their HACCP plan. The plan should include a **recall strategy**. Staff should be **trained** on the points of the strategy. The strategy should be tested regularly, in the form of a **practical drill**. Since potential threats, the physical facility itself, and the operations within the facility may change over time, the food defense plan should be **examined and tested at least once a year**.

- **Decrease availability of potential contaminants.**
  When training employees, managers need to stress the importance of storing all potential contaminants, such as cleaning and pest control chemicals, in **secure storage areas** that are locked. Supplies of contaminants stored on the premises should be limited to only what is needed. You should not keep a large inventory of these products. It is critical that these products are **stored away from food properly labeled, and kept in a locked area**. Access to storage areas for these potential contaminants should be limited to those who need access, based on their job function.

These storage areas should be accessed by **employees only**, and should be far away from the public areas in your establishment. Large amounts of cleaning/chemical products added to the inventory must be controlled and managed. Proper inventory control helps management easily identify any missing products. Additionally, any unneeded items should be properly disposed of to prevent misuse. Keep in mind: readily available cleaning and pest control chemicals are often the contaminant of choice for a disgruntled employee who may want to get back at a manager or coworker by contaminating the food.

Management Must Identify Possible Inside Threats

Insider compromise occurs when an employee (an insider) takes deliberate action to contaminate food or assists outsiders in deliberately contaminating food. In other words, it's an "inside job." The best way to prevent this is **constant supervision** of people working in your establishment. This includes all employees, new and long-term, cleaning or maintenance staff, and vendors. Managers should be particularly aware of a person's unexplained:

- Hours (coming in early or staying late);
- Use of camera phones, cameras, or video recorders at work;
- Probing with inappropriate questions;
- Admission to areas where they do not belong and for no reason; and
- Removal of standard operating procedures, documents, and policies from the facility.

In addition, managers should do the following:

- **Conduct employee background checks.**
  All current and potential employees, especially those with the most access to all areas of your establishment, should be screened. Based on the screening of their record and past behaviors, you can predict possible future behaviors. The first line of defense is a comprehensive employment screening policy that is clearly written by human resources and checked through a legal counsel to make sure that it complies with local laws, and is applicable to all employees. A policy is only good if it is followed; therefore, when checking employment history, follow the company SOPs.

- **Keep track of employees.**
  Management should also keep track of who is and who should be on duty, and where each employee should be working by paying close attention to the prepared schedule (schedules, people charts, deployment charts, etc.). If a disgruntled employee plans to contaminate a product, he or she may plan the attack in an area not normally associated with his or her job. Be vigilant for employees found in an area outside of their normal work station without explanation.

- **Restrict personal items at the workplace.**
  Personal items should always be restricted in your establishment. Not only do personal items increase the risk of unintentional contamination, but a disgruntled employee might plan to intentionally contaminate products by bringing the contaminant into the facility using personal items such as a purse, backpack, or knapsack.

Management policy must include the authority to inspect all employee lockers and should do this periodically or if an employee is suspected of foul play. A disgruntled employee with the intention of contaminating food may use his or her locker as a temporary storage location for a contaminant that he or she has managed to bring into the facility. Managers should check with their legal counsel or human resource department for proper procedures and required notifications that must be given to employees.

Management Must Identify Possible Outside Threats

It is important for management to understand, communicate, and train team members to realize the potential for an exterior attack or a deliberate contamination of food initiated by someone working outside the establishment. These people could include vendors, suppliers, and delivery drivers.

To help avoid exterior attacks, managers should establish policies that include the following:

- **Purchase products only from approved licensed sources.**
  An unknown source may claim it is a legitimate business but may offer counterfeit or contaminated food at a reduced price.

- **Encourage suppliers to practice food defense.**
  Where do your suppliers get the products that they deliver to your establishment? Suppliers should be encouraged to practice food defense. Contamination of food can occur at a supplier's facility, and the contaminated food can then be delivered to your establishment. You should require that specific security measures are part of every supplier's contract.

- **Inspect delivery vehicles.**
  Delivery vehicles should be properly inspected and secured. Locked and/or sealed vehicles keep food from being contaminated while en route to your

establishment. A sealed container that is broken could indicate a shipment has been altered or tampered with. When seals are used, compare the seal numbers on the truck or package with the invoice. They should match. Reject the delivery if the seal numbers do not match, if the lock has been removed, or if there is a potential security breach. Always err on the side of caution.

- **Know in advance when deliveries are being made.**
  Management should create pickup and delivery schedules in advance. **Unscheduled pickups or deliveries should be questioned**. Delivering counterfeit or contaminated food may result in a delay of delivery, due to switching or tampering with the load and/or replacing the original driver (i.e., a hijacked load). The manager should know when a delivery is due, as well as the name of the driver. Management should question anything out of the ordinary.

- **Supervise deliveries.**
  A designated employee or member of management should **supervise offloading of deliveries**. There are a number of reasons to have such a policy; contamination can occur during offloading, especially if it occurs after hours; establishing a policy insures the food product does not violate time temperature control for safety, and ensuring that the proper products are delivered in the proper quantities and safely. The food type and quantity received should **match** what is listed on the invoice.

- **Inspect deliveries.**
  A designated employee or member of management should **inspect food, packaging, and paperwork** when accepting a delivery. Those attempting to contaminate food may leave signs of contamination on the food. Such indicators are abnormal powders, liquids, stains, or odors that accompany the food or evidence that tamper-resistant packaging has been resealed. Counterfeit food may contain improper or mismatched product identity, labeling, or coding. In other words, you may open a can that is supposed to contain peaches, but it contains pizza sauce instead. You should also be aware of invoices with suspicious changes, as these may accompany counterfeit or contaminated loads.

- **Put fencing up around nonpublic areas.**
  Perimeter fencing should be place around nonpublic areas of your establishment. This is the first line of defense against an attack by an intruder. The establishment should take measures to protect doors, windows, roof and vent openings, and other access points, including access to food storage (portable refrigeration units, walk-ins, tanks, and bins) outside the building(s). Locks, alarms, video surveillance, and guards can also keep intruders out.

- **Secure access to all utilities and systems.**
  All utilities including gas, electric, water, and airflow systems should be secured. The greatest concern is the water supply because hazards introduced to water can be passed on to the food.

- **Provide sufficient lighting.**
  Good interior and exterior lighting will deter those who want to cause harm. A brightly lit establishment will help prevent an attack. It will also be easier to detect intruders before they can contaminate any of the products.

- **Create a system of identification.**
  Management should provide a means of employee identification, such as a **uniform and name tag**. Requiring employees to wear identification will help in identifying any intruders.

- **Restrict entry.**
  Entry to nonpublic areas of the establishment should be restricted. Ladders accessing the roof of your facility must be locked at all times. **Security checkpoints** should be created, and designated employees should walk with all visitors through nonpublic areas of the establishment. You should make sure those visitors are whom they claim and that their visit has a valid purpose. This will prevent those with criminal intent from entering the establishment. Always check identification!

- **Examine packages or briefcases.**
  Since a visitor may conceal a contaminant in a package or briefcase that he or she brings into the establishment, management should examine packages that are left in nonpublic areas. If you see a package or briefcase that seems suspicious, follow your corporate policies and procedures.

- **Monitor public areas.**
  Public areas should be monitored for suspicious activity. A customer who wants to contaminate food may return food that he or she has already contaminated to a shelf. Other suspicious activities include a customer spending a considerable amount of time in one part of the establishment contaminating food. Self-service areas (i.e., salad bars, product display areas, etc.), in particular, should be monitored. As mentioned earlier in this chapter, intentional contamination of a self-service location has already occurred in the United States.

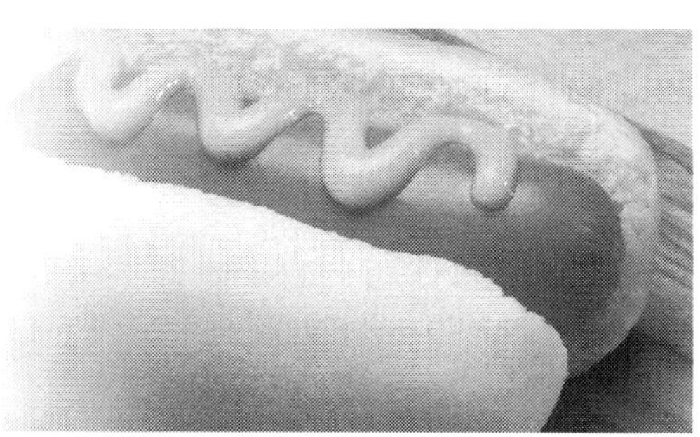

Star Knowledge Exercise:

Food Defense Reality Check

Read the scenario below and answer the questions regarding food defense concerns that relate to this situation. While reading the scenario, keep in mind if there are some actions that Rich or Dan can take to run a safer operation.

Reality Check

Rich figured that his pounding headache and slight nausea were the result of rooting for the winning team in last night's big game. After celebrating with a beer and squeezing in 4 hours of sleep, he opened the restaurant at 6:00 a.m. this morning. Not only was it a rainy morning, but he was late, so he missed the delivery truck. Since Rich wasn't at the restaurant when the driver arrived, the order was left outside in the pouring rain. Once Rich dragged the delivery inside, he quickly realized that last night's crew rushed to close the restaurant so they could all go home to watch the big game. They had done an unacceptable cleaning job. Food was not put away, floors were not swept, and they forgot to "jimmy" the broken door handle on the walk-in with the screwdriver. (Rich makes a mental note to get that repaired.)

Later, Rich checked the phone messages:

- **Message 1.** His closer from last night told him to call a plumber—all the restroom toilets are clogged.
- **Message 2.** His assistant, Christine, who was at the same party as Rich, called to say she was very ill and couldn't come into work today.
- **Message 3.** The printing company said the new menus were printed with the old prices and they will not be ready until late next week.

Needless to say, Rich's headache was getting worse. As the day progressed, Rich encountered disgruntled customers who had to wait too long for their food because several workers called in sick. He told his staff to do whatever it took to get the orders out. In the meantime, another delivery arrived and Rich tipped the driver to put the food away for him, since he was just too busy to check it in himself. Then, two customers complained about cold food.

Eventually, Rich begged his brother-in-law, Dan, to come in and help. Dan never worked in a restaurant before, but he caught on very quickly. He helped put deliveries away, served customers, bused tables, and made sandwiches. Dan thought it was really nice of the new pest control sales representative to leave some samples of a new product for them to test when he stopped by for a visit. He put them on the worktable so Rich could see them later. Since Dan wasn't used to working in such a hot kitchen, he left the back door open to give everyone some relief. As he opened the door, he overheard Rich and a recently fired employee arguing outside. Dan told a waitress to take over making sandwiches so he could talk to them and attempt to break up the fight. Rich would not let the hostile employee inside to get his last paycheck. Instead he let his girlfriend come into the office and pick it up.

Rich then had to excuse himself because he was still feeling ill. He returned to sign the check. The girlfriend walked through the kitchen, into the dining room, and out the front door to her awaiting boyfriend. He yelled some obscenities before driving off in a rage and crashing into three parked cars, disrupting traffic.

Rich's headache was not getting any better. The police and local news crew came in for information. Apparently, the recently terminated employee had an outstanding arrest warrant from a neighboring state. Rich pleaded with the news crew to stay outside while he talked to the police privately in his office. Rich removed a strange large black duffel bag from the chair in his office and sat down to give as much information as possible. Meanwhile, the news crew was getting plenty of footage from the chaos in front of the restaurant, and from wary customers who said things like "I knew something was wrong today," "The service and the food were terrible," and "This place probably does the 'breath test' and hires any one that breathes." Rich was sure he would be feeling much worse before he started feeling any better. Based on the situation described, answer the following two questions.

1. What food safety standard operating procedures should be put in place so Rich can run a safer operation?

____

____

____

____

2. What food defense standard operating procedures can Rich initiate to run a safer operation?

____

____

____

____

Training Employees in Food Defense

As a leader, you need to coach and train your employees as to why it is important to prepare, serve, and sell safe food. All those who work in the food industry must understand that food defense not only protects you but also your family, your business, and the food service or retail industry. Proper training helps develop a culture in your business that promotes proper food defense. The FDA recommends that you take food defense steps to ensure the safety of your customers, your coworkers, and ultimately the country. When you, as the leader, train your employees, it's important to cover the following:

- Employee Awareness SOP
- Customer Awareness SOP
- Vendor Awareness SOP
- Facility Awareness SOP

The Food Defense Employee Training Form is provided for you to train your employees in applying food defense. This ready-to-use form will assist you in covering all of the necessary food defense standard operating procedures.

Food Defense Employee Training Form

Establishment's Name: ______________________________

Employee Name: ______________________ Employee ID#: ______________

Employee Awareness SOP:	*Employee Initials:* ________
• Be a responsible employee. Communicate any potential food defense issues to your manager.	________
• Be aware of your surroundings and pay close attention to customers and employees who are acting suspiciously.	________
• Limit the amount of personal items you bring into your work establishment.	________
• Be aware of who is working at any given time and where (in what area) they are supposed to be working.	________
• Monitor the salad bar and food displays.	________
• Make sure labeled chemicals are in a designated storage area.	________
• Make sure you and your coworkers are following company guidelines. If you have any questions or feel as though company guidelines are not being followed, ask your manager to assist you.	________
• Take all threats seriously, even if it is a fellow coworker blowing off steam about your manager and what he or she wants to do to get back at your manager or your company; or if he or she is angry and wants to harm the manager, the customer, or the business.	________
• If the back door is supposed to be locked and secure, **make sure it is!**	________
• If you use a food product every day and it is supposed to be blue but today it is green, stop using the product and notify your manager.	________
• If you know an employee is no longer with your company and this person enters an "employees only" area, notify your manager immediately.	________
• Cooperate in all investigations.	________
• Do not talk to the media. Refer all questions to your corporate office.	________
• If you are aware of a hoax, notify your manager immediately.	________
Customer Awareness SOP:	
• Be aware of any unattended bags or briefcases customers bring into your operation.	________
• If a customer walks into an "employee only" area of your operation, ask the customer politely if he or she needs help, then notify a member of management.	________

Vendor Awareness SOP:

- Check the identification of any vendor or service person that enters restricted areas of your operation and do not leave him or her unattended. ________
- Monitor all products received and look for any signs of tampering. ________
- When a vendor is making a delivery, never accept more items than what is listed on your invoice. If the vendor attempts to give you more items than what is listed, notify your manager. ________
- When receiving deliveries:

  Step 1. Always ask for identification. ________

  Step 2. Stay with the delivery person. ________

  Step 3. Do not allow the person to roam freely throughout your operation. ________

Facility Awareness SOP:

- Report all equipment, maintenance, and security issues to your manager. ________
- Document any equipment, maintenance, and security issues. ________
- Be aware of the inside and outside of your facility, including the dumpster area, and report anything out of the ordinary. ________

Establishment Specific Food Defense Procedures

(Optional):____

____

____

____ ____
Employee Signature Owner/Manager Signature

____ ____
Date Date

- When it comes to food defense, the best defense is a properly written food defense policy and a proactive, properly trained and motivated staff. Food defense does not just happen.
- Be aware of what to do if any acts of food terrorism or suspected hoaxes occur. Instruct your employees to always report any potential threats. Follow the Food Defense SOPs established by your company.
- **Remember that doing nothing at all is still taking action!** By doing nothing you are allowing hazardous situations to occur.

Crisis Management

Whether you are experiencing issues related to food safety, food defense, or food recalls, you should have a crisis management plan in place to prepare for unpredictable situations. Like HACCP, crisis management is a proactive rather than reactive approach to a problem.

If you prepare for a crisis before it happens, the correct and best decisions will have been well thought out in advance. You will be able to respond more quickly with correct decisions if a crisis occurs. If you take measures to ensure food safety and practice food defense throughout all the steps of food preparation, ideally, you will avoid a crisis with the exception of a natural disaster. Many people believe that a crisis will never happen to them because they never had a problem before. They think, why should we worry now? The data and the experts tell us; the question is not whether a crisis will occur, but when will it occur?

Crisis management is an organized and systematic effort to:

- Restrict the possibility of a likely crisis.
- Manage and conclude an existing crisis.
- Evaluate and learn from a crisis incident.

There are several types of crises that can be associated with the food service and retail industry:

- Foodborne illness complaints
- Foodborne illness outbreaks
- Product recalls
- Food defense issues
- Hoaxes
- Robbery, which may involve the following:
  Theft
  Break-ins
  Murders
  Bomb threats
- Natural disasters, including, the following:
  Floods
  Earthquakes
  Electrical storms
- Other crises, which may include the following:
  Fires
  Power outages
  Water failures
  Injuries

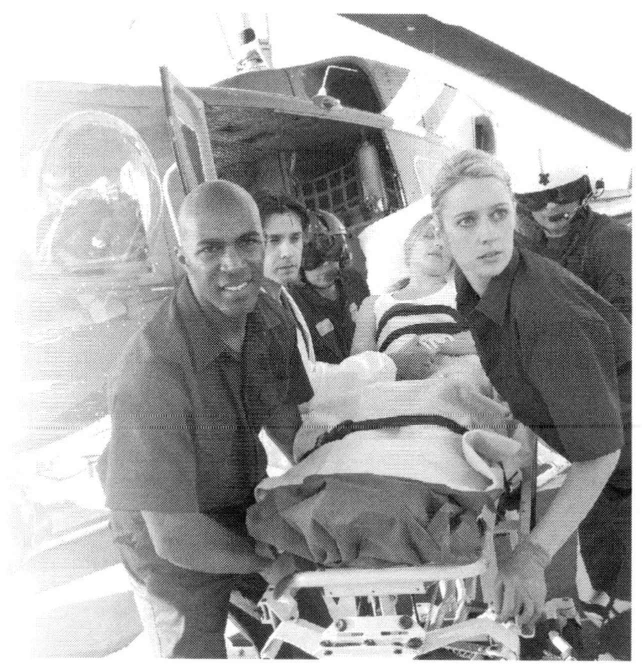

Preparing a Crisis Management Plan

It is essential that every food service or retail operation develops a plan to respond to a potential crisis. The following examples are plans for a foodborne illness crisis and a food recall crisis.

Crisis Management: Foodborne Illness Complaints

When a HACCP plan is implemented successfully, foodborne illnesses typically do not occur. However, if any part of the HACCP plan breaks down, the likelihood of foodborne illnesses occurring increases. If a complaint does occur, a rapid response will help reduce the effect of the complaint on the operation's reputation. A proper response must include the following:

- Obtain complete, reliable information;
- Evaluate the complaint;
- Cooperate with regulatory agencies and the media; and
- Reapply HACCP standards to initiate corrections, prevent recurrence, and reduce liability of the establishment.

Step 1: Plan and develop policies and procedures.

The objectives of the plan should be to preserve human life and prevent property damage. Further, a plan must identify and correct whatever it is that brought about the crisis. By planning in advance, you will be able to respond quickly and make better and more intelligent and informed decisions during a crisis.

An effective plan includes the following:

- Having a "First Responder Emergency Contact Information" form. An example can be found in Appendix 3.
- A method by which employees report emergencies or potential problems to management;
- Identification of potential areas where a crisis is most likely to occur;
- Methods to avoid a crisis before it begins;
- Methods and resources available to management to control and resolve a crisis; and
- A method to evaluate the success of strategies utilized to control the crisis both during and after it is over.

Step 2: Designate a specific person or a "crisis team."

Refer all food illness complaints to the person or team designated to respond to a food-related crisis. If it is a single person, it should be the manager or someone with the responsibility and authority to implement the crisis plan. If a team is utilized, areas of responsibility and lines of communication must be understood and someone must be in charge. Every employee should be trained in the policies and procedures for obtaining basic information. Most often, it is a customer who should be carefully questioned to obtain as many facts as possible. All employees must be trained to report even suspected incidents to their supervisor and ultimately to the "crisis person" or "crisis team" for handling.

The designated crisis person or team should be given the authority to act and to direct other employees to act and utilize necessary resources. All statements made to complainants, regulatory authorities, or the media on behalf of your food service or retail establishment should come only from the crisis person or team to ensure consistent information is being dispersed.

Step 3: Take the complaint and obtain information. Use standardized forms and procedures. A sample foodborne illness complaint form can be found in Appendix 3.

Whoever is designated to handle recording the complaints should follow these guidelines:

- Get all pertinent information possible, without "pressuring" the complainant. Use standardized forms to avoid omitting any information. Be as detailed as possible.
- Remain polite and concerned. Use your interpersonal skills. Do not argue or admit liability. For example, you might say, "I'm sorry you are not feeling well," **NOT** "I'm sorry our food made you sick." Do not offer to pay medical bills or other costs, except with proper approval from your corporation or on the advice of your establishment's attorney or insurance agent.
- Let the person tell his or her own story so you do not introduce symptoms. People tend to be suggestible about illnesses, and if you inquire about a symptom, they may report that symptom, because they think they should. You should only record what the person tells you.
- Note the time the symptoms started. This is very helpful in identifying the disease and can work to clear your involvement.
- Try to get a recent food history from the complainant. Most people blame illness on the last meal they ate, but many diseases have longer incubation periods. Again, this could clear your involvement. However, do not press—most of us can't remember what we ate for more than a few hours. If applicable, try to include food eaten before and after the person was in your establishment or during the last 48 hours.
- Do not play doctor! Avoid the temptation to interpret symptoms or advise on treatment. Simply gather the information, remain polite and concerned, and tell the complainant you will be in touch with him or her in the near future. Then contact the complainant when you have something to report.

Be careful what you write! Remember whatever you write on the form may be read by supervisors, regulators, medical personal, or the media and may wind up in court! Do not write funny words or phrases that you will be sorry for later.

Step 4: Evaluate the complaint.

- Evaluate the complaint, so that it can be handled appropriately and that the correct response is provided by the designated manager.
- Evaluate the complainant's attitude. If he or she is belligerent and demanding, it may be a bluff, or it could reflect a sincere feeling that you have caused. Note the facts on your standardized form.
- Resist the urge to argue with or to "pay off" the complainant.
- Analyze data to determine whether the complainant is describing a legitimate illness. Do not provide a diagnosis; however, examine the reported information for consistency.
- Did the complainant eat all of the implicated serving or just a bite? Severity and duration of illness is often dose-related.
- Did anyone else in the party have the same food?
- Did the symptoms occur immediately?

Remember that most illnesses require several hours of incubation before symptoms occur. Compare the complainant's meal with other meals served during the same time period. Was anything different about the complainant's meal? Was this the only complaint you received?

Most establishments have a policy for isolated events, such as the single person report, that may or may not be related to your establishment. If this complaint is an isolated case, follow your food service or retail establishment's policies regarding small tokens (meal coupons, etc.) to soothe the customer and win back patronage through goodwill.
Be careful to avoid admitting liability. Even in an isolated event, you must review your processes and records for any possible unsafe practices, make needed corrections, and file a complaint form for future reference. One should never assume that and isolated event is simply a one-time occurrence. It may be a sign that shows your company's policies and procedures need corrections or your staff needs additional training.

If your evaluation indicates that the complaint is valid, obtain outside resources to help with your investigation. Contact your local health department or regulatory agency, your attorney, your media spokesperson, and your insurance agent promptly.

Regardless of whether you decide to handle the complaint privately or get involved with regulators and outside advisors, you should investigate the complaint by reapplying the principles of HACCP. First, create a flowchart to represent the activity of the implicated food. Determine whether critical control points were properly controlled, by reviewing the following records:

- Menus and relevant forms and logs;
- Numbers of implicated meals served, and other complaints;
- Recent changes in suppliers, employees, processes, and volume;
- Equipment operating correctly;
- Recent employee illnesses (before and after the implicated meal); and
- Any indication that requirements for critical control points were not met.

If you still have the item which you or the customer suspected or claimed to be the cause, remove it from food preparation and distribution and isolate it by wrapping it securely. Mark it "**Do Not Use.**" If the item is frozen, it should remain frozen. Otherwise, refrigerate it pending further instructions from a food-testing laboratory. Consult with your attorney about the effects of lab-tested samples on liability. Samples could either clear you or confirm diagnosis.

The health department may request its own samples. If it does, you should take duplicate samples and arrange to have the second sample analyzed separately for comparison. For your samples, it is preferable to contract with a private laboratory to compare the results.

Use all the information to assess the operation and make any needed changes to prevent recurrence (or use the data to clear your establishment of any wrongdoing). Resolve the complaint in accordance with your policies and advice from your attorney and insurance agent regarding the issuance of coupons or payments. Keep all complaints filed and indexed for future reference.

Crisis Management: Food Recalls

A **food recall**, as defined by the FDA, is "an action by a manufacturer or distributor to remove a food product from the market because it may cause health problems or possible death."

Recall Classification General Definition and Example

- **Class I** - This classification involves a health hazard situation where there is a **reasonable** probability that consuming the product will cause adverse health problems or death. For example, a Class I would be a ready-to-eat product such as luncheon meat or hot dogs contaminated with a pathogen. Another example is a product that is found to contain an allergen, such as dry milk, that is not mentioned on the label. Undeclared allergens are considered a Class I recall.

- **Class II** - This involves a potential health hazard situation where there is a **remote** probability of adverse health problems from consuming the product. A Class II example would be a product found to have small pieces of plastic in it. Another example is a product that is found to contain a food product (non- allergen) that is not mentioned on the label.

- **Class III** - This involves a situation when consuming the product will not cause adverse health problems. For example, a product that has a minor ingredient missing from the label that is not an allergen, such as labeled processed meat in which added water is not listed on the label as required by federal regulations.

- **Withdrawal** - Only the FDA uses this classification. The situation occurs when a product has a minor violation that would not be subject to FDA legal action. The company removes the product from the market or corrects the violation. A withdrawal example would be a product removed from the market due to tampering, without evidence of manufacturing or distribution problems.

- **Hold** - A time period used for investigation after a USDA commodity food has been identified as potentially unsafe. The hold time for commodity foods is no longer than 10 days.

- **Release** - When the product on hold has been found safe and can be used.

For more information on recall classifications, visit:

- www.fsis.usda.gov/OA/pubs/recallfocus.htm
- www.cfsan.fda.gov/~lrd/recall2.html

Remember: A food recall requires immediate action! There is a limited amount of time to perform the tasks necessary to guard the safety of customers when a food recall occurs. It is best to have a standard operating procedure in place before being notified of a food recall.

Food Recall SOP

To ensure that the Food Recall SOP will be handled properly and without incident if a food recall should occur, the manager should:

- **Take action immediately when you receive notice of a recall!**
- Conduct a mock food recall to assist in teaching employees the appropriate steps within this particular process.
- Appoint a responsible person to coordinate food safety in the establishment. The manager also appoints a backup food safety coordinator in case the principle food safety coordinator is unavailable during the time of crisis.

Certain steps must be taken in the event of a food recall. Here are the twelve steps:

1. Develop a SOP before being notified of a food recall. A sample Food Recall SOP can be found in Appendix 2.

The best time to plan for a recall is **before** the recall occurs. The standard operating procedure must include a list of steps that should be taken, those who are responsible for each step, and detailed procedures to be followed at each step. For the procedures to be effective, personnel must be trained to implement the hold and recall process.

Warning:
Product placed on hold must be identified by:
(Describe the product identifier: A large sign, not less than 8-1/2 x 11 inches, with the words **"DO NOT USE"** and **"DO NOT DISCARD"** will be securely attached to the product placed on hold.)

2. Review the recall notification report when it is received.

- Determine what the problem is according to the recall.
- Review all instructions issued in the recall.
- Determine what actions must be taken.
- Gather recall information following the FDA form #3177. This form can be found at: http://www.docstoc.com/docs/575879/FORM-FDA-RECALL-AUDIT-CHECK-REPORT

The form, FDA form #3177, found in the appendix, will be generated and completed by the FDA. In the event of a food recall, the establishments affected will receive a recall notification report from the State Distributing Agency. This report will identify the name of the product, affected lot numbers, and any other information about the product. Establishments affected must return information to the State Distributing Agency. This information will include where the product listed on the recall has been stored, the quantity being stored, the quantity of the product that was already used, and documentation of the received product so that those involved can be reimbursed. The following report is the result of the initial recall investigation. Food service and retail operations will take actions based on the information given to them from this report. Products under authority of the United States Department of Agriculture will have recall information provided as exampled below in the USDA Recall Notification Report.

3. **Communicate information about the food recall immediately.**

The manager of the food service and retail establishment must communicate the information to everyone involved in the recall. These agencies and individuals include; federal, state, and/or local regulators, manufacturer, processor, distributor, and company/organization leaders involved in the recall. The manager must also do the following:

- Clarify all issues related to the food recall by speaking directly to the person responsible for the recall;
- Document and confirm receipt of all communication;
- Immediately notify all sites of the recall;
- Identify the location of all products affected by the recall;
- Verify that the food items have the product identification codes listed in the recall;
- Isolate and label the food products to avoid accidental use; and
- Take an accurate inventory by location.

4. **Collect health-related information needed for public communications.**

Recall classification is determined by the seriousness of the health risk involved. For Class I or Class II recalls, the following should be documented:

- If any of the affected food was served;
- To whom it was served;
- The dates it was served; and
- Any health problems reported that could be related to the recalled food product.

5. **Work closely with all public communication contact persons.**

Notify the communications contact person/media spokesperson associated with your establishment so that this person is aware of the nature and scope of the problem. This ensures that they are prepared to handle all public communications with health agencies and local media. Provide the public communications contact person with all the correct information so he or she is well-informed of the situation, including:

- Copies of the food recall notice;
- Press releases;
- Any related recall information;
- Information on whether the product has been used and served, to whom it has been served, and on what dates it has been served; and
- Any health risk reports related to the recalled product.

The extent of the information communicated to the public will depend on the type of recall and whether any of the food products have been consumed. If the food product has been served to customers and there is the risk of an adverse health effect, the persons potentially affected should (ethically and legally) be notified. If there is no potential adverse health risk associated with serving the product or if the product has not been served, there is no reason to report the recall to the customer.

6. **Locate the recalled food product.**

- Determine where any of the affected food product listed in the recall notice is located.
- Make sure the codes on the affected product match the code(s) listed in the recall notice.

7. **Count the inventory of the recalled food product.**
   Accurately conduct an inventory count to determine how much of the recalled food product has already been used and the amount of the recalled food that is still being stored.

8. **Account for all of the recalled food.**
   Check all records to verify that all recalled food has been accounted for and has been removed from potential use.

9. **Separate and secure the recalled food product from food that is not listed on the recall.**
   Keeping the affected food properly labeled and separated from food not listed on the recall, will prevent instances of cross contamination from occurring.

10. **Take action to conform to the recall.**
    - To receive reimbursement or replacement of the recalled product, and to have the affected product removed from your establishment, you must submit information to the manufacturer, distributor, or state agency. This information must describe the quantity of the product in stock and where it has been stored. The information must be submitted within 10 days of the first recall notification.
    - Determine if the product should be returned to someone, if the product needs to be destroyed, who is responsible for destroying it, and how will it be destroyed. Note that in nearly all food recalls, the distributor or vendor will collect and/or destroy the recalled food products.
    - Determine which employees will be responsible for obtaining this information and following the standard operating procedures involved with such actions.
    - Notify all parties involved of the procedures, dates, and relevant information that must be followed in the recall or destruction of the recalled food product.
    - Work with the state distributing agency and the contracted warehouse/distributor to determine how and when to collect the recalled food product. The recalled product should be collected as soon as possible, and no later than 30 days after the date of the recall notice.
    - Do not destroy any product without official written notification from USDA (United States Department of Agriculture), FSIS (Food Safety and Inspection Service), or the FDA (United States Food and Drug Administration). Once notified by one of these agencies, if you destroy the food on-site, you must determine how the food should be destroyed, who should be there, and who must know about the process. Due to the potential health risk to humans or animals, some state public health departments require notification of all recalled food products to be destroyed before any action is taken.

11. **Consolidate documentation from all sites for inventory counts.**
    This will help the manager/director account for a recalled product that has been served as well as the product that is still at the food service or retail operation.

12. **Document any reimbursable costs.**
    Determine what recalled food items you should be reimbursed for by the manufacturers and/or distributors, and submit the necessary paperwork for the reimbursement of food costs. Complete and maintain all necessary documentation related to the recall. The FDA recommends keeping records for 3 years, plus the current year.

These examples of crisis management plans have been provided to help prepare you for such crises in your food service or retail operation. Keep in mind if you practice the 7 HACCP principles, you can reduce or even prevent the risk of a crisis from occurring. Hopefully, you will never have to use a crisis management plan, since your facility has implemented a HACCP plan and are practicing food safety. However, it's extremely important to have a crisis management plan, in place, just in case a crisis occurs.

Sample Follow Up Schedule

This chart is provided by the U.S. Department of Agriculture to assist in the managing of crisis follow-up items.

Monitoring Schedule for Items that Require Follow-Up Action					
Task to monitor or follow-up	When will follow-up begin?	How often will follow-up occur?	Who is responsible?	Results of follow-up	Check when completed

Pop Quiz:

Food Defense SOPs

What four food defense standard operating procedures should food service and retail employees receive training on at their facility?

1. ____________________________________

2. ____________________________________

3. ____________________________________

4. ____________________________________

Regulatory Agency as a Valued Partner

The role of regulatory agencies is to protect the consumer by helping support and educate food service and retail operators. Regulatory agencies are valued partners to food service and retail operators. Regulators provide plan reviews and third-party audits on a regular basis. Additionally, regulators provide resources such as; support during a food recall or a foodborne illness outbreak, food defense checklists, self-audit checklists, and HACCP forms. Often operators will seek support from regulatory agencies when they suspect they are experiencing a foodborne illness outbreak. This is why these relationships are important and need to be developed prior to any crisis. The first time you interact with your regulators should not be during a crisis!

All operators, from farm to table, are encouraged to build relationships, establish communication, and take part in educational opportunities with regulators by participating in the International Association for Food Protection (www.foodprotection.org) and the Association of Food and Drug Officials (AFDO; www.afdo.org). AFDO is an international nonprofit organization that has six regional affiliates that serve as resources for you and your food service or retail operation. The six regional affiliates are:

- CASA—Central Atlantic States Association of Food and Drug Officials; www.casafdo.org
- AFDOSS—Association of Food and Drug Officials of the Southern States; www.afdoss.org
- MCAFDO—Mid-Continental Association of Food and Drug Officials; www.mcafdo.org
- NCAFDO—North Central Association of Food and Drug Officials; www.ncafdo.org
- WAFDO—Western Association of Food and Drug Officials; www.wafdo.org
- NEFDOA—North East Food and Drug Officials Association; www.nefdoa.org

When should you contact the health department? The best practice is to call the health department and any other regulatory agencies (such as the USDA or the FDA) to assist you if you believe the complaint is valid, and certainly, if there are more than two complaints or hospitalizations involved. It is to your benefit to establish a cooperative stance by involving these regulatory agencies from the start of when the complaint is first lodged against your food service or retail establishment.

It is important to consult with your attorney about the specific laws in your jurisdiction concerning your rights and responsibilities. Ideally, this should be accomplished before a crisis so you understand your rights. Generally, however, the health department is authorized to:

- Take reasonable samples of suspect foods;
- Prevent the sale of suspect foods;
- Require medical and laboratory examinations of employees;
- Exclude suspect employees from food-handling duties; and
- Order the facility to be closed due to "imminent health hazards" present in your facility in extreme cases.

In the Food Code, the definition of an **imminent health hazard** is, "a significant threat or danger to health that is considered to exist when there is evidence sufficient to show that a product, practice, circumstance, or event creates a situation that requires correction or cessation of operation to prevent injury based on:

- The number of potential injuries; and
- The nature, severity, and duration of the anticipated injury."

Operations must be discontinued in an Imminent Health hazard exists. These include:

- Fire,
- Flood;
- Extended interruption of electrical service or water service, including boil water advisories/notices;
- Sewage backup;
- Onset of an apparent foodborne illness;
- Gross unsanitary conditions; and
- Anything that may endanger public health.

Regulatory agency may allow continuation of an operation involved in an extended electrical or water service interruption if a written emergency operation plan has been approved; immediate corrective action is taken to eliminate, prevent or control any food safety risk and hazard associated with the electrical of water serviced interruption; and the regulatory agency is informed upon implementation of the written emergency operation plan.

Think positive! An inspection by health department investigators may help to show that there are no problems with your facility and clear you in a dispute. You should always be frank and candid; do not get caught in what appears to be a "cover-up." When dealing with these investigators you should:

- Be cooperative;
- Provide appropriate records (customer charge slips and dealer invoices) and make these records available for review; and
- Provide investigators reasonable access to observe whatever they request.

Dealing with the Media

In today's world, technology ensures that the media and public are notified of a crisis within minutes of it being reported. The speed at which bad news can travel can destroy a brand, company, or business if the information is not managed properly. You must be prepared to handle the media in case of any crisis, especially if foodborne illness occurs in your food service or retail establishment.

When communicating with the media, you should be cautiously cooperative. Have your facts straight before you speak. It is best to make a statement and not answer questions. This way you control the conversation. If you must, answer questions with a simple straight forward response and do not be moved from your message. Avoid using words that are known in the industry as "jargon" but may be misunderstood by the media. Remember, it is best to give a statement and politely tell the press that there will be additional information if and when available. Remain professional, stay calm, and do not allow yourself to be provoked. Keep your answers positive, not defensive.

Do not answer hypothetical questions. Do not answer a question you do not understand. If you must answer questions; one planning technique suggests that you imagine your worst nightmares being described in the newspapers or on television, then practice answering those potentially embarrassing questions until you feel and act comfortable.

Do not guess at an answer. It is acceptable to say, "I do not know and I will find out." Do not bluff. Also, remember that "no comment" tends to sound like an admission of guilt. Sometimes, if you have nothing good to say, it is better to say nothing at all. Managers **must** tell employees they are not permitted to speak with the press and be reminded of that often. Instruct all employees that all requests made of employees by the media should be referred to management or the corporation. A sample model press release with example provided by the FDA ORA/Office of Enforcement Division of Compliance Management and Operations (www.fda.gov/ora/compliance_ref/recalls/ecoli.htm) can be found in the Appendix.

Star Point 2 Conclusion

In Star Point 1, we covered the need for good retail practices, active managerial control, prerequisite programs, and SOPs in great detail. Now, having read through Star Point 2, it is clear that in addition to food safety SOPs, a food service or retail establishment needs food defense SOPs in place to prevent a deliberate and accidental act of food contamination from occurring. Your food service or retail establishment must have standard operating procedures in place for food defense or food safety, before your organization begins to implement the first HACCP principle: Conducting a Hazard Analysis.

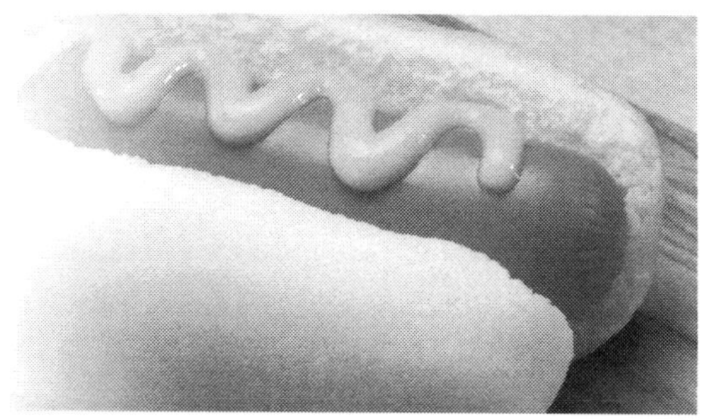

Star Knowledge Exercise:

Food Defense - What Should I Do If

Consider the following...Should you get involved if you suspect something is not quite right in your food service or retail operation? Yes or No? Think about the following situations. Is the scenario a food defense concern? If it is, what would you do?

Situation	Is the situation a concern? Yes or No?	If so, what do you do to fix the problem?
1. A newly hired employee approaches you and tells you he saw your best employee contaminating food.	❑ Yes ❑ No	
2. You enter an "employees only" area of the food service or retail establishment and find an ex-boyfriend of one of your co-workers walking around.	❑ Yes ❑ No	
3. An employee tells you that the employee you wrote up yesterday is upset and was heard talking to another co-worker about how unfair this was and that "I'm going to get even" was overheard.	❑ Yes ❑ No	
4. A customer with shopping bags asked permission to use the toilet facilities and was escorted. This person is observed outside the building after you close for the day.	❑ Yes ❑ No	
5. An ex-employee returns only one uniform after she had been terminated. Your paperwork indicates she had been given three uniforms.	❑ Yes ❑ No	

Situation	Is the situation a concern? Yes or No?	If so, what do you do to fix the problem?
6. An incident happened in your operation causing many customers to become seriously ill. A customer approaches you and starts asking very specific questions about the incident.	❑ Yes ❑ No	
7. A vendor, in addition to your order, wants to leave a case of product as a free sample as part of a promotional effort to introduce a new product the company has begun to distribute.	❑ Yes ❑ No	
8. You walk by the food bar and notice what looks like salt on a portion of the food bar. You do not have any granular products at the food bar.	❑ Yes ❑ No	
9. A vendor who has been delivering to you for years walks through the back door with a delivery of raw chicken wings. You notice the cases are dripping an odd liquid.	❑ Yes ❑ No	
10. An employee tells you there seems to be a dimple in the center of the ketchup bottle seals that were being opened prior to placement on the customer's tables.	❑ Yes ❑ No	

Resources: www.gao.gov • www.fda.gov • www.dhs.gov • www.fsis.usda.gov • www.usda.gov • www.epa.gov

Did you know... By not taking any action, you are allowing such situations to occur and are risking the health of your customers, fellow employees, and the public. Further, you run the risk of damage to your brand, loss of business, and financial ruin.

Star Point 2 Check for Understanding

(Circle one.)

1. Which scenarios could affect the safety of the food in your facility?

- **a.** Leaving the back door open
- **b.** Allowing a service person to roam freely in the facility
- **c.** Not reporting suspicious activity
- **d.** a and c only
- **e.** all of the above

2. Food defense is ______________________________.

- **a.** preventing accidental contamination of food
- **b.** preventing intentional contamination of food
- **c.** having a 2 year supply of food
- **d.** having a strong military

3. Food security is ______________________________.

- **a.** preventing accidental contamination of food
- **b.** preventing intentional contamination of food
- **c.** having a 2 year supply of food
- **d.** having a strong military

4. When a vendor arrives, you should always ________.

- **a.** say hello and let him in the door
- **b.** check his identification
- **c.** stay with him while he is in the facility
- **d.** tell him to put the supplies in the storage area
- **e.** both b and c

5. Food Defense SOPs do not include ______________.

- **a.** Employee awareness
- **b.** Facility awareness
- **c.** Employee health awareness
- **d.** Vendor awareness
- **e.** Customer awareness

6. When should you call the Health Department or regulatory agency?

- **a.** If you believe the complaint is valid
- **b.** If there are more than two complaints or hospitalizations involved
- **c.** When one person complains
- **d.** both a and b

7. When dealing with the media you should _________.

- **a.** have a spokesperson
- **b.** stick to the truth
- **c.** be cautiously cooperative
- **d.** remain as professional as possible
- **e.** all of the above

8. Like HACCP, crisis management is______________.

- **a.** proactive rather than reactive
- **b.** based on measurements
- **c.** revolved around consumer complaints
- **d.** something only managers need to understand

9. In response to the attack on September 11, 2001, congress passed the ________________________.

- **a.** Food Defense Law and Bio-terrorism Preparedness Law
- **b.** Public Health Security and Bioterrorism Preparedness and Response Act
- **c.** Public Safety Response Act
- **d.** Public Health Security and Food Security Act

10. Food terrorism can potentially occur when there is a ____________________________.

- **a.** lack of awareness
- **b.** limited budget for food defense measures
- **c.** lack of training
- **d.** all of the above
- **e.** none of the above

HACCP Star Point 3: HACCP Principles 1 & 2 – Evaluate Hazards and Critical Control Points

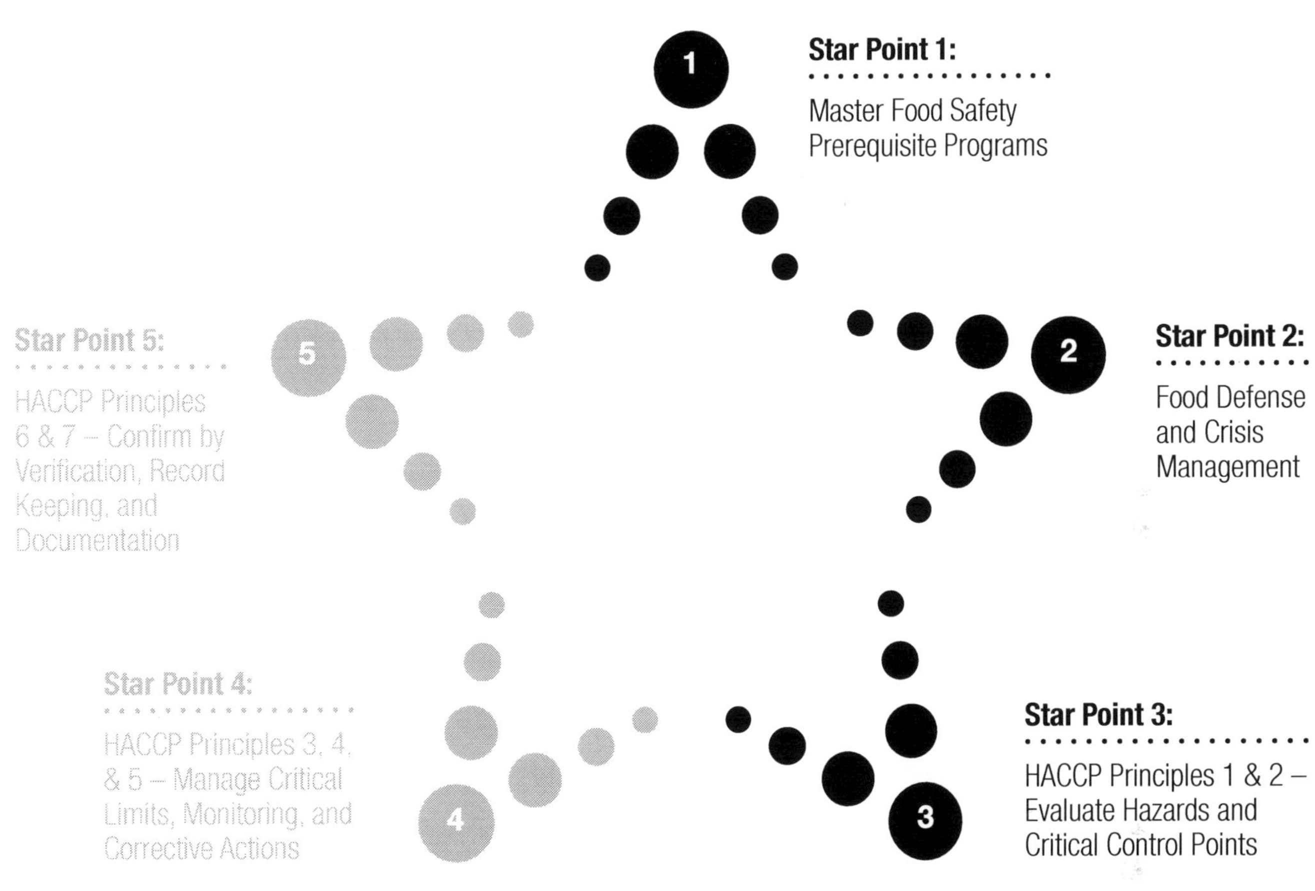

Star Point 3 Myth or Fact (Check one.)

1. A HACCP plan must identify potential biological, chemical, and physical hazards in the flow of food.
___**Myth** ___**Fact**

2. In a hazard analysis capacity must be evaluated to determine if the facility, equipment, and people are able to safely execute the desired menu.
___**Myth** ___**Fact**

3. Traceability is the ability to trace the history, application, or location of an item or activity with the help of documentation.
___**Myth** ___**Fact**

4. Every recipe or food must be considered in the hazard analysis and placed in the proper food preparation process.
___**Myth** ___**Fact**

5. Some points in the flow of food are more critical than others they are called Control Points (CP).
___**Myth** ___**Fact**

Star Point 3 Goals: You will learn to

- Define HACCP and describe its importance to your food service or retail operation.
- Understand the importance of the Codex Alimentarius Commission
- Describe the HACCP philosophy and define your role.
- Practice a hazard analysis (HACCP Principle 1).
- Describe the preliminary steps and the flow of food.
- Determine critical control points (HACCP Principle 2).

This third point of the HACCP Star examines HACCP Principles 1 (Conducting a Hazard Analysis) and 2 (Determining Critical Control Points). Once the prerequisite programs for food safety and food defense have been established for your operation, you have a solid foundation on which you can build an effective HACCP plan. Remember, simply having a HACCP plan, no matter how well written, is useless without training and monitoring employees in food safety and food defense basics. These are vital to making HACCP successful. This means that each employee must do their part to understand and maintain prerequisite program basics that include facility design, equipment, pest control, chemical control, cleaning and sanitizing procedures, responsible employee practices, purchasing practices, food specifications, and food temperature control. This Star Point also addresses the importance and philosophy of HACCP, as well as, the international implications and the Codex Alimentarius Commission.

HACCP Introduction

HACCP ("has-sip") is an abbreviation for Hazard Analysis and Critical Control Point. HACCP food safety management systems provide an easily understood, systematic, and common sense approach to preventing food safety disasters such as foodborne illness outbreaks. HACCP food safety management systems provide the food production and service team with clear and precise actions needed to achieve active managerial control of food safety hazards which, in turn, minimizes the risks.

A foodborne illness occurs when someone eats food and it makes them sick. As we learned earlier, the CDC lists the five most common risk factors that create foodborne illness:

Food From Unsafe Sources

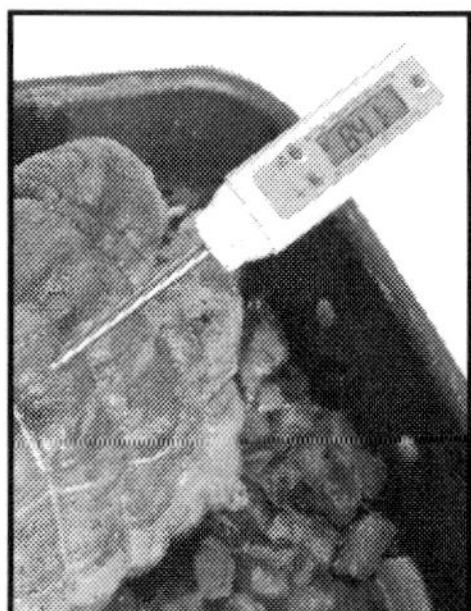

Inadequate Cooking

Improper Holding Temperatures

Contaminated Equipment

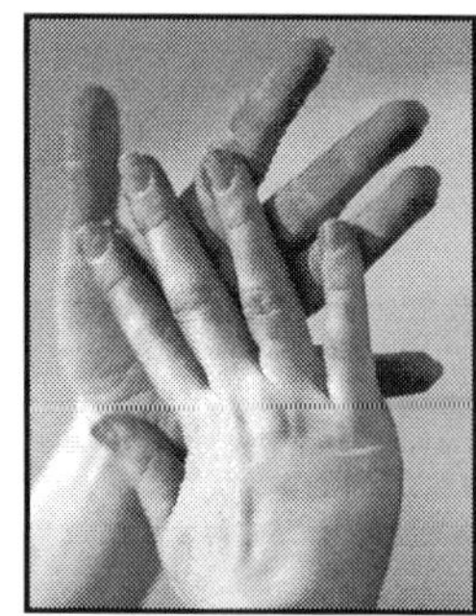

Poor Personal Hygiene

An outbreak occurs when two or more people eat the same food and get the same illness. HACCP helps prevent foodborne illness outbreaks because HACCP is a proactive approach to controlling every step in the flow of food. Simply stated, the **HACCP goal is to prevent, eliminate, and reduce problems that impact the safety of food.**

A well written HACCP food safety plan identifies food safety hazards and the steps needed to implement practices and procedures that will ensure the selling and serving of safe food. Star Point 1 (prerequisites programs) and Star Point 2 (food defense) have laid the foundation for developing a HACCP plan. The next three Star Points explore creating, working, and checking a HACCP plan. **The HACCP food safety system has 7 principles. You will learn about these 7 principles in the next three Star Point sections.**

Star Point 3—Create the HACCP Plan:

HACCP Principle 1: Conducting a Hazard Analysis

HACCP Principle 2: Determining Critical Control Points

Star Point 4—Work the Plan:

HACCP Principle 3: Establish Critical Limits

HACCP Principle 4: Monitoring

HACCP Principle 5: Taking Corrective Actions

Star Point 5—Checks and Balances:

HACCP Principle 6: Verification

HACCP Principle 7: Record Keeping and Documentation

No matter what your job responsibilities and duties are, you will benefit from understanding and knowing the HACCP plan. In many operations, such as food manufacturers and public schools a HACCP plan is mandated by law. Though most states do not mandate retail HACCP, it is just as important to this industry as it is to other regulated food industries.

Importance of HACCP

Based upon the combined efforts of the Food and Agriculture Organization (FAO) concentrating on global nutrition, and the **World Health Organization (WHO)** focusing on preventing disease and promoting general well-being, in 1963 the **United Nations** established the **Codex Alimentarius Commission**. Codex Alimentarius means food law or code in Latin. The Codex Alimentarius Commission has more than 180 member countries that represent 97 percent of the world population. Its mission is to develop worldwide standards for food safety and nutrition. The Codex Alimentarius Commission is instrumental in developing, maintaining, and coordinating international food safety guidelines, procedures, and standards to protect the health and safety of consumers and in encouraging fair international trade. This allows the consumer to be better protected and to enjoy more varieties of food products, while at the same time promoting healthy and safe choices.

The United States' position regarding food imports is that any company in a foreign country exporting food to the United States must have a food safety management system, or HACCP plan, that is equal to or better than the requirements expected of a company in the United States. This establishes the standards and expectations for food importers and gives countries that comply the opportunity to sell their food products in the United States, as long as these rules are followed. Countries that need to improve their food safety system can look at these regulations as a measure to stop lower quality and possibly tainted imported products from entering their countries.

International cooperation also helps in traceability if food product contamination occurs. Member countries can work together to identify, control, eliminate, and then recover from the adulteration, whether deliberate or accidental. **Traceability** is the ability to trace the history, application, or location of an item or activity with the help of documentation. Without using a precise tracking system, it would be difficult, if not impossible to track defective wheat from a loaf of bread back to the farm or the contaminated hamburger patty back to a specific cow.

Additional benefits of traceability are improved supply management initiatives with electronic coding systems, increased inventory control, and methodical tracking. Retail operators, in an effort to prove the effectiveness of their HACCP plan, often require reputable suppliers to use third-party certification and documentation to verify their traceability system. If this tracking is in place, the supplier can isolate quality issues and, more importantly, the source and extent of any food safety concerns. Examples of tracking system control measures to facilitate traceability from farm to table include:

- Providing country-of-origin labeling;
- Requiring written recall processes to be in place.
- Requiring all manufacturers and processors to register and identify sources.

These controls help to ensure the safety of the flow of food starting at the very source of the food chain. Further, these controls will help identify and isolate potentially dangerous food. Without these screening tools, substandard (or adulterated or deleterious) foods will make their way to consumers. Controls and safeguards cannot be implemented only at the last step in the flow of food—the selling or serving. Ensuring safe food requires a global team that implements controls and safeguards from farm to table.

To better understand the importance of HACCP it is necessary to become familiar with its history. Early in the 1960s, recognizing the need to minimize the possibility of astronauts becoming sick while in space, the Pillsbury Company, with the cooperation and participation of the **National Aeronautic and Space Administration** (NASA), Natick Laboratories of the U.S. Army, and the U.S. Air Force Space Laboratory Project Group, developed HACCP for the U.S.

space program. **Yes, the HACCP program was actually developed by rocket scientists!** The problem was that it was not easy to get help to a sick astronaut. Imagine an astronaut in space who shows signs of a foodborne illness (vomiting and diarrhea)? "Houston, we have a problem!"

Since all food contains microorganisms, NASA needed a food safety system that would prevent, eliminate, and reduce the number of microorganisms, to safe levels, to stop the astronauts from being stricken with a foodborne illness, while in space. The United States space programs goal was 100 percent assurance against contamination by bacterial and viral pathogens, toxins, and chemical or physical hazards that could cause illness or injury to astronauts. This was done by developing and implementing a successful HACCP plan. As a result, HACCP replaced end product testing and provided a preventive system for producing safe food that had universal application.

After NASA successfully incorporated HACCP plans, the military, manufacturers, schools, and in some jurisdictions, retailers have recognized the importance and developed their own plans. In the succeeding years, the HACCP system has been recognized and widely accepted worldwide as an effective system of controls. In the last fifty years, the HACCP system has undergone considerable analysis, refinement, and testing.

The National Advisory Committee on Microbiological Criteria for Foods (NACMCF) is an advisory committee chartered under the U.S. Department of Agriculture (USDA) and composed of participants from the USDA (Food Safety and Inspection Service), Department of Health and Human Services (U.S. Food and Drug Administration and the Centers for Disease Control and Prevention), Department of Commerce (National Marine Fisheries Service), Department of Defense (Office of the Army Surgeon General), academia, industry, and state employees. NACMCF, established in 1988, provides guidance and recommendations to the Secretary of Agriculture and the Secretary of Health and Human Services regarding the microbiological safety of foods.

In November 1992, NACMCF defined seven widely accepted HACCP principles that should be considered when developing a HACCP plan. In 1997, the NACMCF requested that the HACCP Working Group reconvene to review the committee's November 1992 HACCP document and compare it to current HACCP guidelines prepared by the Codex Alimentarius Committee on Food Hygiene. As a result of this 1997 committee meeting, HACCP was defined as a systematic approach to the identification, evaluation, and control of food safety hazards based on the following 7 principles:

HACCP Principle 1: Conducting a Hazard Analysis

HACCP Principle 2: Determining Critical Control Points

HACCP Principle 3: Establish Critical Limits

HACCP Principle 4: Monitoring

HACCP Principle 5: Taking Corrective Actions

HACCP Principle 6: Verification

HACCP Principle 7: Record Keeping and Documentation

In the United States, the **FDA Model Food Code** applies to food service and retail food safety. It was created by the Food and Drug Administration (FDA), the Centers for Disease Control and Prevention (CDC) of the U.S. Department of Health and Human Services (HHS), and the Food Safety and Inspection Service (FSIS) of the U.S. Department of Agriculture (USDA). The FDA Model Food Code is updated every four years and it is updated every two years with a supplement. It is critical for all food safety management systems, especially your HACCP plan, to have the most current scientific information. The FDA Food Code provides practical, science-based guidance and manageable, enforceable provisions for mitigating risk factors known to cause foodborne illness. Food service operations, retail food stores, institutions, such as schools, hospitals, nursing homes, child care centers, and regulatory agencies incorporate the FDA Model Food Code as reference to ensure food safety. Most state and local food regulatory agencies have adopted the FDA Model Food Code, or some modified version thereof, as their food safety regulatory standard.

The HACCP Philosphy

HACCP is internationally accepted. The **Codex Alimentarius Code of Practice** recommends a HACCP-based approach wherever possible, to enhance food safety. It is important to recognize that the development and implementation of a HACCP plan is not a process conducted by an individual at one point in time. This process involves an entire team. In making the decision to take this training, you have become one of the important team members. Whether developing a HACCP plan or executing one, your company or institution is counting on you to do your part in preventing foodborne illness in your food service or retail operation.

It is critical that each facility assembles a HACCP team. Assembling the HACCP team is a preliminary step required for a HACCP plan. The ideal size of the HACCP team should not be larger than six members, including the team leader. However, some food service or retail operations may need to enlarge the team temporarily with personnel from other departments to provide support such as purchasing, finance, marketing, and research and development. The HACCP team leader needs to assign responsibilities, train employees, and ensure the initiatives are being accomplished. In addition, the team leader needs to coordinate with management to make sure the appropriate resources are provided. This enables a successful development and implementation of the HACCP plan.

The ideal candidates for a HACCP team should be skilled at identifying hazards, determining critical control points, monitoring, and verifying the prerequisite programs and implementing the HACCP plan. HACCP team members should include people who have an understanding of the equipment used, aspects of the food operation, food microbiology, and HACCP principles. The first responsibility of the HACCP team should be to determine the scope of the HACCP plan. The team should:

- Define the flow of food to be studied;
- Be specific with the processes, products, intended use, and consumers; and
- Identify the biological, chemical, and physical hazards to be included.

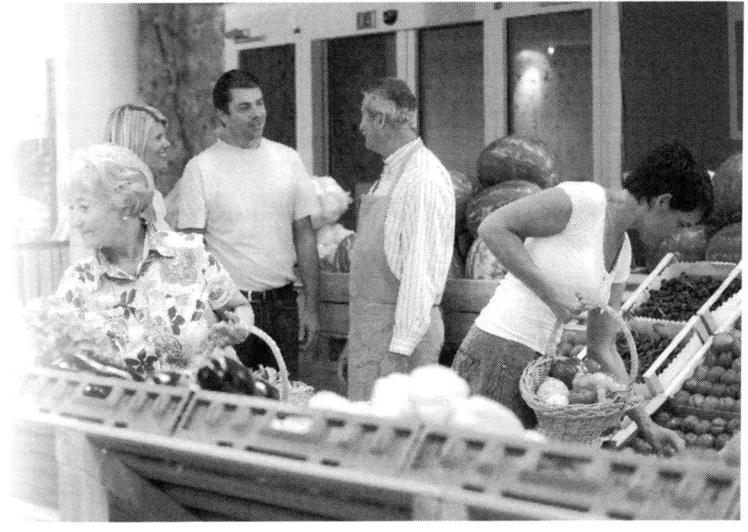

As you now know, our food supply is globalized and the eating habits of people around the world have also changed. Customers living in areas with cold winters want fresh produce year round. People are consuming more exotic foods that are imported from around the world. People eat more ready-to-eat foods (RTE) and enjoy more ethnic dishes and food varieties than ever before. The more food products are touched by people or machines, the greater the opportunity for contamination, or, even worse, the greater the opportunity to spread a foodborne illness. These demands make it increasingly important for food establishments to apply HACCP plans to their food service or retail operations to ensure the safe consumption of their menu items. The more food establishments consistently apply HACCP principles and create HACCP plans, the more likely food will be safer for all consumers throughout the world. This is why HACCP is so important!

Traditionally, food service and retail establishments have been reactive to food safety problems rather than developing programs to prevent these food safety problems from occurring in the first place. In the past, food safety concerns within establishments had not been addressed unless someone has become sick or an employee, disgruntled customer, or an inspection by a regulatory agency has brought the issue to the management's attention. Preventing dangers is always better than having to react to the consequences.

HACCP food management systems require monitoring and system checks that comprise of a continual self-inspection process. As a result, when a problem does occur or a regulatory agency performs an inspection, the establishment will have ready access to the documentation that will prove food safety is practiced at all times. Inspections will confirm that procedures are in place to maintain active managerial control of food safety hazards. The significance is that the regulatory inspection is a confirmation that the HACCP food safety management plan is in place and functioning properly and will also alert management of out-of-control conditions.

In order to complete the hazard analysis, the HACCP team must complete some basic preliminary steps. These preliminary steps are documented on two forms the **Hazard Analysis Worksheet Form** and the **HACCP Plan Form**, both of which can be found in Appendix 4 of this book. The HACCP team must answer the following preliminary questions:

1. What is the business concept? Retail? Casino? Military? Grocery? etc.

2. What is the company's name and address?

3. Who is the company's target market? Who is the target consumer? Are they a highly susceptible population?

4. What is the intended use for the consumer?

5. What products is the company planning to sell? What is the product description? Is there a recipe for each product?

6. What is the process description? What is the process flow chart including the steps in the flow of food?

7. What is the method of distribution?

Biological Hazards - (microorganisms) - bacteria, viruses, parasites and fungi. Biological Hazards are the greatest threat to food safety and human health. These hazards also receive the greatest attention in HACCP plans.

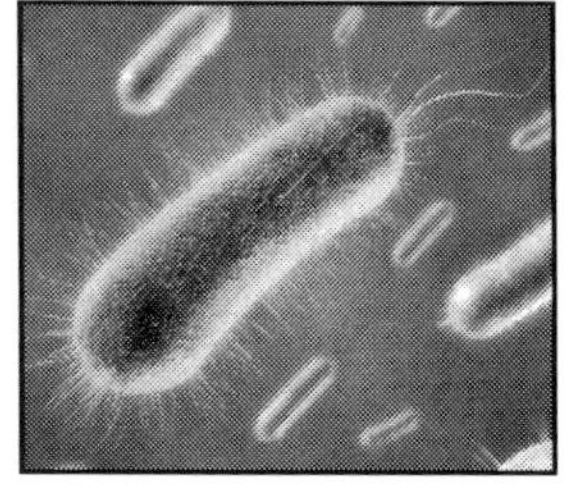

Bacteria

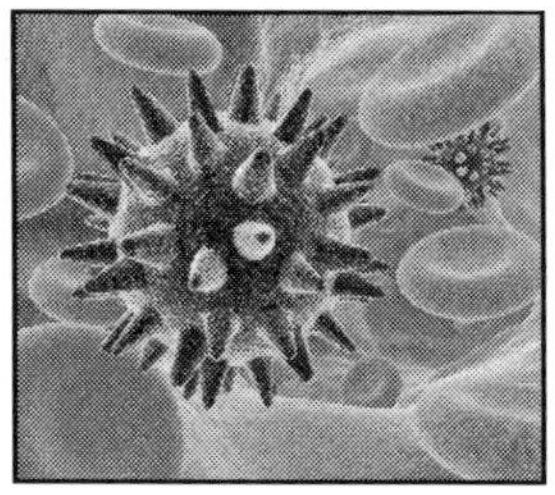

Viruses

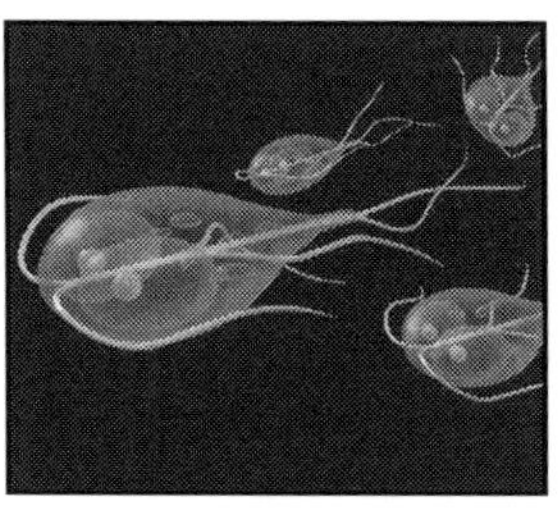

Parasites

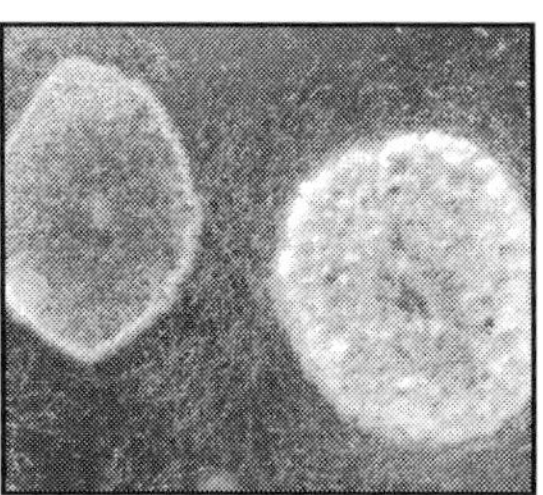

Fungi

Chemical Hazards - pesticides, unapproved additives or food colors, toxic metals, natural poisons, and cleaning chemicals.

Physical Hazards - foreign objects that do not belong in food. Some common examples are; hair, dirt, fake fingernails, plastic wrap, band aids, cherry pits and fish bones.

HACCP Principle 1: Conduct a Hazard Analysis

A **hazard analysis** is the first principle in evaluating foods in your operation. The analysis looks for food safety hazards (biological, chemical, and physical) that are likely to occur in your operation and are reasonably likely to cause injury or harm if not effectively controlled. According to the Food Code, a hazard is a biological, chemical, or physical property that may cause a food to be unsafe for human consumption. **The following are several questions that should be asked when assessing the food safety of your operation:**

- What has been the safety record for the product in the marketplace?
- Is the food from a safe source?
- Are there natural toxins that are associated with this food?
- Does the preparation procedure or process include a step that destroys pathogens or their toxins?
- Have bare hands touched the food, or otherwise cross contaminated it?
- What chemical hazards could exist with this food?
- What physical hazards could be present?
- Does the food permit survival or multiplication of pathogens and/or toxin formation in the food before or during preparation?
- Will the food permit survival of pathogens and/or toxin formation during subsequent steps of preparation?
- Will the food permit multiplication of pathogens and/or toxin formation during subsequent steps of preparation?
- Is there an epidemiological history associated with this food?
- Is the food served to a highly susceptible population?
- What is known about the time/temperature exposure of the food?
- What is the water activity (a_w) and acidity (pH) of the food?
- Do food workers practice good personal hygiene, including frequent and effective hand washing?
- Has the food been exposed to unclean or unsanitized equipment?
- Is the product subject to recontamination after cooking?

By answering these questions, you are assessing potential hazards to determine the likelihood that a foodborne illness or injury will occur.

Biological Hazards

As you might recall from Star Point 1, biological hazards include bacterial, viral, and parasitic microorganisms. These microorganisms are of the most significant concern with regard to food safety. The CDC has identified more than 250 foodborne illnesses. The majority of these foodborne infections are caused by bacteria, viruses, and parasites.

The following tables from the Food and Drug Administration will assist you in the evaluation of specific foods that you may sell or serve, and identify potential biological hazards that you must control to provide your customers with safe food.

Selected Biological Hazards Found at Retail, Associated Food, and Control Measures

Associated Foods	Hazard	Control Measures
	Bacteria	
Meat, poultry, starchy foods (rice, potatoes), puddings, soups, cooked vegetables	*Bacillus cereus* (intoxication caused by heat stable, performed emetic toxin and infection by heat labile, diarrheal toxin)	Cooking, cooling, cold holding, hot holding
Poultry, raw milk	*Campylobacter jejuni*	Cooking, handwashing, preventing cross contamination
Vacuum-packed food, reduced oxygen packaged foods, under-processed canned foods, garlic-in-oil mixtures, time/temperature abused baked potatoes and sautéed onions	*Clostridium botulinum*	Thermal processing (time + pressure), cooling, cold holding, hot holding, acidification and drying, etc.
Raw ground beef, raw seed sprouts, raw milk, unpasteurized juice, food contaminated by infected food workers via fecal-(hand) oral route	*E. coli* 0157:H7 (other shiga toxin-producing E. coli)	Cooking, no bare-hand contact with RTE foods, employee health policy, handwashing, prevention of cross contamination, pasteurization, or treatment of juice.
Raw meat and poultry, fresh soft cheese, pate, smoked seafood, deli meats, deli salads	*Listeria monocytogenes*	Cooking, date marking, cold holding, handwashing, preventing cross contamination, pasteurization, or treatment of juice.
Meat and poultry, seafood, eggs, raw seed sprouts, raw vegetables, raw milk, unpasteurized juice	*Salmonella* spp.	Cooking, use of pasteurized eggs, employee health policy, no bare-hand contact with RTE foods, handwashing, pasteurization, or treatment of juice.
Raw vegetables and herbs, other foods contaminated by infected workers via fecal-(hand)-oral route.	*Shigella* spp.	Cooking, no bare-hand contact with RTE foods, employee health policy, handwashing
RTE TCS foods touched by bare hands after cooking and further time/ temperature abuse	*Staphylococcus aureus* (preformed heat stable toxin	Cooling, cold holding, no bare-hand contact with RTE food, hand washing
Seafood, shellfish	*Vibrio* spp.	Cooking, approved source, preventing cross contamination, cold holding

Associated Foods	Hazard	Control Measures
	Parasites	
Various fish (cod, haddock, fluke, pacific salmon, herring, flounder, monkfish)	*Anisakis simplex*	Cooking, freezing
Beef and pork	*Taenia* spp.	Cooking
Pork, bear, and seal meat	*Trichinella spiralis*	Cooking
	Viruses	
Shellfish, any food contaminated by infected worker via fecal-(hand)-oral route	Hepatitis A and E	Approved source, no bare-hand contact with RTE food, minimizing bare-hand contact with foods not RTE, employee health policy, handwashing

RTE = ready-to-eat TCS = time/temperature control for safety food Source: FDA Code

Foods That May Be Served Raw or Undercooked

Raw Animal Food	Menu Items	Hazards
Beef	Steak tartare Carpaccio	*Salmonella* spp. *Eschericha coli 0157:H7*
Poultry	Duck	*Salmonella* spp. *Campylobacter jejuni*
Eggs	Quiche, hollandaise sauce, Eggs Benedict, homemade mayonnaise, meringue pie, some puddings and custards, Monte Cristo sandwich, mousse, tiramisu, chicken croquettes, rice balls, stuffing, lasagna, french toast, crab cakes, egg nog, fish stuffing, Caesar salad, ice cream	*Salmonella enteritidis*
Raw Fish / Finfish	Lightly cooked fish, sushi, raw-marinated, cold-smoked fish, ceviche, tuna carpaccio	*Anisakis simplex* *Diphyllobothrium* spp. *Pseudoterranova decipiens* *Vibrio parahaemolyticus*
	Reef fish: (barracuda, amberjack, horse-eye jack, black/jack, other large species of jack, king mackerel, large groupers, large snappers)	Ciguatera toxin
Shellfish	Oysters, Clams	*Vibrio vulnificus* *Vibrio* spp. Hepatitis A Norovirus
Raw Dairy Products	Raw or unpasterized milk, some soft cheeses like Camembert, Brie, etc.	*Listeria monocytogenes* *Salmonella* spp. *Campylobacter jejuni* *E.coli* 0157:H7

Source: Managing Food Safety: A Manual for the Voluntary Use of HACCP Principles for Operators of Food Service Retail Establishments (Food and Drug Administration, U.S. Department of Health and Human Services).

Common Parasites in Seafood[1]

Parasites[2]	Species of fish likely to be used on a menu that may not be fully cooked to 145°F		Control Measures
Nematodes or roundworms Cestodes or tapeworms Trematodes or flukes	Sea bass Capelin & roe Cod Flounder -Dab -Fluke Grouper Halibut Herring Jack Jobfish Kahawai Mackerel Monkfish Mullet	Chilean Sea Bass Ocean Perch Plaice Pollock Rockfish Sablefish Salmon & roe (aquacultured and wild) Seatrout Sole Sprat/Bristling Trout/steelhead/rainbow Tuna, small Turbot Wolffish	Purchase from a processor, require the raw fish to have been: • Frozen and stored at -4°F (-20°C) or below for 7 days; or • Frozen at -31°F (-35°C) or below and stored at -31°F (-35°C) for 15 hours; or • Frozen at -31°F (-35°C) or below until solid and stored at -4°F (-20°C) for 24 hours. Freezing can be done in your operation if it is done in accordance with the Food Code Chapter 3.

[1] Fish and Fishery Products Hazards and Controls Guide, Third Edition, June 2011

[2] Some food products that have been implicated in human parasite infection are: ceviche, lomi lomi, poisson cru, salmon roe, sashimi, sushi, green herring, drunken crabs, cold smoked fish, undercooked grilled fish

Source: Managing Food Safety: A Manual for the Voluntary Use of HACCP Principles for Operators of Food Service Retail Establishments (Food and Drug Administration, U.S. Department of Health and Human Services).

Chemical Hazards

Chemical hazards may also cause foodborne illness. Chemical hazards can occur naturally or be introduced during any stage of food production. Dangerous, naturally occurring chemicals can be found in some species of fish (scombroid, ciguatera, puffer fish) or shellfish (molluscan, lobsters, red rock crabs), and in some plant foods (red kidney beans or mushrooms). Allergens are considered naturally occurring chemical hazards in the Food Code.

Common Chemical Hazards at Retail, Along with their Associated Foods and Control Measures

Associated Foods Naturally Occurring:	Chemical Hazards	Hazards Control Measures
Primarily associated with tuna fish, mahi-mahi, bluefish, anchovies bonito, mackerel; Also found in cheese	Scombrotoxin	Check temperatures at receiving; store at proper cold holding temperatures; buying specifications: obtain verification from supplier that product has not been temperature abused prior to arrival in facility.
Reef finfish from extreme Southeast US, Hawaii, and tropical areas; barracuda, amberjacks, king mackerel, large groupers, and snappers	Ciguatoxin	• Purchase fish from approved sources • Fish should not be harvested from an area that is subject to an adverse advisory
Puffer fish (Fugu, Blowfish)	Tetrodotoxin	Do not consume these fish.
Corn and corn products, peanuts and peanut products, cottonseed, milk, and tree nuts such as Brazil nuts, pecans, pistachio nuts, and walnuts. Other grains and nuts are susceptible but less prone to contamination. Apple juice products	Mycotoxins Aflatoxin Patulin	Check condition at receiving; do not use moldy or decomposed food. Buyer specification; obtain verification from supplier or avoid the use of rotten apples in juice manufacturing.
Numerous varieties of wild mushrooms	Toxic mushroom species	Do not eat unknown varieties from unapproved sources.
Molluscan shellfish from NE and NW coastal regions; mackerel, viscera of lobsters and Dungeness, tanner, and red rock crabs Molluscan shellfish in Japan, western Europe, Chile, NZ, eastern Canada Molluscan shellfish from Gulf of Mexico Molluscan shellfish from NE and NW coasts of NA; viscera of Dungeness, tanner, red rock crabs and anchovies.	Shellfish toxins Paralytic shellfish poisoning (PSP) Diarrhetic shellfish poisoning (DSP) Neurotoxin shellfish poisoning (NSP) Amnesic shellfish poisoning (ASP)	Ensure molluscan shellfish are: • from an approved source; and • properly tagged and labeled.
Plant food containing these alkaloids. Most commonly found in member of the Borginaceae, Compositae, and Leguminosae families.	Pyrrolizidine alkaloids	Do not consume foods contaminated with these alkaloids.

Associated Foods	Chemical Hazards	Hazards Control Measures
Raw red kidney beans (undercooked beans may be more toxic than raw beans)	Phtyohaemmagglutinin	Soak in water for at least 5 hours. Pour away the water. Boil briskly in fresh water, with occasional stirring, for at least 10 minutes
Foods containing or contacted by: Milk Egg Fish Crustacean shellfish Tree nuts Wheat Peanuts Soybeans	Allergens	Use a rigorous sanitation regime to prevent cross contact between allergenic and non-allergenic ingredients.
Added Chemicals:		
Any food may become contaminated.	Environmental contaminants: Pesticides, fungicides, fertilizers, insecticides, antibiotics, growth hormones	Follow label instructions for use of environmental chemicals. Soil or water analysis may be used to verify safety.
Fish	PCBs	Comply with fish advisories.
Numerous substances are prohibited from use in human food; no substance may be used in human food unless it meets all applicable requirements of the FD&C Act.	Prohibited substances (21 CFR 189)	Do not use chemical substances that are not approved for use in human food.
Fish exposed to organic mercury: shark, tilefish, king mackerel, and swordfish. Grains treated with mercury based fungicides.	Toxic elements/compounds Mercury	Pregnant women/women of childbearing age/nursing mothers, and young children should not eat shark, swordfish, king mackerel, or tilefish because they contain high levels of mercury. Do not use mercury-containing fungicides on grains or animals.
High acid foods and beverages.	Cooper	Do not store high acid foods in copper utensils; use backflow prevention device on beverage vending machines.
High acid foods and beverages.	Lead	Do not use vessels containing lead.

Associated Foods Naturally Occurring:	Chemical Hazards	Hazards Control Measures
Fresh fruits and vegetables Shrimp Lobster Wine	Preservatives and Food Additives: Sulfiting agents (sulfur dioxide, sodium and potassium bisulfite, sodium and potassium metabisulfite)	Sulfiting agents added to a product in a processing plant must be declared on labeling. Do not use on raw produce in food establishments.
Cured meats, fish, any food exposed to accidental contamination, spinach Meat and other foods to which sodium nicotinate is added	Nitrites/Nitrates Niacin	Do not use more than the prescribed amount of curing compound according to labeling instructions. Sodium nicotinate (niacin) is not currently approved for use in meat or poultry with or without nitrates.
Asian or Latin American food	Flavor enhancers Monosodium glutamate (MSG)	Avoid using excessive amounts.
Any food could become contaminated	Chemicals used in retail establishments (e.g., lubricants, cleaners, sanitizers, cleaning compounds, and paints)	Address through SOPs for proper labeling, storage, handling, and use of chemicals; retain Safety Data Sheets (SDS) for all chemicals.

Source: 2017 Food Code

Physical Hazards

A physical hazard is any physical material or foreign object not normally found in a food that can cause illness and injury. These physical hazards may be the result of intentional contamination, carelessness, mishandling, or implementing poor procedures. Physical hazards can be introduced at any point in the food chain; from harvest to consumer, including those within the food establishment. These hazards are usually the easiest to identify because someone, usually the consumer, finds the foreign object and reports the incident. Refer to the chart located on page 128 for the main materials of concern as physical hazards and common sources.

Main Materials of Concern as Physical Hazards and Common Sources[a,b]

Material	Injury Potential	Sources
Glass fixtures	Cuts, bleeding; may require surgery to find or remove	Bottles, jars, light, utensils, gauge covers
Wood	Cuts, infection, choking; may require surgery to remove	Fields, pallets, boxes, buildings
Stones, metal fragments	Choking, broken teeth Cuts, infection; may require surgery to remove	Fields, buildings, machinery, wire, employees
Insulation	Choking; long-term if asbestos	Building materials
Bone	Choking, trauma	Fields, improper plant processing
Plastic	Choking, cuts, infection; may require surgery to remove	Fields, plant packaging materials, pallets, employees
Personal effects	Choking, cuts, broken teeth; may require surgery to remove	Employees

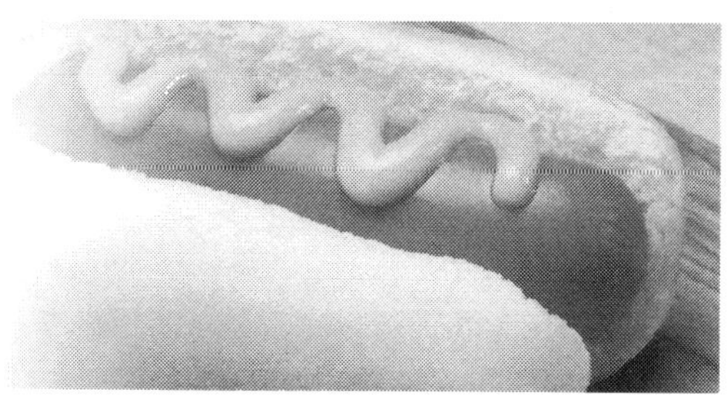

Star Knowledge Exercise:

Biological Contamination Exercise
Kevin's Story

Dedicated to Patricia Buck and her grandson, Kevin Kowalcyk

Answer the question at the end of this story on prevention, using your knowledge of biological hazards and the Biological Hazards Chart.

Controlling biological hazards can make a difference in the health and lives of people around the world. The following is a true story of how this kind of tragedy can strike anywhere and at any time. Hopefully not but someday, you may meet a person who has experienced a tragedy as the result of a foodborne illness.

Patricia Buck is a Grove City, Pennsylvania grandmother, whose two-and-a-half-year-old grandson Kevin Kowalcyk died from a fatal disease that was found to be in undercooked hamburger. He became a statistic because of his death from E. coli 0157:H7 in 2001. That precious child was more than a statistic to Patricia Buck. She began and continues to crusade for food safety by working to have laws passed to enforce safety and standards in meat and poultry plants around the United States. It's important to Patricia Buck that HACCP is mandated. She has personally thanked food safety trainers (including Tara Cammarata, one of this book's authors) for teaching food service and retail employees about the importance of doing their jobs correctly to avoid food contamination. Watching an innocent child suffer for 12 days as the E. coli ravaged his body, resulting in a painful, horrifying death, should not be what happens when someone eats a hamburger.

According to the Biological Hazards Chart, what control measures could have prevented this senseless death?

____

____

____

Hazard Analysis: A Two-Stage Process

It is important to remember that **hazard analysis** focuses on food safety, not food quality. The focus on HACCP is serving food which is safe to eat. Consider the following: one or more reheating steps might dry out a certain food. Can this food still be served? According to HACCP standards, the answer is yes. While it may have lost some of its appeal to a customer, it is still safe to eat. Also consider that food may seem appealing and taste good but, if not properly handled and prepared may contain a deadly toxin! The process of conducting a hazard analysis involves two stages, neither involves food quality. Food quality ≠ Food safety.

Stage 1 is Hazard Identification and Stage 2 is Hazard Evaluation of the foods that are used in your establishment. Managers should focus on the two stages in the hazard analysis.

Overview of Stage 1: Hazard Identification

This stage focuses on identifying the food safety hazards that might be present in the food following the food preparation process used, the handling of the food, the facility, and general characteristics of the food itself. During this stage, there is a review of the following; ingredients used and the activities conducted at each step in the process, the equipment used, and the final product itself. Further, there should be an examination of the methods of storage and distribution, as well as the intended use of the product by consumer. Based on this review, a list is made of potential biological, chemical, or physical hazards at each stage in the food preparation process.

Stage 1: Hazard Identification

- **A. Intended Use.** Analyze your customers and the consumers of the product.
- **B. Menu Evaluation.** Determine general characteristics of the food; identify ingredients and determine if the food requires time/temperature control for safety is an allergen; and the associated hazards.
- **C. Flow of Food.** List preparation process and activities conducted at each step. Understand the flow of food to determine where hazards may be controlled.
- **D. Food Processes and Handling.** Evaluate your menu. Divide your menu items into three categories based on how the food is prepared: Simple/No-Cook recipes, Same-Day recipes, and Complex recipes.
- **E. Capacity.** Evaluate the facility and equipment needs, as well as, personnel training and knowledge requirements.

Overview of Stage 2: Hazard Evaluation

In Stage 2, the Hazard Evaluation, each potential hazard is evaluated based on the severity of the potential hazard and the likelihood of an occurrence. The purpose of this stage is to determine which of the potential hazards listed in Stage 1 warrants control in the HACCP plan. The answers to these three questions help in determining the status of any hazard.

Stage 2: Hazard Evaluation Questions

- What is the likelihood of a hazard to occur here?
- What is the risk if the hazard does occur?
- Is there a way for this hazard to be controlled or eliminated?

Severity is the seriousness of the consequences if exposure to the hazard occurs. When determining the severity of a hazard, you must recognize the impact of the medical condition caused by the illness, as well as the magnitude and duration of the illness or injury. The severity of a likely occurrence is usually based upon a combination of experience, epidemiological data, and information in technical literature. During the evaluation of each potential hazard, the food, its method of preparation, transportation, storage, and persons likely to consume the product, should be considered to determine how each of these factors might influence the likely occurrence and severity of the hazard being controlled. For example, E. coli 0157:H7 is definitely a potential hazard in raw ground beef; it is likely to occur. However, when properly cooked to 155°F (68.3°C) for 17 seconds, the likelihood of E. coli 0157:H7 presenting a severe hazard is reduced. Also, the presence of E. coli 0157:H7 in precooked frozen hamburger patties has already been reduced, so the likelihood of a severe hazard is minimal for E. coli 0157:H7 exposure. The patty that is commercially processed, hermetically sealed, or provided in an intact package from a food processing plant must still be reheated to 135°F (57.2°C) for 15 seconds to reduce other microorganisms that may have been introduced to the food via food handlers, preparation, or packaging.

Here is more detailed information on completing these two stages.

Stage 1: Hazard Identification

A. Intended Use:

Analyze your customers and the consumers of the product.

Do you serve the general population? Or do you serve a highly susceptible population? Highly susceptible people are those who, if contract a foodborne illness, are more likely to have far greater medical problems. They are more vulnerable to foodborne illnesses. Schools, hospitals, day-care sites for children and adults, and assisted-living centers all serve highly susceptible persons and require very strict standards of operation because of the high vulnerability of these customers. You must be aware of those you serve such as infants and children, pregnant women, people on medications, or senior citizens when conducting hazard identification. Serving food to highly susceptible population groups will require an operator to manage health issues differently or make changes to handling certain foods. It is important to recognize that similar foods can involve very different handling procedures based upon the characteristics of the consumer, the operation style and type of service.

Pop Quiz:

Analyze Customers
Stage 1: Hazard Identification, Intended Use

Mark an "X" in the box that analyzes the customer bases as examples of general population or a highly susceptible population. Note: Operations can serve both types of customers.

Customer Base	General Population	Highly Susceptible Population
Convenience store		
Middle school		
Quick service restaurant		
Senior care facility		
Hospital		
Casual dining restaurant		
Fine dining restaurant		
Day care		
Institutional foodservice		
Tavern		

B. Menu Evaluation:
Determine general characteristics of the food being produced. Identify ingredients, potentially hazardous foods, that requires time/temperature control for safety, and allergens.

When analyzing the food in your establishment, one of the first things to do is to identify all TCS foods. Hazard Analysis of the food to be handled is conducted to identify associated biological, chemical, and physical hazards. Additional research or expertise may be required depending upon specific products or processes. When conducting the hazard analysis, identifying whether products are raw, processed, used as an ingredient, or contain allergen proteins further characterize the potential hazard.

Using the sample menu and the recipes provided, can you identify any time/temperature control for safety food as well as any "Big 8" allergen concerns? Remember, not all foods are potentially hazardous or need time/temperature control for safety. Complete the Star Knowledge exercise on the next page to test your skills on identifying TCS foods and allergens.

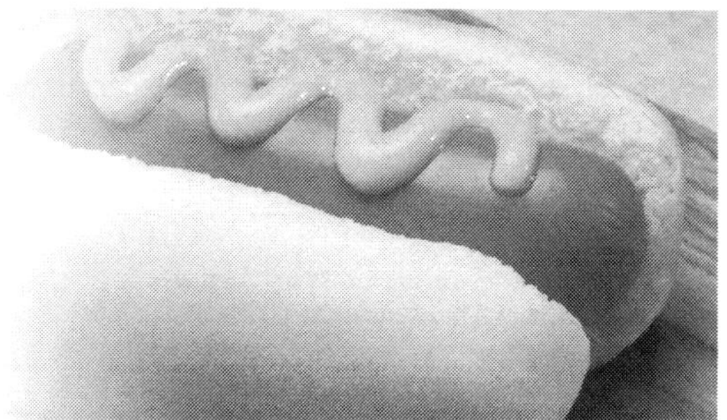

Star Knowledge Exercise:

TCS and Allergen Identification Stage 1: Hazard Identification, Menu Evaluation

Analyze the menu items below and identify TCS foods and the "Big 8" allergens from each recipe.
Note: Keep these recipes handy, they will be used throughout the book with other exercises. **Please consider all canned foods to be opened when evaluating them.**

Sample Menu

Mixed Fruit Cup	Roasted Chicken Club	Banana Smoothie	Chili
Spanish Rice Bake	Chicken Pasta Primavera	Pork Barbeque	Tuna Melt

Mixed-Fruit Crisp

TCS	Allergen	Food Item
☐	☐	1 15-ounce can (443.6 ml) mixed fruit
☐	☐	1/2 cup (118.29 ml) quick rolled oats
☐	☐	1/2 cup (118.29 ml) brown sugar
☐	☐	1/2 cup (118.29 ml) all-purpose flour
☐	☐	1/4 teaspoon (1.24 ml) baking powder
☐	☐	1/2 teaspoon (2.45 ml) ground cinnamon
☐	☐	1/4 cup (59.15 ml) butter or margarine

(Recommendation: prepare a day in advance.)

1. Preheat oven to 350ºF (176.6ºC).
2. Drain mixed fruit and set aside.
3. Lightly grease an 8- or 9-inch (20.32- or 22.86-cm) baking pan. Place the mixed fruit on the bottom of the pan.
4. In a smaller bowl, combine all of the dry ingredients. Cut in the butter or margarine with a pastry blender. Sprinkle mixture over mixed-fruit filling.
5. Bake for 30 to 35 minutes in conventional oven to a minimum internal temperature of 135ºF (57.2ºC) for 15 seconds.
6. Cool properly. Cool hot food from 135°F to 70°F (57.2°C to 21.1°C) within 2 hours; you then have an additional 4 hours to go from 70°F to 41ºF (21.1ºC to 5°C) or lower for a maximum total cool time of 6 hours.
7. Store in refrigeration at 41ºF (5°C) or lower.
8. Reheat 165°F (73.9°C) for 15 seconds within 2 hours, serve warm.

Banana Smoothie

TCS	Allergen	Food Item
☐	☐	1 cup (236.59 ml) evaporated milk
☐	☐	1 ripe banana
☐	☐	1 teaspoon (4.91 ml) lemon juice
☐	☐	2 cups (473.18 ml) ice
☐	☐	1 tablespoon (14.79 ml) honey or sugar
☐	☐	optional nutmeg

1. Mix evaporated milk, banana, lemon juice, and honey together in a blender on high speed. Add ice gradually; process until slushy. Sprinkle with nutmeg, if desired.

Chili

TCS	Allergen	Food Item
☐	☐	12 ounces (340.19 grams) ground beef
☐	☐	1 cup (236.59 ml) onion, chopped (1 large onion)
☐	☐	1⁄2 cup (118.29 ml) green bell pepper, chopped
☐	☐	2 cloves garlic, minced
☐	☐	1 15.5-ounce can (458.39 ml) tomatoes, cut up (do not drain the liquid from the can)
☐	☐	1 15.5-ounce can (458.39 ml) dark red kidney beans, rinsed and drained
☐	☐	1 8-ounce can (236.59 ml) tomato sauce
☐	☐	2 to 3 teaspoons (9.82–14.73 ml) chili powder
☐	☐	1⁄2 teaspoon (2.45 ml) dried basil, crushed
☐	☐	1⁄4 teaspoon (1.24 ml) pepper

1. In a large saucepan, cook ground beef, onion, bell pepper, and garlic until meat is brown and onion is tender. Drain fat.
2. Stir in the tomatoes, kidney beans, tomato sauce, chili powder, basil, and pepper.
3. Cook to minimum internal temperature of 165ºF (73.9ºC).
4. Hold on stove for 1 hour.
5. Cool properly. Cool hot food from 135°F to 70°F (57.2°C to 21.1°C) within 2 hours; you then have an additional 4 hours to go from 70°F to 41°F (21.1°C to 5°C) or lower for a maximum total cool time of 6 hours.
6. Store the chili in refrigeration at 41°F (5°C) or lower to allow the flavors to blend.
7. Properly reheat the next day to 165°F (73.9°C) for 15 seconds within 2 hours, hot hold and serve.

Spanish Rice Bake

TCS	Allergen	Food Item
☐	☐	1 pound (453.59 grams) lean ground beef
☐	☐	1⁄2 cup (118.29 ml) onion, finely chopped
☐	☐	1⁄4 cup (59.15 ml) green bell pepper, chopped
☐	☐	1 15.5-ounce can (458.39 ml) tomatoes
☐	☐	1 cup (236.59 ml) water
☐	☐	3⁄4 cup (177.44 ml) uncooked long-grain rice
☐	☐	1⁄4 cup (118.29 ml) chili sauce
☐	☐	1 teaspoon (4.91 ml) salt
☐	☐	1⁄2 teaspoon (2.45 ml) Worcestershire sauce
☐	☐	1 pinch ground black pepper
☐	☐	1⁄2 cup (118.29 ml) shredded cheddar cheese
☐	☐	1⁄2 teaspoon (2.45 ml) ground cumin (optional)
☐	☐	2 tablespoons (29.57 ml) chopped fresh cilantro (optional)

1. Preheat oven to 375ºF (190.55ºC).
2. Brown the ground beef in a large skillet over medium-high heat. Drain excess fat and transfer beef to a large pot over medium-low heat. Stir in the onion, green bell pepper, tomatoes, water, rice, chili sauce, salt, brown sugar, cumin, Worcestershire sauce, and ground black pepper.
3. Simmer for about 30 minutes, stirring occasionally, and then put into a 2-quart (1.892-liter) casserole dish. Press down firmly and sprinkle with the shredded cheddar cheese.
4. Bake product to a minimum internal temperature of 165ºF (73.9ºC). Garnish with chopped fresh cilantro, if desired. Hot hold and serve.

Chicken and Pasta Primavera

TCS	Allergen	Food Item
☐	☐	1-1/2 cups (354.88 ml) uncooked bow tie pasta (or any other type of pasta)
☐	☐	1 10.75-ounce can (317.92 ml) condensed cream of mushroom soup
☐	☐	3/4 cup (177.44 ml) milk
☐	☐	1/8 teaspoon (.62 ml) ground black pepper
☐	☐	2 cups (473.18 ml) broccoli florets
☐	☐	1/8 teaspoon (.67 ml) garlic powder
☐	☐	2 carrots, sliced thinly
☐	☐	1/3 can (about 10 ounces) (295.74 ml) canned chicken, drained
☐	☐	1/4 cup (59.15 ml) grated parmesan cheese (optional)

1. Cook pasta in boiling water. Drain.
2. While the pasta is cooking, prepare the cream sauce. In a medium saucepan, stir together soup, milk, pepper, broccoli, garlic powder, carrots, and parmesan cheese (optional). Reduce heat to low and cover. Simmer for 10 minutes, or until vegetables are tender. Stir occasionally.
3. Stir pasta and chicken into cream sauce and heat thoroughly to a minimum internal temperature of 165°F (73.9°C). Serve.

Pork BBQ Sandwich

TCS	Allergen	Food Item
☐	☐	1 teaspoon (4.91 ml) vegetable oil
☐	☐	1 large onion, chopped
☐	☐	2 cups (473.18 ml) canned pork
☐	☐	3/4 cup (177.44 ml) prepared barbecue sauce
☐	☐	5 hamburger rolls

1. In large skillet, heat the oil on low heat.
2. Add onion and cook until tender, about 5 minutes.
3. Mix in pork and barbecue sauce and cook to a minimum internal temperature of 135°F (57.2°C) for 15 seconds.
4. Spoon barbecue mixture on bottom half of opened hamburger bun.
5. Serve.

Tuna Melt Sandwich

TCS	Allergen	Food Item
☐	☐	1 12-ounce can (354.88 ml) tuna, drained and flaked
☐	☐	1⁄3 cup (78.86 ml) low-fat mayonnaise/mayonnaise
☐	☐	1⁄4 teaspoon (1.24 ml) dry mustard
☐	☐	3 tablespoons (44.36 ml) minced fresh onion
☐	☐	1⁄2 cup (118.29 ml) finely diced celery
☐	☐	1⁄3 cup (5 ounces) (78.86 ml) shredded American cheese
☐	☐	5 English muffins, split

1. In a bowl, combine the dry mustard and mayonnaise.
2. Stir in the onions, celery, and drained tuna. Toss lightly to mix.
3. Mix in half of the shredded cheese.
4. Lay out split English muffins onto a baking pan. Spread 1⁄4 cup (59.15 ml) of tuna salad to the edge of each muffin.
5. Sprinkle the top with 1 tablespoon (14.79 ml) of remaining shredded cheese.
6. Bake at 350°F (176.6°C) for 5 minutes until cheese is melted.
7. Serve.

Remember... It is important to evaluate each food menu item and its ingredients to ensure that you know what foods you are serving and the risk associated with serving those foods! This step is vital in conducting a hazard analysis.

Pop Quiz:

Evaluate Your Menu - Hazard Analysis Stage 1: Hazard Analysis, Menu Identification

Roasted Chicken Club

In this exercise, the Chicken Club will be evaluated.
Mark of any TCS foods or "Big 8" allergens from each recipe.

TCS	Allergen	Food Item
☐	☐	Pre-Cooked Roasted Chicken
☐	☐	Fresh Cured Bacon
☐	☐	Pepper Jack Cheese
☐	☐	Mayonnaise
☐	☐	Shredded Lettuce
☐	☐	Sliced Raw Tomato
☐	☐	Salt
☐	☐	Pepper
☐	☐	Wheat Bread

1. Cook raw bacon to 145°F for 15 seconds and set aside for sandwich assembly.
2. Assemble sandwich on wheat bread using pre-cooked roasted chicken, cooked bacon, pepper jack cheese, mayonnaise, lettuce, tomato, salt and pepper.
3. Cover and store in refrigeration at 41°F (5°C) or lower until served.

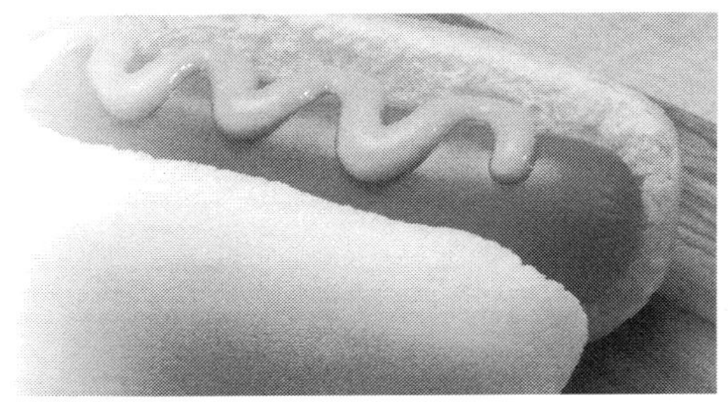

Star Knowledge Exercise:

Roasted Chicken Club
Stage 1: Hazard Analysis,
Menu Evaluation

Roasted Chicken Club

Evaluate the menu item by identifying the food characteristics and hazards associated with the ingredients. Use the knowledge you gained in Star Point 1 and the charts and tables provide in this chapter to complete the chart.

Food Item	Component Ingredients	TCS	Biological Hazard Bacteria, Fungi, Parasites	Chemical Hazard Cleaners, sanitizers, pesticides,		Physical Hazard Metal, Glass, Wood	Raw Food	Processed Food
				Allergen	Other			
Pre-Cooked Roasted Chicken	Chicken, salt, pepper, allspice							
Bacon (uncooked, cured)	Pork, salt, sugar, sodium nitrite, sodium phosphate, sodium erythorbate							
Pepper Jack Cheese	Pasteurized milk, red & green jalapeno peppers, cheese culture, salt, enzymes							
Shredded Lettuce								
Sliced Tomato								
Mayo	Soybean oil, water, whole eggs, egg yolk, vinegar, salt, sugar, lemon juice							
Salt								
Pepper								
Wheat Bread Roll	Wheat Flour, cellulose fiber, wheat gluten, yeast, salt, sugar, wheat bran, molasses, mono-and diglycerides, calcium propionate (preservative), grain vinegar, calcium sulfate, mono-calcium phosphate, soy lecithin, sucralose, soy flour							

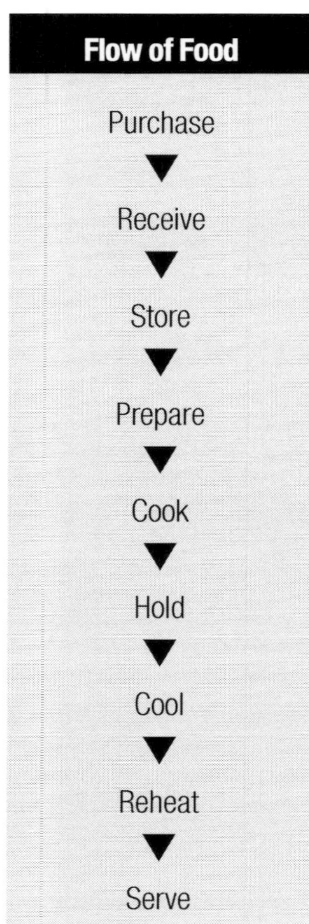

C. Flow of Food:

The flow of food refers to each stage in the food service or retail process. In order to determine where hazards may be controlled, you need to understand the flow of food. All the food we eat goes through what we call the flow of food. Most flows start with the purchasing of food from approved sources. Sometimes food is grown or raised on site, but that is rare. In any case, food is received, stored, prepared, cooked, held, cooled, reheated, and served.

The flow of food is best described by looking at, as an example, how you make a pot of homemade soup. First, you **purchase** the ingredients, hopefully from a clean, safe grocery store. You take the food you purchased and **receive** the food into your home. Then, you need to **store** the food properly either in dry storage (your cabinets or pantry) or cold storage (your refrigerator or freezer). Once the food is stored properly, you then **prepare** the food (slicing vegetables, portioning meats, etc.). After preparation, the product is **cooked**. To cook your homemade soup properly, the meat must reach a minimum internal cooking temperature of 165°F (73.9°C). Once the soup has reached 165°F (73.9°C), and then you can **hold** the soup. The correct hot-holding temperature for your delicious homemade soup is 135°F (57.2°C).

If not consumed immediately, the next step in the flow of food is to **cool** the soup for storage, in your refrigerator. The proper procedure for cooling soup is to cool it as quickly as possible to 41°F (5°C) (follow the cooling process you learned in Star Point 1) and place it in the refrigerator. The next day, you decide to **reheat** the soup. To be safe, the soup must be reheated to 165°F (73.9°C) for 15 seconds within 2 hours. The final step is to **serve** the soup and enjoy!

Roasted Chicken Club

Purchase
↓
Receive
↓
Store
↓
Prepare
↓
Cook
↓
Prepare/Assemble
↓
Cold Storage
↓
Serve

In summary, the flow of food included the purchasing, receiving, storing, preparing, cooking, holding, cooling, reheating, and serving process of a product. **HACCP helps you ensure that at each step in the flow of food, the food remains safe.** In our example, no one became sick from eating the homemade soup because prerequisite programs and SOPs were properly followed in the flow of food. It is necessary for all food service and retail establishments to set the same goal—to serve safe food!

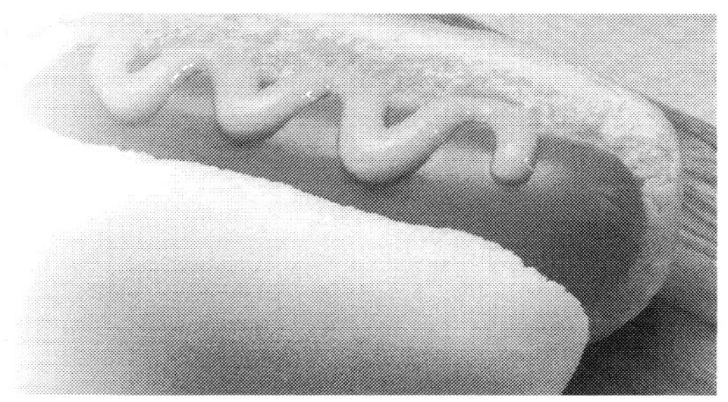

Star Knowledge Exercise:

Stage 1: Hazard Analysis, Flow of Food

In this activity, using the recipes provided earlier on pages 132-137, identify the steps in the flow of food for each of the items in the sample menu. Some items will have more steps than others.

Sample Menu

Mixed Fruit Cup	Roasted Chicken Club	Bananna Smoothie	Chili
Spanish Rice Bake	Chicken Pasta Primavera	Pork Barbeque	Tuna Melt

Mixed Fruit Crisp	Roasted Chicken Club	Banana Smoothie	Chili	Spanish Rice Bake	Chicken and Pasta Primavera	Pork Barbeque	Tuna Melt

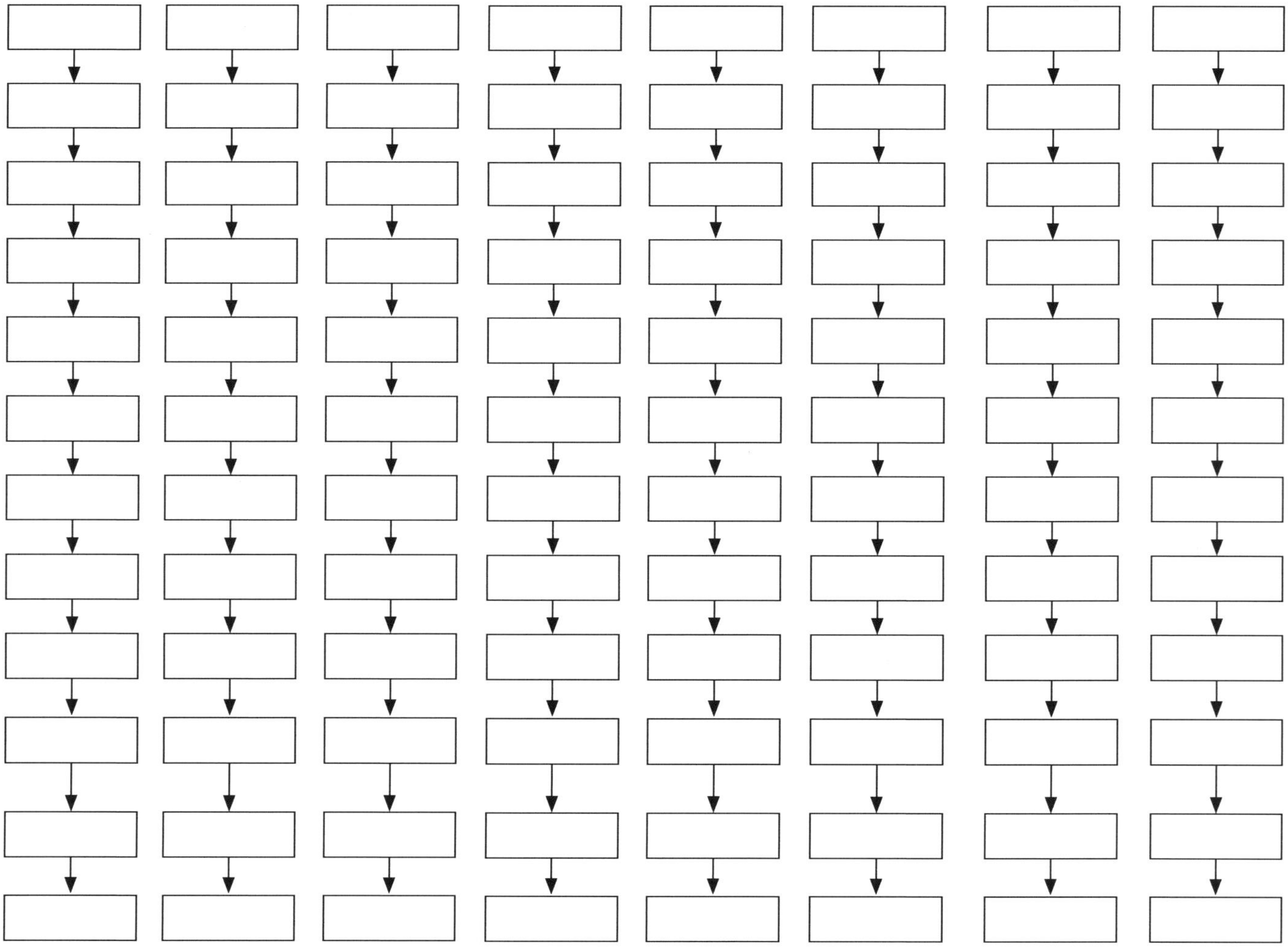

D. Food Processes and Handling:

Once the flow of food is determined for your menu items, you then divide the menu items into one of three categories. The three categories are Simple/No-Cook, Same-Day, and Complex. Every food item is placed in one of these categories. This is determined by **how the item is prepared and the number of times the food moves through the TDZ**.

Simple/No-Cook

A Simple/No-Cook recipe means exactly that. There is no cooking involved. For example, when tuna salad is prepared, a can or bag of tuna is opened, drained of the juice, placed in a bowl, and mayonnaise and seasonings are added. It is then mixed well, chilled, and served. These foods make no complete trips through the TDZ. Since there is no-cook step to reduce harmful microorganisms, good hygiene is a very important control measure. **Control Measures** are activities and actions that are used by food service and retail operators to prevent, eliminate, or reduce food safety hazards to an acceptable level.

Other foods your HACCP plan might identify as Simple/No-Cook recipes may include the following:

Retail sales of raw meat, steak, poultry, etc. • Vegetable tray • Deli meat • Salad

Cheese • Raw oysters • Cole slaw • Sashimi • Yogurt • Fresh fruit

You will need to determine the control measures that should be implemented to **prevent the occurrence of risk factors** in each food preparation process. Additional control measures include: preventing cross contamination, cooking, hot holding, cold holding, cooling, reheating, drying, pasteurization, and acidification.

Same-Day

A Same-Day Recipe means a food product is prepared for same-day service or has some Same-Day cooking involved. The food will pass through the TDZ once before it is served or sold. For example, a hamburger requires that you take the frozen raw hamburger patty from the freezer, place the hamburger on the grill, cook the hamburger to 155°F (68.3°C) for 17 seconds, place the cooked hamburger on a bun, and serve.

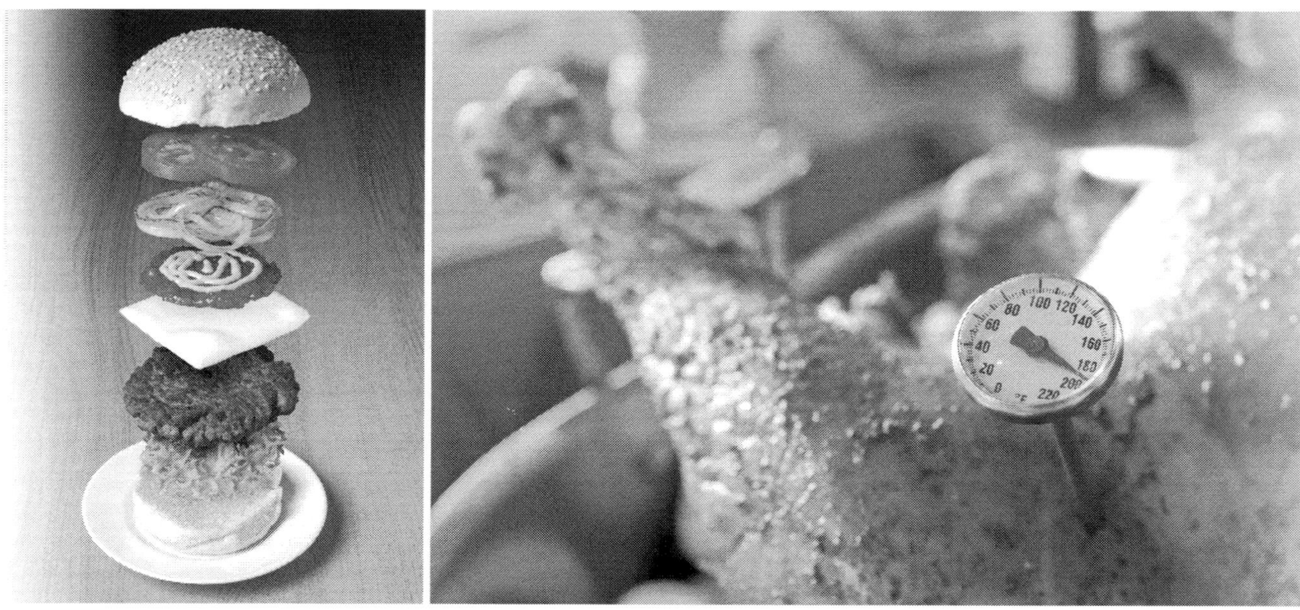

Foods your HACCP plan might identify as Same-Day Recipes include the following:

Hamburger • Baked chicken • Baked meatloaf • Chicken wrap • Fried chicken • Cheesesteak

Popcorn shrimp • Grilled cheese • Scrambled eggs • Grilled vegetables • Beef fajita • Shrimp stir-fry

Complex

A Complex Recipe calls for food to be prepared, cooled, stored, and then reheated. If a food moves through the temperature danger zone two times or more, it is considered a Complex Recipe. The homemade soup described earlier is an example of a Complex Recipe. When using a Complex Recipe you must:

1. Determine the potential for microorganisms to:
    a. Survive a heat process (cooking or reheating); and
    b. Multiply at room temperature and during hot and cold holding.
2. Find sources and specific points of contamination that are not covered in the food safety and food defense standard operating procedures.

Foods your HACCP plan might identify as Complex Recipes include the following:

Potato salad • Lasagna • Twice-baked potatoes • Chili • Casserole

Homemade meatballs • Chicken Armando (chicken stuffed with grilled eggplant)

Application of the Three Food Preparation Processes

Pictured below are the Simple/No-Cook, Same-Day, and Complex recipes as each one proceeds through the TDZ.

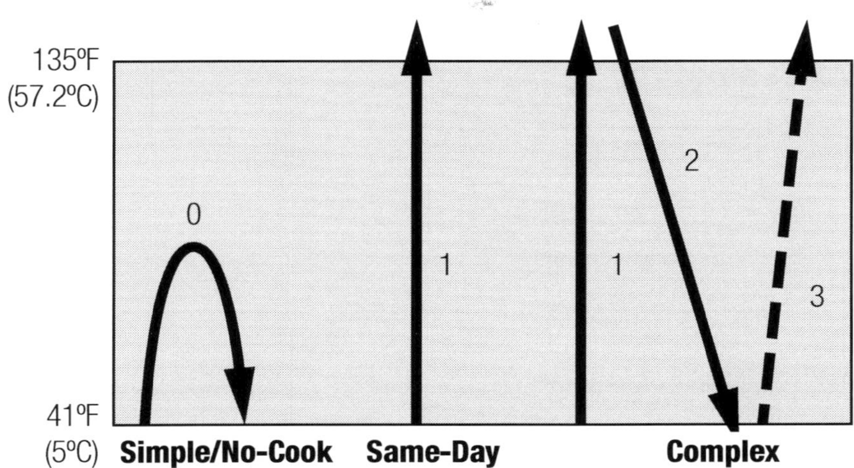

Pop Quiz:

Menu Categories
Stage 2: Menu Evaluation, Food Preparation Processes

Check the appropriate process for each food item using the recipes provided earlier on pages 132-137 in the sample menu.

Menu Item	Simple/No-Cook	Same-Day	Complex
Mixed Fruit Crisp			
Roasted Chicken Club			
Banana Smoothie			
Chili			
Spanish Rice Bake			
Chicken and Pasta Primavera			
Pork BBQ Sandwich			
Tuna Melt Sandwich			

E. Capacity:
Evaluate your menu including the facility and equipment that is used. Is the facility and equipment in your operation capable of producing the foods you want on your menu?

Next compare your menu to the ability of your employees to maintain a HACCP plan. Do you have employees who are capable of handling complex menu items and procedures? Or do you need to train or hire people with more advanced skills and culinary training? In evaluating these situations, you may need to refine, reduce, or simplify your menu. It is advantageous to address such questions now, as **re-purchasing**, **re-designing**, and **re-hiring** are expensive alternatives to a failed plan.

Stage 2: Hazard Evaluation

Hazard analysis questions:

- What is the likelihood of a hazard to occur here?
- What is the risk/severity if the hazard does occur?
- Is there a way for this hazard to be controlled or eliminated?

What is the likelihood for a hazard to occur?

Most hazards are biological (bacteria, viruses, and parasites). Biological hazards are the most common cause of foodborne illnesses. Most of these hazards can be controlled by adequate cooking, cooling, and storage of potentially hazardous foods. Other hazards might be chemical (cleaning products, sanitizers, and pesticides) or physical (metal shavings, foreign objects, and hair).

In the tuna salad, hamburger, and chicken soup examples used earlier, what is the likelihood for these hazards to occur? What are the chances these hazards could contaminate the food? Is a preventative measure needed to reduce the hazard to a safe level?

What is the severity if the hazard does occur?

If there is a high risk of contamination, it leads to an unacceptable heath risk that can be life threatening. An unacceptable health risk increases the likelihood of injury, illness, or death. If the risk of contamination is low, the risk may be considered acceptable. Acceptable risks are those that present little or no chance of injury, illness, or death. The FDA recommends that a scientist should assist your company in analyzing the hazards and completing the risk assessments. Experts use scientific data to determine if the risk is high, medium, or low in each hazard that is analyzed. In April 2004, the FDA updated these hazards associated with food. The table that follows is a **Risk Severity Assessment Chart** based on the rating system of high, medium, or low.

High **Severe Hazards**	**Medium** **Moderate Hazards: Potential Extensive Spread**	**Low** **Moderate Hazards: Limited Spread**
Clostridium botulinum	*Listeria monocytogenes*	*Campylobacter jejuni*
Salmonella typhi	*Salmonella non-typhoidal*	*Bacillius cereus*
Shigella dysenteriae	*Shigella spp.*	*Staphylococcus aureus*
Hepatitis A	*E. coli* 0157:H7	*Clostridium perfringens*
Vibrio cholerae, 01	Norovirus/Norwalk virus group	*Vibrio cholerae*, non-01
Vibrio vulnificus	Rotavirus	*Yersinia*
Trichinella spiralis	*Streptococcus pyogenes*	*Giardia*

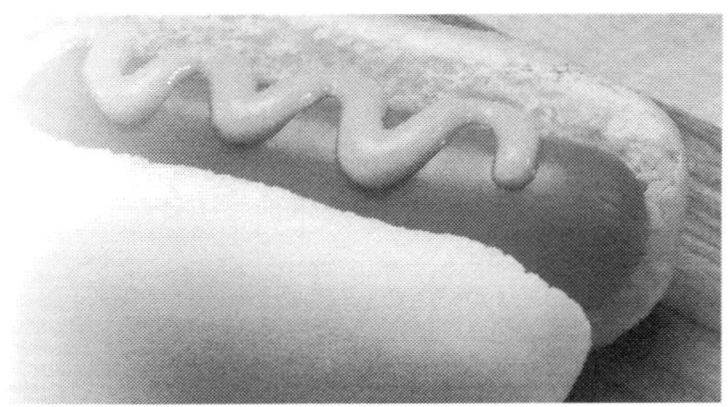

Star Knowledge Exercise:

Assess the Hazards
Stage 2: Hazard Evaluation, Hazards and Severity

This Star Knowledge Exercise provides an overview of the process used in the hazard analysis. Using the foodborne illness severity charts provided on page 146, identify one or two potential biological hazards that are likely to occur and place in the chart in the column marked Hazards Likely to Occur. Then rate the risk severity as low, medium, or high and place your answer in the table marked Severity of Illness.

Menu Item	Biological Hazards Likely to Occur	Severity of Illness
Mixed Fruit Crisp		
Roasted Chicken Club		
Banana Smoothie		
Chili		
Spanish Rice Bake		
Chicken and Pasta Primavera		
Pork BBQ Sandwich		
Tuna Melt Sandwich		

Examples of How the Stages of Hazard Analysis are Used to Identify and Evaluate Hazards*				
Product being analyzed		Frozen cooked beef patties produced in a manufacturing plant	Product containing eggs prepared for food service	Commercial frozen pre-cooked, boned chicken for further processing
Stage 1 Hazard Identification (Biological)	Determine potential hazards associated with product	Enteric pathogens (i.e., E. coli 0157:H7 and Salmonella)	Salmonella in finished product	Staphylococcus aureus in finished product
Stage 2 Hazard Evaluation	Determine likelihood of occurrence of potential hazard if not properly controlled.	E coli 0157:H7 is of very low probability and salmonellae is of moderate probability only in raw meat. This product is cooked.	Product is made with liquid eggs, which have been associated with past outbreaks of salmonellosis. Recent problems with Salmonella serotype Enteritidis in eggs cause increased concern. Probability of salmonella in raw eggs cannot be ruled out.	Product may be contaminated with S. aureus due to human handling during boning of cooked chicken. Enterotoxin capable of causing illness will only occur as S. aureus multiplies to about 1,000,000/g. Operating procedures during boning and subsequent freezing prevent growth of S. aureus; thus the potential for enterotoxin formation is very low.
	Using information above, determine if this potential hazard is being addressed in the HACCP plan.	The HACCP team decides that pathogens are hazards for this product since E. coli and Salmonella have a moderate risk severity level. **Hazards must be addressed in the plan.**	HACCP team determines that if the potential hazard is not properly controlled, consumption of product is likely to result in an unacceptable health risk with moderate risk severity. **Hazard must be addressed in the plan.**	The HACCP team determines that the potential for toxin formation is very low. However, it is still desirable to keep the initial number of S. aureus organisms low. Employee practices that minimize contamination, rapid carbon dioxide freezing and handling instructions have been adequate to control this potential hazard. **Potential hazard does not need to be addressed in the plan.**

*For illustrative purposes only, The potential hazards identified may not be the only hazards associated with the products listed. The responses may be different for different establishments.
Source: Food and Drug Administration 2009 Model Food Code, Source: Hazard Analysis and Critical Control Point Principles and Application Guidelines, **U.S. Food and Drug Administration**
http://www.fda.gov/Food/FoodSafety/HazardAnalysisCriticalControlPointsHACCP/ucm114868.htm

Control Measures

The Food Code requires that upon the completion of the hazard analysis, a list of significant hazards must be listed in the HACCP plan, along with any control measure(s) that can be used to prevent, eliminate, or reduce the hazards to a safe level. As mentioned earlier, these measures are called **control measures**. These are actions or activities that can be used to prevent, eliminate, or reduce a hazard. Some control measures are not essential to food safety, while others are. Control measures are essential to food safety, such as, proper cooking, cooling, and refrigeration of ready-to-eat foods. The term control measure is used because not all hazards can be prevented, but virtually all can be controlled. More than one control measure may be required for a specific hazard. Likewise, more than one hazard may be addressed by a specific control measure, such as proper cooking. The following chart illustrates examples of hazards and control measures for same-day service menu items.

Examples of Hazards and Control Measures for Same-Day Service Items

Example Products	Baked Meatloaf	Roasted Chicken
Example Biological Hazards	• *E. coli* 0-157:H7 • *Clostridium perfringens* • Various fecal-oral route pathogens	• *Salmonella spp.* • *Campylobacter* • *Clostridium perfringens* • Various fecal-oral route pathogens
Example Control Measures	• Refrigeration at 41°F (5°C) or below • Cooking at 155°F (68.3°C) for 17 seconds • Hot Holding at 135°F (57.2°C) or above or Time Control • Good personal hygiene (No bare hand contact with RTE food, proper handwashing, exclusion/restriction of ill employees)	• Refrigeration at 41°F (5°C) or below • Cooking at 165°F (73.8°C) • Hot Holding at 135°F (57.2°C) or above or Time Control • Good personal hygiene (No bare hand contact with RTE food, proper hand-washing, exclusion/restriction of ill employees)

Source: 2017 Food Code, U.S. Food and Drug Administration

The key to a successful HACCP program is to conduct a thorough hazard analysis. If the hazards are not correctly identified, the risks to your operation increase significantly and the program will not be effective.

HACCP Principle 2: Determine Critical Control Points

HACCP Principle 2 is to determine critical control points by first identifying all the control points in the flow of food. Once all the control points are identified, then you can determine which points are more critical than others. If a critical step is not controlled, then the risk of people contracting a foodborne illness increases. Before determining control points and critical control points, you need to have a clear understanding of what they are.

1. **Control Point (CP).** A **control point** is **any** point, step, or procedure in the flow of food where biological, chemical, or physical factors can be controlled. If loss of control occurs at this point and there is only a minor chance of contamination **and** there is not an unacceptable health risk, then the control point is not critical. It is simply a control point in the flow of food. Control point examples can be operational steps such as purchasing, receiving, storing, and preparing the food. If loss of control occurs, there are additional operational steps that can prevent, eliminate, or reduce the hazard to a safe level.

2. **Critical Control Point (CCP).** A **critical control point** is an **essential** step in the product handling process where controls can be applied and food safety hazards can be prevented, eliminated, or reduced to acceptable levels. A **critical control point** is **one of the last** chances you have to ensure the food is safe. This may include cooking, cooling, hot/cold holding, maintaining specific sanitation procedures, preventing cross contamination, or ensuring employee hygiene. It is the critical step that prevents or slows microbial growth. Every operation is different, so critical control points will vary from one operation to another. While not every step in the flow of food will be a CCP, there will be a CCP in at least one or more steps whenever a time/temperature control for safety of foods (TCS foods) is in the recipe. Lack of hazard control at this point could lead to an **unacceptable health risk**, which is why it is critical. Common examples of CCPs include cooking, cooling, hot holding, and cold holding of ready-to-eat TCS foods. Due to vegetative, spore- and toxin-forming bacteria that are associated with raw animal foods, the proper execution of control measures at each of these operational steps is essential to prevent or eliminate hazards or reduce them to acceptable levels.

Critical Control Point (CCP) Guidelines

To identify critical control points, in the flow of food, consider the following important questions. If you answer yes to any of these questions at any stage in the preparation process, you have identified a critical control point.

- Can the food you are preparing become contaminated?
- Can contaminants multiply at this point?
- Does this step eliminate or reduce the likely occurrence of a hazard to an acceptable level?
- Can you take corrective action(s) to prevent this hazard?
- Is this the last chance you have to prevent, eliminate, or reduce the hazard before you serve the food item to a customer?

Decision Tree to Determine Critical Control Points

To identify the critical control points of a food item, we must identify the most critical food safety procedures. The Codex Alimentarius Commission recommends using the decision tree table to determine if the operational process is or is not a critical control point. The HACCP team can use the decision tree to give each operational step a complete evaluation to determine if it is a critical control point.

CCP Decision Tree Table

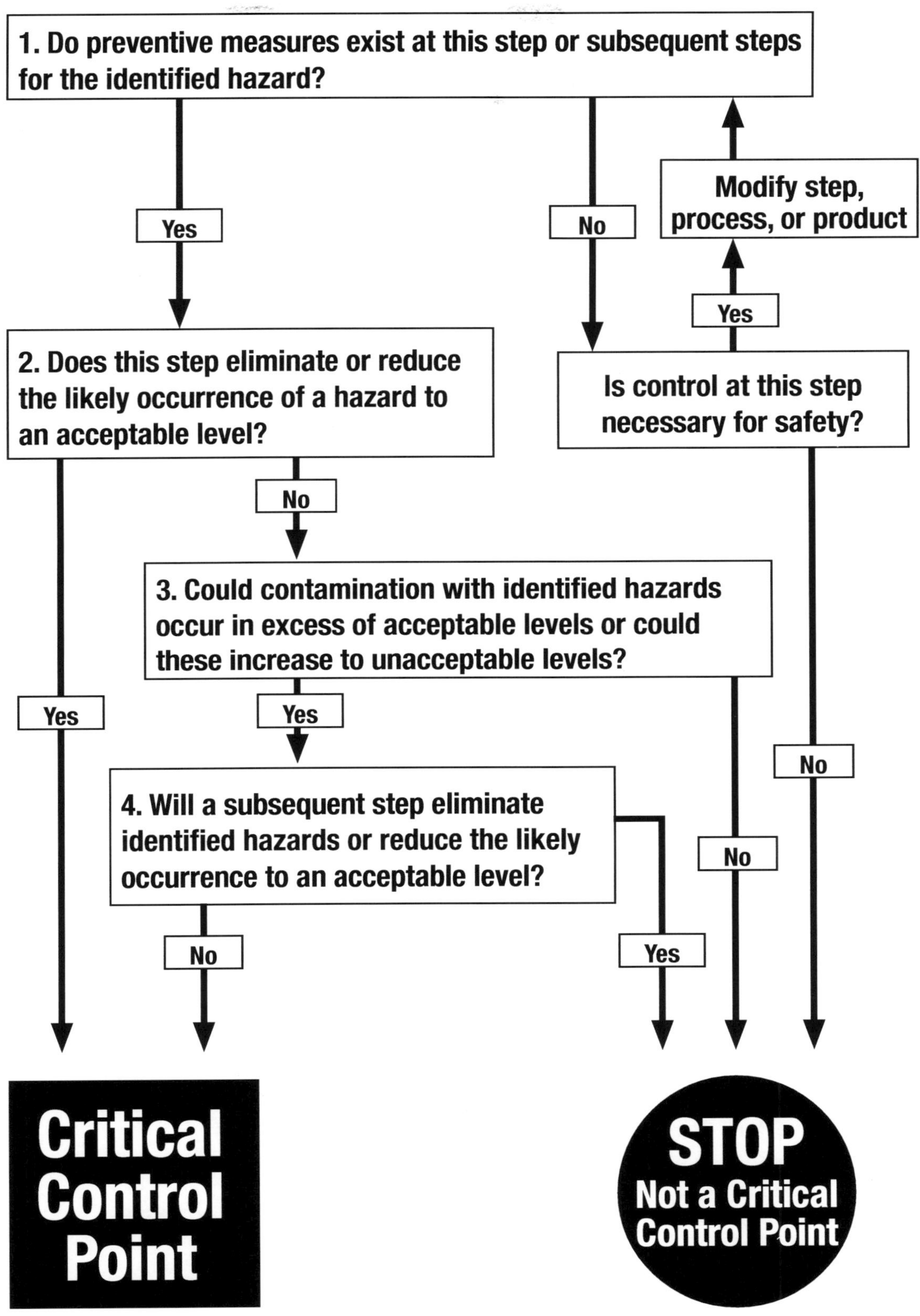

Decision Tree adapted from NACMCF.

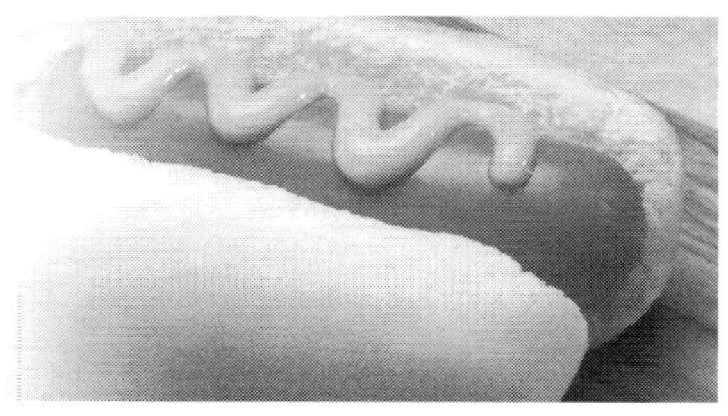

Star Knowledge Exercise:

Identify Control Points (CPs) and Critical Control Points (CCPs)

Using the recipes provided earlier on pages 132-137 to determine if each step is either a control point (CP), critical control point (CCP), or not applicable (N/A). Simple identify each step by placing a circle around the correct answer.

			Mixed-Fruit Crisp
CP	CCP	N/A	**Purchase**
CP	CCP	N/A	**Receive**
CP	CCP	N/A	**Store**
CP	CCP	N/A	**Prepare**
CP	CCP	N/A	**Cook**
CP	CCP	N/A	**Hold (Hot)**
CP	CCP	N/A	**Hold (Cold)**
CP	CCP	N/A	**Cool**
CP	CCP	N/A	**Reheat**
CP	CCP	N/A	**Serve**

			Banana Smoothie
CP	CCP	N/A	**Purchase**
CP	CCP	N/A	**Receive**
CP	CCP	N/A	**Store**
CP	CCP	N/A	**Prepare**
CP	CCP	N/A	**Cook**
CP	CCP	N/A	**Hold (Hot)**
CP	CCP	N/A	**Hold (Cold)**
CP	CCP	N/A	**Cool**
CP	CCP	N/A	**Reheat**
CP	CCP	N/A	**Serve**

			Roasted Chicken Club
CP	CCP	N/A	**Purchase**
CP	CCP	N/A	**Receive**
CP	CCP	N/A	**Store**
CP	CCP	N/A	**Prepare**
CP	CCP	N/A	**Cook**
CP	CCP	N/A	**Hold (Hot)**
CP	CCP	N/A	**Hold (Cold)**
CP	CCP	N/A	**Cool**
CP	CCP	N/A	**Reheat**
CP	CCP	N/A	**Serve**

			Chili
CP	CCP	N/A	**Purchase**
CP	CCP	N/A	**Receive**
CP	CCP	N/A	**Store**
CP	CCP	N/A	**Prepare**
CP	CCP	N/A	**Cook**
CP	CCP	N/A	**Hold (Hot)**
CP	CCP	N/A	**Hold (Cold)**
CP	CCP	N/A	**Cool**
CP	CCP	N/A	**Reheat**
CP	CCP	N/A	**Serve**

Chicken/Pasta Primavera

CP	CCP	N/A	**Purchase**
CP	CCP	N/A	**Receive**
CP	CCP	N/A	**Store**
CP	CCP	N/A	**Prepare**
CP	CCP	N/A	**Cook**
CP	CCP	N/A	**Hold (Hot)**
CP	CCP	N/A	**Hold (Cold)**
CP	CCP	N/A	**Cool**
CP	CCP	N/A	**Reheat**
CP	CCP	N/A	**Serve**

Pork Barbeque Sandwich

CP	CCP	N/A	**Purchase**
CP	CCP	N/A	**Receive**
CP	CCP	N/A	**Store**
CP	CCP	N/A	**Prepare**
CP	CCP	N/A	**Cook**
CP	CCP	N/A	**Hold (Hot)**
CP	CCP	N/A	**Hold (Cold)**
CP	CCP	N/A	**Cool**
CP	CCP	N/A	**Reheat**
CP	CCP	N/A	**Serve**

Star Point 3 Conclusion

In this Star Point, we discussed how to begin setting up a HACCP plan and how to identify the hazards associated with preparing food. After learning how to identify these hazards, which is HACCP Principle 1, then we learned to divide a menu into Simple/No-Cook, Same-Day, and Complex recipes. This then laid the foundation to understanding the flow of food, control points, and critical control points in HACCP Principle 2. To better assess your knowledge of these concepts, please answer the following questions in the Star Point 3 Check for Understanding.

Star Point 3 Check for Understanding

(Circle one.)

1. Any step in the flow of food where hazard can be controlled is called a ____________________.
   - **a.** critical control point
   - **b.** hazard evaluation
   - **c.** control point
   - **d.** hazard identification

2. HACCP stands for ______________________.
   - **a.** Hazard Analysis Critical Control Points
   - **b.** Hazard Analysis and Critical Control Point
   - **c.** Hazard Analysis and Control Critical Points
   - **d.** Hazard Analysis Critical Control Point

3. HACCP Principle 2 is ____________________.
   - **a.** Hazard Identification
   - **b.** Hazard Evaluation
   - **c.** Preparation Process Activities
   - **d.** Determine Critical Control Points

4. A critical control point is __________________.
   - **a.** a point where you check invoices
   - **b.** one of the last steps where you can prevent, eliminate, or reduce a food safety hazard
   - **c.** the point where food is cooled and then reheated
   - **d.** a step in the process where you can control a hazard.

5. Which of the following is not a TCS?
   - **a.** Sprouts
   - **b.** Raw broccoli
   - **c.** Sliced tomatoes
   - **d.** Cut leafy greens
   - **e.** Cut watermelon

6. What are the first and last steps in the flow of food?
   - **a.** Purchase and Store
   - **b.** Preparation and Serve
   - **c.** Purchase and Serve
   - **d.** Preparation and Cook
   - **e.** Receiving and Reheating

7. Which is a critical control point for hamburgers served to school children?
   - **a.** Purchase
   - **b.** Store
   - **c.** Thaw
   - **d.** Cook
   - **e.** Serve

8. What type of recipe category are grilled vegetables for immediate consumption?
   - **a.** Simple/No-Cook
   - **b.** Same-Day
   - **c.** Complex

9. What type of hazard is the most common cause of foodborne illnesses?
   - **a.** Biological
   - **b.** Chemical
   - **c.** Physical
   - **d.** Radiological

10. If the risk of contamination is ________________, the risk may be considered acceptable.
    - **a.** Low
    - **b.** Medium
    - **c.** High

You have successfully completed the third point of the HACCP Star. It is now time to begin Star Point 4 and learn about HACCP Principles 3, 4, & 5!

HACCP Star Point 4: HACCP Principles 3, 4, & 5 – Manage Critical Limits, Monitoring, and Corrective Actions

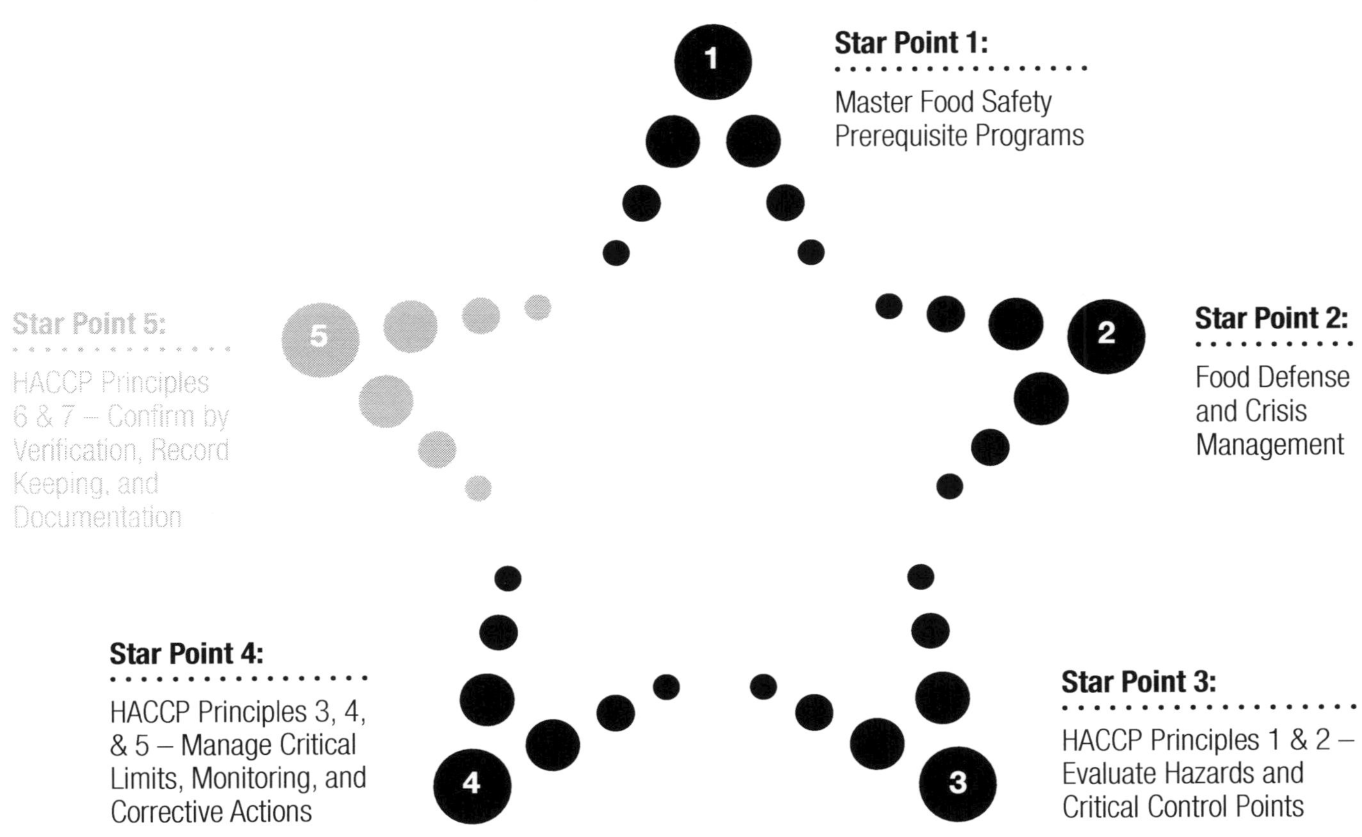

Star Point 4 Myth or Fact (Check one.)

1. There is a critical limit for every control point, and this must be met.
___**Myth** ___**Fact**

2. Visual observation involves using an appropriate tool to obtain an accurate reading.
___**Myth** ___**Fact**

3. Corrective actions are acts taken by employees when critical limits are not met.
___**Myth** ___**Fact**

4. Critical limits are not based on scientific research and proven fact.
___**Myth** ___**Fact**

5. Monitoring is the act of observing and making measurements to ensure team members are meeting the established critical limit.
___**Myth** ___**Fact**

Star Point 4 Goals: You will learn to

- Establish critical limits (HACCP Principle 3).
- Understand time and temperature critical limits.
- Define monitoring procedures (HACCP Principle 4).
- Recognize the difference between continuous and intermittent (non-continuous) monitoring.
- Determine corrective actions (HACCP Principle 5).
- Develop a Risk Control Plan.

In Star Point 4, we will discuss HACCP Principles 3 (Critical Limits), 4 (Monitoring), and 5 (Corrective Actions). This is the most important Star Point for your employees because this is where they "work the plan." By knowing and understanding the critical limits, then monitoring the critical limits, the plan is put to use. Finally, when a critical limit is not met, your employees must have the knowledge and training to take the appropriate corrective actions to keep food safe.

HACCP Principle 3: Establish Critical Limits

Now that you have completed the hazard analysis and identified control points and critical control points, the next step is to understand critical limits. A **critical limit** is the specific **scientific measurement** that must clearly indicate what needs to be done and must be met at each critical control point. Critical limits must be attainable and realistic, and they must be established for each preventive measure. If the critical limit is not met, a corrective action must be performed. Corrective actions are discussed later in this Star Point. A critical limit is like a traffic speed limit on a major highway. There is always a minimum or maximum speed. If you do not drive the minimum speed or if you exceed the maximum speed both are dangerous and you could get stopped and receive a ticket. Critical limits are the same in food preparation; if you do not hold the food to a specific minimum temperature or maximum temperature, people may be stopped with a foodborne illness.

Critical limits determine if the food is safe or unsafe, and depending on your operation, they may consist of physical dimensions, sensory information, acidity (pH), water activity (a_w), time, and temperature.

In food service and retail operations, the Food Code emphasizes critical limits for time and temperature, acidity (pH), water activity (a_w), sensory information, and physical dimensions. Some examples of critical limits in food service and retail operations are:

- **Physical dimensions.** Hamburger patty thickness: _____in. (cm). The physical dimension and product specifications are directly related to standard operating procedures. If the supplier delivers uncooked hamburger patties, which are thicker than usual, your employees will follow the current cooking procedures for the thinner patties. This is dangerous because customers who order these burgers are at risk for contracting E. coli 0157:H7. Since the thickness of the hamburger patties is thicker than normal and they were not cooked to a temperature high enough to meet the critical control point.

- **Sensory information.** The sensory tools used in evaluating critical limits are your nose, eyes and hands. Your nose is good for detecting odors, eyes for visual confirmation of quality, and hands to touch non-RTE food to feel for abnormalities. For instance, if a recipe calls for fresh fish, touching the texture to feel for sliminess or stickiness will help to determine whether the fish is still fresh enough to be cooked. The smell of the fish can help to determine if it is safe to prepare. Does the fish smell fishy or does it smell like the ocean? A strong odor of fish is an indication that the fish should not be cooked. The visual appearance of the fish is also an indication of whether or not the fish is safe to use. Are the fish eyes dull, sunken in, and cloudy (bad), or are they clear and full (good)? This sensory information is necessary to determine if the fish is safe to serve to customers.
- **pH.** Acidified or acidic foods have a pH of 4.6 or below. For example, cooked white rice has an acidity of 6.00 to 6.70, making it neutral on a 14-point acidic scale, which is an ideal range for microorganisms (especially *Bacillus cereus*) to grow. By adding rice vinegar to the cooked rice, the acidity is lowered to 4.6 or below. This deters the growth of microorganisms. Monitoring this process with a pH meter ensures that this rice is a non-potentially hazardous food. Additional examples of acidifiers are acetic acid, citric acid, lactic acid, tartaric acid, and phosphoric acid.
- **Time and temperature.** The most common critical limit that is used in schools, contract food services, retail operations, and independent and franchise operations is controlling time and temperature. Proper equipment and operational steps will help to prevent, reduce, or eliminate pathogens in the flow of food. Clocks with a second hand or timers in conjunction with calibrated, cleaned, and sanitized thermometers are the tools needed to measure time and temperature.

Time and Temperature Critical Limits

Time and temperature is the most common critical limit or measurable standard used in the food service and retail industry. Most operational steps in the flow of food have some measurable critical limit. Below are examples of some critical limits for various food service and retail operations followed by a few more detailed examples of critical limits for various steps in a food flow.

Operational Steps

- **Receiving of products.** Meat, fish, poultry, and dairy are received at 41°F (5°C) or below; crustacean and shellfish 45°F (7.2°C) and alive; and fresh shell eggs ambient 45°F (7.2°C).
- **Storing of products.** Meat, fish, poultry, and dairy are stored at 41°F (5°C) or below; crustacean and shellfish 45°F (7.2°C) and alive; and fresh shell eggs ambient 45°F (7.2°C).
- **Preparation of items.** The maximum amount of time most food can remain in the TDZ is 4 hours. This is cumulative, combining all times in the TDZ throughout the flow of food (receiving, storing, prep, etc.) until the food is thoroughly cooked. When the food is reheated, the 4 hour time frame begins again. Proper thawing of food is a core category preparation step in the Food Code, and has critical limits.
- **Cooking items.** See the Critical Limits: Minimum Cooking Temperatures in the example to follow.
- **Cooling products.** Quickly cool from 135ºF to 70ºF (57.2ºC to 21.1ºC) within 2 hours, and from 70ºF to 41ºF (21.1ºC to 5ºC) within 4 hours, for a maximum total of 6 hours. Cool food as quickly as possible.
- **Reheating products.** Reheat to 165°F (73.9°C) for 15 seconds within 2 hours.
- **Holding items.** Hold cold food at 41°F (5°C) or below; hold hot food at 135°F (57.2°C) or above.
- **Set up, assembly, and packing.** This may involve wrapping food items, assembling these items on trays, and packing them in a transportation carrier or a display case. Again, the maximum amount of time most food can spend in the TDZ is 4 hours.

- **Serving and selling.** The last operational step before the food reaches the customer is serving and selling. Proper personal hygiene and hand-washing procedures must be implemented with the water temperature for hand washing at 100°F (37.7°C) for a minimum of 20 seconds.

Example: Critical Limits - Cooking Temperatures

If cooking is identified as the critical control point, the food must reach a minimum internal cooking temperature and held for 15 seconds to ensure that it is able to be consumed safely. If a recipe for baked chicken says "cook until done" or "cook until juices run clear," that is not time and temperature specific.How do we know if the product is really safe to eat? The correct critical limit should be explained as "cook to an internal temperature of 165°F (73.9°C) for 15 seconds." Why? Scientific data, found in the Food Code, provides documented evidence that proves customers will not become sick if chicken is cooked to this designated temperature for the specific amount of time.

Below is a list of cooking critical limits for familiar items to help reinforce the important minimum times and temperatures. By using these critical limits, operators can destroy the pathogens on food or, at a minimum, reduce them to a safe level to lessen the risk of foodborne illness or worse, an outbreak. As the manager, supervisor, or leader of a food service or retail operation, it is essential to train team members on the importance of the critical limits, particularly cooking times and temperatures for various foods to ensure that the food served and sold is safe to eat.

Critical Limits: Minimum Internal Temperatures

165°F (73.9°C) for < 1 Second

- Reheat all leftover foods and reheated foods (for 15 seconds holding time).
- Cook all poultry and wild game.
- Cook all stuffed products, including pasta.
- Cook all foods cooked in a microwave; then let sit for 2 minutes.
- Cook when combining already cooked and raw TCS products (casseroles).
- Cook all raw animal foods that have been partially cooked (no longer than 60 minutes and properly cooled).

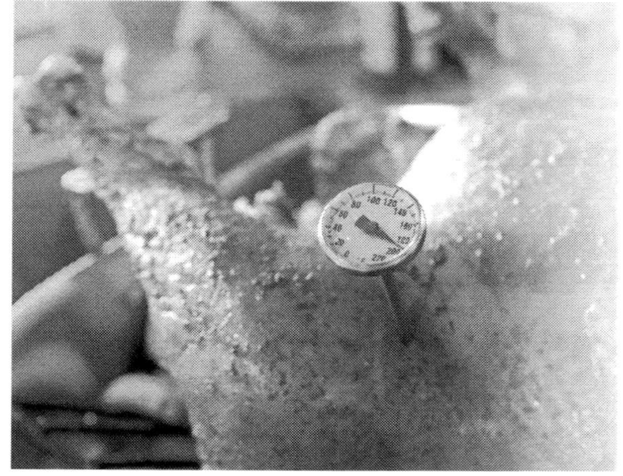

155°F (68.3°C) for 17 Seconds

- Cook all ground foods: fish, beef, commercially raised game animals, ratites (emu and ostrich), and pork.
- Cook all flavor-injected and mechanically tenderized meats.
- Cook all eggs for hot holding and later service (buffet service).

145°F (62.8°C) for 15 Seconds

- Cook all fish and shellfish.
- Cook all intact meats including, chops/steaks of veal, beef, pork, commercially raised game animals, and lamb.
- Cook fresh eggs and egg products for immediate service.
- Cook roasts to 145°F for **4 minutes**. (Roasting temperatures vary; know the proper procedure in your food service or retail establishment.)

135°F (57.2°C)

- Commercially processed products for hot holding.
- Cook vegetables and fruits for hot holding.

Example: Critical Limits - Properly Thaw Foods

Often we need to thaw food prior to starting the cooking process. How many times have you seen turkeys removed from the freezer and left sitting on a work table to thaw? Sitting frozen food on the counter to thaw is not a safe food handling practice. Food needs to move safely through the TDZ as it thaws.

The operational step of thawing has measured limits to assure food safety. There are four safe methods for thawing food:

Method 1: Thaw in a refrigerator at 41°F (5°C) or below. As foods thaw, they may produce extra liquid. When thawing TCS foods in a refrigerator, be sure to place them in a pan or on a tray to avoid cross contamination.

Method 2: Thaw in running water. Food thawed under running water must be placed in a sink with running water at 70°F (21.1°C) or cooler. The sink must be open to allow the water to push the microorganisms off the food and flow down the drain. Do not allow the sink to fill with water. Also, do not allow food to exceed 41°F (5°C) for more than 4 hours total time.

Method 3: Cooking. Frozen food can be thawed by following the cooking directions for the product. Food will thaw and then move directly into the cooking process where it will cook to the required Food Code cooking temperatures. Frozen food may take longer to cook depending on the size and type of product.

Method 4: Microwave. Food can be thawed using the microwave if it will then be immediately cooked to the required cooking temperatures in the Food Code. When thawing food in the microwave, remember that there will be uneven thawing and some of the food may have started to cook, taking some of the food into TDZ. This is why you must finish the cooking process immediately after microwave thawing.

Example: Critical Limits - Equipment

Equipment used in the food service or retail industry also has critical limits, which are the measurable standards that must be met to assure food safety. If not kept at the proper temperature or calibration, equipment may directly impact a critical control point consequently producing unsafe foods. Here are examples of equipment critical limits:

- Conveyor belt time—rate of heating and cooling (conveyor belt speed in): ____ft/min ____cm/min
- Freezer temperature: ____° F or ____°C
- Refrigerator temperature: ____° F or ____°C
- Oven temperature: ____° F or ____°C
- Broiler temperature: ____°F or ____°C
- Cold-holding unit temperature: ____° F or ____°C
- Hot-holding unit temperature: ____° F or ____°C

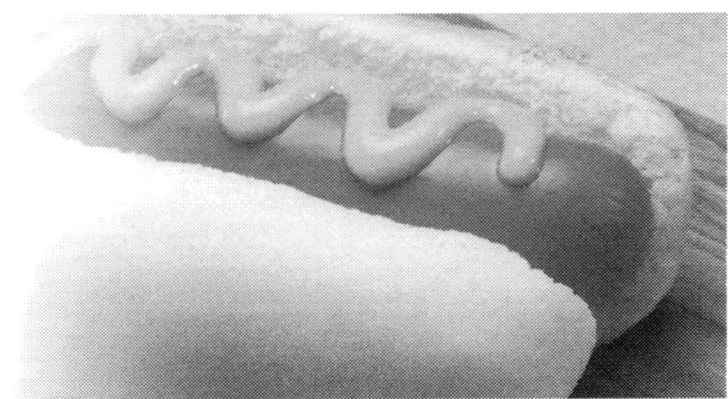

Star Knowledge Exercise:

Critical Limits

Match the critical limit to the CCP by placing the letter that is most correct in the space provided.

a. The critical limit is 165°F (73.9°C) for $<$ 1 second.

b. The critical limit is 165°F (73.9°C) for 15 seconds within 2 hours.

c. The critical limit is 155°F (68.3°C) for 17 seconds.

d. The critical limit is 145°F (62.8°C) for 15 seconds.

e. The critical limit is 135°F to 70°F (57.2°C to 21.1°C°) within 2 hours; you then have an additional 4 hours to go from 70°F to 41°F (21.1°F to 5°C) or lower for a maximum total cool time of 6 hours.

f. The critical limit is 41°F (5°C) or below.

g. The critical limit is 135°F (57.2°C) or above.

1. If holding is the CCP for a cold roasted chicken club, what is the critical limit? __________

2. If cooking is the CCP for a roasted chicken club, what is the critical limit? __________

3. If hot holding is the CCP for chili, what is the critical limit? __________

4. If cooking is the CCP for chicken noodle soup, what is the critical limit? __________

5. If cold holding is the CCP for mixed-fruit crisp, what is the critical limit? __________

6. If cooling is the CCP for mixed-fruit crisp, what is the critical limit? __________

7. If reheating for hot holding is the CCP for chili, what is the critical limit? __________

8. If cooking in the microwave is the CCP for a pork chop, what is the critical limit? __________

9. If hot holding is the CCP for pork chops, what is the critical limit? __________

10. If cooking is the CCP for fish, what is the critical limit? __________

HACCP Principle 4: Establish Monitoring Procedures

Monitoring Procedures, the foundation for HACCP Principle 4, ensure that team members are meeting established critical limits. Taking measurements (pH, water activity [a_w], time and temperature) and making observations are two typical tasks of monitoring. Measurements involve using an appropriate tool to obtain an accurate reading. Visual observation occurs when you look carefully at products to determine if there are any signs that they may be hazardous. An example is the observation of frozen foods to make sure that they show no signs of previous temperature abuse, such as ice crystals and stains. There is a critical limit for every critical control point, and this must be met. If you do not check the CCPs of your food service or retail operation regularly, you do not know if the plan is being followed and there is no way of determining if the food being served and sold is safe. In that case, your HACCP plan can easily fail.

Monitoring enables the manager to determine if the team members are doing their part to serve and sell safe food. Monitoring provides tracking for your food safety management system throughout the operation. These concerns vary from faulty equipment (refrigeration that will not maintain temperature), to training deficiencies (employees who continually make errors), or product specification issues (receiving goods that are incorrect). You make the difference in terms of whether or not your operation is serving or selling safe food.

How to Monitor

Records are proof you are doing things correctly. Make sure you take and record measurements accurately. You never know when these records may be reviewed or needed for verification of the HACCP plan.

It is important to know your role and the roles of other team members and employees. When monitoring, these questions must be considered:

- Who will monitor the CCP(s)? Managers could, but perhaps a different team member would be better.
- What equipment and materials are needed to monitor? Equipment could be thermometers, test strips, logs, clipboards, and pens.
- How will the CCP(s) be monitored? What is the SOP? Precise directions must be given.
- Is every team member following SOPs? Everyone, no matter what his or her job description, has duties that impact food safety.
- When should monitoring take place? It should be built into schedules.
- How often should monitoring take place? Some monitoring is necessary on a continuous basis or intermittently—for example, every 2 hours, every 4 hours, once per shift, once daily, or once weekly.
- Is there an accurate and permanent record of the previous monitoring that can be used for future verification? You cannot determine deviations or patterns without maintaining a log.

As touched on in the preceding list, there are two kinds of monitoring:

- Continuous; and
- Intermittent (non-continuous).

Continuous monitoring is preferred because it provides constant monitoring of a CCP. This is done with built-in measuring equipment that records items such as; pH measurement, or time and temperatures. Computerized equipment systems are an example of continuous monitoring.

Intermittent (non-continuous) monitoring occurs at scheduled intervals or on a per-batch basis and is performed often to ensure critical limits are met. This type of monitoring is primarily what the majority of food service or retail operations use. An example of intermittent monitoring is using a properly calibrated, cleaned, and sanitized thermometer to measure the temperature of chicken soup every 2 hours.

When monitoring, it is critical to consider the following best practices:

- **Assign appropriate staff to monitor items.** The appropriate person should have the most contact with the food being monitored. It might be a manager, but it might also be the chef who is preparing the food. It could also be the team member in charge of the salad bar. These individuals must be properly trained in using the monitoring equipment designated to measure the critical limits and in following the standard operating procedures (SOPs). They should ensure the results are reported accurately. If monitoring food items and procedures is not an assigned duty to an individual, you run the risk of no one monitoring that food. If no one monitors the food, it is likely that the food is unsafe.
- **Know how to use monitoring tools—thermometers, visual observations, and pH testing kits.** Taking the temperature of food is useless if the thermometer is not properly calibrated, cleaned, and sanitized or in the food for the appropriate amount of time. It can cause inaccuracy and cross contamination. If one does not know how to properly conduct a pH test, it may not be done accurately. Different foods require different measuring devices. Monitoring the sell by, consume by, or discard by dates is an example of visual inspection or observation. Proper training is required for food employees to perform these functions effectively.
- **Know the proper temperatures.** The reason for monitoring is not just to get a temperature reading, but to make sure the product is safe. It is a good idea to have critical limits printed on monitoring logs, recipes, posters, and job aids so the employee preparing and/or cooking the food has the standards right in front of him or her.
- **Know ALL critical limits.** All TCS foods have a critical control point; therefore, you must know the correct critical limit to meet for the CCP. Simply posting cooking limits falls short since it is specific to the step in the flow of food that will prevent, eliminate, and reduce the item to a safe level. As discussed earlier in this chapter, there are other critical limits to monitor as well. Training, charts, or other means of communicating these standards to employees are important.
- **Record monitoring results in logs.** Recording the results in logs provides the documentation necessary for verification, evaluation, adjustment. It also provides documentation if standards have not been met which will help determine if employees need more training or coaching. These logs will help better manage your employees and ensure that safe food is served and sold!
- **Perform scheduled and random monitoring tasks.**
  (For example, every 2 hours or every 4 hours, at a minimum) Consistent monitoring of food items definitely keeps them safe. However, there are also benefits to random checks. Checking items at precisely the same time every day may not alert you of fluctuations in equipment that could affect food safety. Varying monitoring schedules may allow employees to gain more monitoring experience and expertise regarding critical limits, which will make them even more valuable to your food service or retail establishment.

Use Monitoring Forms

In the HACCP system, proper documentation must be maintained throughout the operational food flow. Effective use of monitoring forms when receiving, preparing, cooking, cooling, reheating, and storing a food item provides a product history. This verifies that a product meets standards or indicates when adjustments to the system are needed. It also provides documentation that you have done all you can do to keep the food safe if a foodborne illness outbreak occurs. These records provide your documentation to the Department of Health, the media, and local, county, state, and federal food inspectors.

Equipment temperatures during meal preparation and service should be monitored at least every 4 hours. This includes all refrigeration, cooking, and holding equipment. If necessary, adjust the equipment thermostats so products meet the required temperature standards. If, when temperature monitoring is done, the product is not at the correct temperature, fix the equipment and consider discarding the food.

Every food service and retail operation must establish standard operating procedures for specific documentation on approved forms when monitoring. These SOPs include sanitation practices, employee practices, and employee training. Each of these SOPs may consist of an informal notation of observations concerning what is working well and what is not working well. This documentation helps to identify practices and procedures that may have to be modified and may indicate a need for additional employee training. If the documentation is not kept, there is no proof that it was done.

Sample SOP Receiving Monitoring Instructions

1. Inspect the delivery truck when it arrives to ensure that it is clean, free of putrid odors, and organized to prevent cross contamination. Be sure refrigerated foods are delivered on a refrigerated truck.
2. Check the interior temperature of refrigerated trucks.
3. Confirm the vendor's name, day and time of delivery, as well as the driver's identification before accepting delivery. If the driver's name is different than what is indicated on the delivery schedule, contact the vendor immediately.
4. Check frozen foods to ensure that they are all frozen solid and show no signs of thawing and refreezing, such as the presence of large ice crystals or liquids on the bottom of cartons.
5. Check the temperature of refrigerated foods.
    a. For fresh meat, fish, and poultry products, insert a calibrated, cleaned, and sanitized thermometer into the center of the product to ensure a temperature of 41ºF (5ºC) or below.
    b. For packaged products, insert a food thermometer between two packages, being careful not to puncture the wrapper. If the temperature exceeds 41ºF (5ºC), it may be necessary to take the internal temperature before accepting the product.
    c. For eggs, the interior temperature of the truck should be 45ºF (7.2ºC) or below.
6. Check the dates of milk, eggs, and other perishable goods to ensure safety and quality.
7. Check the integrity of food packaging.
8. Check the cleanliness of crates and other shipping containers before accepting products. Reject foods that are shipped in dirty crates.

Examples of Monitoring Forms

Thermometer Calibration Log: (As Scheduled)

Time	Date: 7/12	Employee Initials	Manager Initials	Date: 7/13	Employee Initials	Manager Initials
6 AM	32°F (0°C) 33°F (.5°C) 32°F (0°C)	KK	CE			
2 PM	36°F (2.2°C) 33°F (.5°C) 32°F (0°C)	HB	SM			
10 PM						

Corrective Actions: At 2pm 36°F (2.2°C) was recalibrated to 32°F (0°C). HB/SM

Cooking Log:

Date: 7/12	Time	Food Product	Internal Temperature °F (°C)	Corrective Action	Employee Initials	Manager Initials
	9 AM	Scrambled Eggs	158°F (70°C)	________	KK	CE
	10 AM	Chili	120°F (48.8°C)	REHEAT	HB	SM
	10:30 AM	Soup	165°F (73.8°C)	________	HB	SM

Corrective Actions: Reheat chili from 120°F (48.8°C) to 165°F (73.8°C) for 15 seconds within 2 hours. HB/ SM

Holding Log:

Date: 7/12	Time	Food Product	Manager Initials	Manager Initials	Date: 7/13	Employee Initials	Manager Initials
	6 AM	Sausage 151°F (66.1°C)	KK	CE			
	10 AM	Scrambled Eggs 138°F (58.8°C)	KK	CE			
	2 PM	Chili 147°F (63.8°C)	HB	SM			
	10 PM	Soup 145°F (62.7°C)	TB	JE			

Corrective Actions: ______________________________

Cooling Log:

Date	Food	Time	°F /°C	Time + 2 Hours	Must be 70°F or lower °F / °C	+ 3 Hours	°F /°C	+ 4 Hours	°F /°C	+ 5 Hours	Time After 6 Hours	°F /°C	Must Be 41°F or lower+ 6 Hours Time
7/12	Chili	9pm	147ºF (63.8°C)	11pm	68ºF (20°C)	12am	52ºF (11.1°C)	1am	39ºF (3.8°C)				
7/12	Soup	11pm	151ºF (66.1°C)										

Corrective Actions: ______________________________

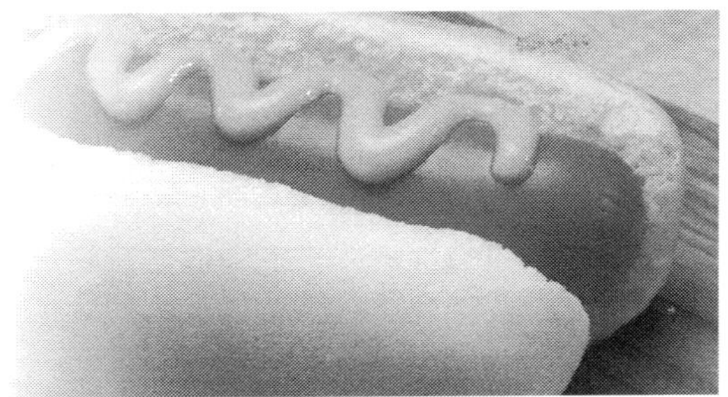

Star Knowledge Exercise:

Monitoring

Monitoring Logs

- **A.** Receiving log or invoice (indicating temperature of frozen and/or refrigerated food as received)
- **B.** Freezer temperature log
- **C.** Refrigerator temperature log
- **D.** Dry storage temperature log
- **E.** Preparation temperature log
- **F.** Cooking log
- **G.** Holding log (Hot or Cold)
- **H.** Cooling log
- **I.** Reheating log
- **J.** Serving line temperature log

Equipment

- **K.** Calibrated thermometers
- **L.** pH meter
- **M.** Display tank
- **N.** Refrigeration unit
- **O.** Cold holding equipment
- **P.** Cold serving equipment
- **Q.** Freezer unit
- **R.** Heat Source: Oven, Grill, Fryer, Microwave, Cooker, Kettle, Stove, etc.
- **S.** Hot holding equipment
- **T.** Hot serving equipment
- **U.** Equipment to quickly cool food—ice bath, ice paddle, pans to reduce product for quicker cooling; or a blast chiller

What type(s) of monitoring logs and food safety equipment would you need to have in place for the following foods? Check the appropriate letter for monitoring logs and equipment.

1. Chili prepared on-site to be served the next day.

Monitoring Logs: ❑ A. ❑ B. ❑ C. ❑ D. ❑ E. ❑ F. ❑ G. ❑ H. ❑ I. ❑ J.

Equipment: ❑ K. ❑ L. ❑ M. ❑ N. ❑ O. ❑ P. ❑ Q. ❑ R. ❑ S. ❑ T. ❑ U.

2. Potato salad prepared on-site for deli case and salad bar.

Monitoring Logs: ❑ A. ❑ B. ❑ C. ❑ D. ❑ E. ❑ F. ❑ G. ❑ H. ❑ I. ❑ J.

Equipment: ❑ K. ❑ L. ❑ M. ❑ N. ❑ O. ❑ P. ❑ Q. ❑ R. ❑ S. ❑ T. ❑ U.

3. Roasted chicken club sandwiches prepared on-site served cold the next day.

Monitoring Logs: ❑ A. ❑ B. ❑ C. ❑ D. ❑ E. ❑ F. ❑ G. ❑ H. ❑ I. ❑ J.

Equipment: ❑ K. ❑ L. ❑ M. ❑ N. ❑ O. ❑ P. ❑ Q. ❑ R. ❑ S. ❑ T. ❑ U.

4. Live lobsters in display tank served today.

Monitoring Logs: ❑ A. ❑ B. ❑ C. ❑ D. ❑ E. ❑ F. ❑ G. ❑ H. ❑ I. ❑ J.

Equipment: ❑ K. ❑ L. ❑ M. ❑ N. ❑ O. ❑ P. ❑ Q. ❑ R. ❑ S. ❑ T. ❑ U.

5. Sushi prepared on-site.

Monitoring Logs: ❑ A. ❑ B. ❑ C. ❑ D. ❑ E. ❑ F. ❑ G. ❑ H. ❑ I. ❑ J.

Equipment: ❑ K. ❑ L. ❑ M. ❑ N. ❑ O. ❑ P. ❑ Q. ❑ R. ❑ S. ❑ T. ❑ U.

HACCP Principle 5: Identify Corrective Actions

Once the minimum and maximum critical limits have been identified and recorded through monitoring efforts, we can utilize the corrective actions necessary to fix any deficiencies. The corrective actions are predetermined steps that are automatically taken if the critical limits are not being met. This is Principle 5 of the HACCP process.

There are five tasks necessary when a corrective action occurs:

1. Establish the exact cause of the deficiency;
2. Determine who corrects the problem;
3. Correct the problem;
4. Decide what to do with the product; and
5. Record the corrective actions that were taken.

The following are examples of approved corrective actions:

- **Reject a product that does not meet purchasing or receiving specifications.** If, upon inspection when receiving a shipment, you find that a substitution has been made to the size, quantity, brand, or other issues related to the food item, do not accept the product. Any of these inconsistencies could affect the quality of your recipe, or compromise the safety of your product.
- **Reject a product that does not come from a reputable source.** Risks when receiving food items from unreliable sources include poor quality food, unsafe food, no recourse if refunds are needed, and the inability to do trace backs in the event of an foodborne illness outbreak.
- **Discard unsafe food products.** If food is identified as **adulterated** (contains any poisonous or deleterious substance), it cannot be eaten or sold. It should be disposed of so it is not mistakenly used.
- **Discard food if cross contamination occurs.** This is especially true if there is no cooking step involved, since there is no possibility of destroying any pathogens. Food that is touched, dropped, or otherwise cross contaminated can introduce any number of unknown risks to the customer. If it cannot be made safe, you cannot serve or sell it.
- **Fix, calibrate, or replace all thermometers throughout the facility including thermometers in refrigerators, freezers, ovens, cold holding carts, hot holding carts.** Without properly functioning thermometers there is no way to ensure the food will remain safe.
- **Train staff to calibrate thermometers and to take temperatures properly.** An un-calibrated thermometer will give a false reading that may lead to serving or selling unsafe foods. Thermometers should be calibrated every shift. Using the wrong thermometer, or one not inserted into the food properly, may also be misleading.
- **Continue cooking food until it reaches the correct temperature.** Monitoring this process can effectively eliminate the risk of serving undercooked food. No one can calculate the temperature of food by looking at it, so calibrated thermometers are the tools that will enable you to ensure foods are cooked to their safe temperatures.

- **Reheat food to 165°F (73.9°C) for 15 seconds within 2 hours.** Monitoring will alert you to any foods that have remained in the temperature danger zone (TDZ), thereby allowing the rapid growth of microorganisms. Quickly raising the temperature to 165°F (73.9°C) for 15 seconds within 2 hours will destroy enough of the microorganisms to make the food safe for consumption. This can apply to foods that are being held on a buffet line or left out to cool.
- **Change methods of food handling.** Monitoring by observation may indicate food employees are not following (or understanding) proper food-handling methods. Retraining might be necessary for food employees who do not wash hands between tasks or when they have touched a dirty surface. Procedures must be explained and enforced to prevent cross contamination by washing, cleaning, and sanitizing food contact surfaces and utensils. Proper food handling also includes practices of safely thawing foods, separating raw and RTE foods, and cleaning and sanitizing the containers, utensils, and hands that have contacted the raw and RTE foods.
- **Document: Write everything down.** Do not forget to record all readings and document what has been done to correct the problems you have observed when monitoring. This practice is important and helpful if a customer is stricken with a foodborne illness. These documents provide evidence that your HACCP system has been implemented.

Did You Know...
It is just as important to document your actions when things do not go according to plan as it is to document them when they do. What corrective actions did you take to resolve a potential problem?

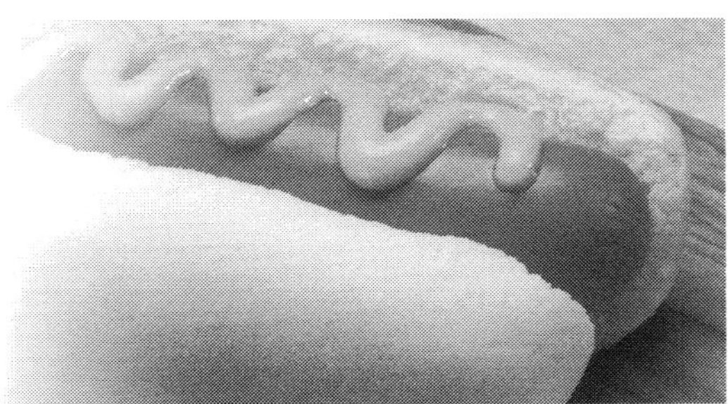

Star Knowledge Exercise:
Corrective Action

Using the food products from our sample menu, take a look at the critical control point, the critical limit, and the monitoring results identified. Based on the monitoring results, what would you determine is the corrective action to perform?

Product	CCP	Critical Limit	Monitoring	Corrective Action
Mixed-Fruit Crisp	Reheat	165°F (73.8°C)	155°F (68.3°C)	
Roasted Chicken Club	Hold (Cold)	41°F (5°C)	48°F (8.8°C)	
Chili	Cook	165°F (73.8°C)	121°F (49.4°C)	
Spanish Rice Bake	Cook	165°F (73.8°C)	157°F (69.4°C)	
Chicken Pasta Primavera	Cook	165°F (73.8°C)	145°F (62.7°C)	
BBQ Pork	Reheat	135°F (57.2°C)	139°F (59.4°C)	
Tuna Melt	Hold (Hot)	135°F (57.2°C)		

For all SOPs, it is mandatory that predetermined steps should be developed **before** the deficiency occurs. This ensures that employees and managers know what to do when the event occurs.

Sample Corrective Actions-Receiving

Here is an example of corrective actions for receiving deliveries.

Corrective Action:

1. Reject the following:

- **a.** Frozen foods with signs of previous thawing;
- **b.** Cans that have signs of deterioration—swollen sides or ends, flawed seals or seams, dents, or rust;
- **c.** Punctured packages;
- **d.** Expired foods; or
- **e.** Foods that are in the temperature danger zone or deemed unacceptable by the established rejection policy.

Sample Corrective Action Logs

Receiving Log:			**Date:**			
Time	**Temp or Condition Upon Receipt**	**Food Product Description**	**Product Code**	**Corrective Action Taken**	**Employee Initials**	**Manager Initials**

Cooling—Corrective Action Log:			**Date:**		
Food Product	**Time**	**Temperature Must: 70°F (21.1°C) – 2 Hours Must: 41°F (5°C) – 6 Hours**	**Corrective Action Taken Must: Reheat Must: Discard**	**Employee Initials**	**Manager Initials**

Refrigeration Log:				**Date:**		
Time	**Type Of Unit**	**Location**	**°F/°C**	**Corrective Action Taken**	**Employee Initials**	**Manager Initials**

Pop Quiz:

HACCP Principle Check

As a quick review, match the five HACCP principles with the corresponding description.

HACCP Principle 1: ______

HACCP Principle 2: ______

HACCP Principle 3: ______

HACCP Principle 4: ______

HACCP Principle 5: ______

a. Establish Critical Limit

b. Corrective Action

c. Conduct a Hazard Analysis

d. Determine Critical Control Points

e. Monitoring

Risk Control Plan (RCP)

Once developed, your HACCP plan is your system for self-inspection. You are responsible for executing the plan. Although you conduct self-inspections, your local regulatory official also inspects your business. The inspection may determine everything is being done appropriately, or may show that some of your procedures do not comply with government regulations or are out-of-control. In an effort to help get your procedures back on track and under control, the regulatory official might request that you complete a **Risk Control Plan (RCP)**. A Risk Control Plan is a written plan developed by you (the food service or retail operator) with input from the regulatory official (your local health inspector) that describes how to manage and correct specific out-of-control risk factors. Below is a chart from the Food Code with specific solutions to assist you in serving and selling safe food.

Out-of-Control Procedure	Associated Hazards	On-Site Correction (COS)	Long-Term Compliance
Bare-hand contact with RTE Food	Bacteria, parasites, and viruses via fecal-oral route	Remove and potentially discard potentially contaminated food. Preform a hazard analysis to make your decision.	Risk Control Plan (RCP), train employees, SOP/ HACCP development
Cold holding	Vegetative bacteria, toxin-forming and spore-forming bacteria, scrombrotoxin (finfish)	Discard or re-chill potentially contaminated food. Preform a hazard analysis to make your decision.	Conduct hazard analysis, train employees, develop SOP/HACCP/recipe
Contaminated equipment	Bacteria, parasites, and viruses	Clean and sanitize equipment; discard or reheat RTE food	Train employees, change equipment or layout, develop SOP

Out-of-Control Procedure	Associated Hazards	On-Site Correction (COS)	Long-Term Compliance
Cooking	Vegetative bacteria, parasites, and possibly viruses	Continue cooking to proper temperature	Change equipment, RCP, train employees, develop SOP/HACCP/recipe
Cooling	Toxin-forming and spore-forming bacteria	Discard or reheat potentially contaminated food. Preform a hazard analysis to make your decision.	Change equipment, RCP, train employees, develop SOP/HACCP/recipe
Cross contamination of RTE foods with raw animal foods	Bacteria, parasites, and possibly viruses	Discard or reheat RTE food. Preform a hazard analysis to make your decision.	Change equipment layout, RCP, train employees, develop SOP/HACCP/recipe
Food source/sound condition	Bacteria/parasites/viruses/ scombrotoxin/ciguatera toxin	Reject or discard	Change buyer specifications, train employees
Freezing to control parasites	Parasites	Freeze immediately; discard; or cook	Change buyer specifications, RCP, develop SOP/HACCP/recipe, change equipment, train employees
Hand washing	Bacteria, viruses, and parasites	Wash hands immediately; Discard or reheat potentially contaminated food. Preform a hazard analysis to make your decision.	Change equipment layout, train employees, RCP, develop SOP/HACCP
Hot holding	Toxin-forming and spore-forming bacteria	Discard or reheat potentially contaminated food. Preform a hazard analysis to make your decision.	Change equipment, RCP, train employees, develop SOP/HACCP/recipe
Receiving temperatures	Scombrotoxin, bacteria	Reject or discard	Change buyer specifications, train employees, develop SOP/ HACCP/invoice
Reheating	Vegetative bacteria; toxin-forming and spore-forming bacteria	Discard or reheat potentially contaminated food. Preform a hazard analysis to make your decision.	Change equipment, RCP, train employees, develop SOP/HACCP/recipe

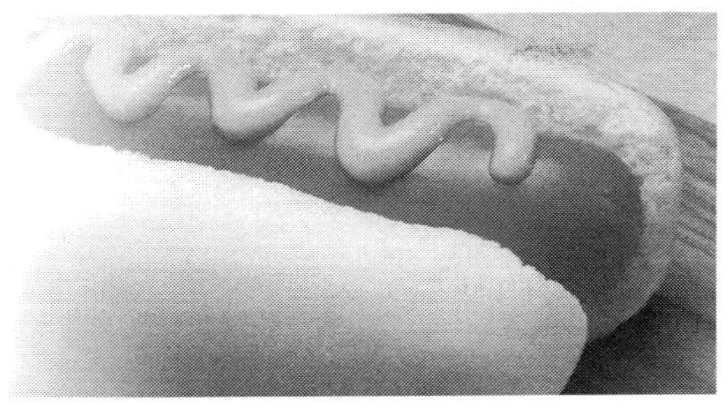

Star Knowledge Exercise:

Risk Control Plan

You are the supervisor of a food service facility for senior citizens. The regulatory inspector (local health inspector) arrives at your facility for an unannounced spot inspection. He goes into the walk-in cooler and observes that the temperature of the turkey vegetable soup is at 65°F (18.3°C) after being in the walk-in cooler for 12 hours. The inspector meets with you immediately and tells you to prepare a Risk Control Plan (RCP) for the turkey vegetable soup. Complete the blank Risk Control Plan form below, for the uncontrolled operational step of cooling the turkey vegetable soup.

Risk Control Plan

Establishment Name: ________________ Type of Facility: ________________

Physical Address: ________________ Person-in-Charge: ________________

City: ________________ State: ____________ Zip: ________________

County: ________________

Inspection Time In: ________________ Inspection Time Out: ________________ Date: ____________

Inspector's Name: ________________

Agency: ________________

Specific observation noted during inspection:

____

____

____

____

____

____

Applicable code violation(s):

____

____

____

____

____

____

____

Risk factor to be controlled:

____
____
____
____
____
____
____

What must be achieved to gain compliance in the future?

____
____
____
____
____
____

How will active managerial control be achieved?

Who is responsible for the control? What monitoring procedures and record keeping is required? Who is responsible for monitoring and completing records? What corrective actions should be taken? When deviations are noted, how long is the plan to continue?

____
____
____
____
____
____
____

How will the results of implementing the RCP be communicated to the inspector?

____
____
____
____
____
____

As the person-in-charge of the _________ located at _________, I have voluntarily developed this Risk Control Plan, in consultation with _________, and understand the provisions of this plan.

____
Establishment Manager: Date:

____
Regulatory Official: Date:

It is important to keep FATTOM in mind when completing a Risk Control Plan.

FATTOM

Food

Acidity

Time

Temperature

Oxygen

Moisture

Example Answer: Risk Control Plan for Turkey Vegetable Soup

Establishment Name: ABC Establishment

Type of Facility: Full Service

Physical Address: 123 Any Street

Person-in-Charge: Johnny Pasta

City: Any City **State:** Any State

Zip: 00000

County: Any County

Inspection Time In: 9:00 a.m.

Inspection Time Out: 12:30 p.m.

Date: 12.01.16

Inspector's Name: Cleo Chloe

Agency: Your jurisdiction

Specific observation noted during inspection:

Temperature of turkey vegetable soup in walk-in cooler was 65°F (18.3°C) after cooling in the walk-in all night (12 hours).

Applicable code violation(s):

Food Code Section 3-501.14 — Soup not cooled from 135°F – 41°F (57.2°C - 5°C) in 6 hours or less.

Risk factor to be controlled:

Improper Holding Temperatures (Cooling)

What must be achieved to gain compliance in the future?

Cool from 135°F to 41°F (57.2°C to 5°C) within 6 hours provided that food is cooled from 135°F to 70°F (57.2°C to 21.1°C) in ≤ 2 hours.

How will active managerial control be achieved?

Attached is the Cooling SOP

Conduct a Trial Run to Determine if Cooling Procedure Works

The head chef will portion soup at a temperature of 135°F (57.2°C) in cleaned and sanitized 3-inch (7.62-cm) metal pans, and when the soup has reached 70°F (21.2°C), place them uncovered in the coolest, protected area of the walk-in cooler. He will record the time on the "Time-Temperature Log." Two hours later, the temperature of the soup will be checked and recorded. If the temperature of the soup is not 70°F (21.1°C) or less, the soup will be reheated to 165°F (73.9°C), and the trial run will be restarted in an ice bath. When the temperature is 70°F (21.2°C) or less within 2 hours, the time and temperature will be recorded, and cooling will continue. Four hours later, the temperature of the soup will again be checked and recorded. If the soup is 41°F (5°C) or less, the cooling procedure will be established. If the soup is not 41°F (5°C) or less, it will be discarded and other cooling options will be used (see below).

Procedure

When there is less than one gallon of soup left over at the end of the day, the head chef will log the volume and disposition of the soup. When the volume is greater than one gallon, the established procedure will be followed. The head chef will complete the Temperature Log daily for 30 days. The general manager will review the log weekly for completeness and adherence to the procedure.

How will the results of implementing the RCP be communicated to the inspector?

The log will be available for review by the regulatory authority upon request.

As the person-in-charge of the ________ located at ________, I have voluntarily developed this Risk Control Plan,

in consultation with ________, and understand the provisions of this plan.

Establishment Manager: ______________________________ Date: ______________

Regulatory Official: ______________________________ Date: ______________

Other options that may be suggested to the operator include purchasing a data logger to record cooling overnight; discarding any leftover soup at the end of the day; using chill sticks/ice paddles; using an ice bath to cool leftovers prior to storage; and purchasing a blast chiller.

Did You Know… No operation is perfect! Mistakes will happen. A properly prepared HACCP plan will help you know what to do when they occur!

Star Point 4 Conclusion

In Star Point 4, "Work the Plan", we discussed why working the plan is the most important Star Point for your food service or retail facility. This is where you make the greatest difference! Working the plan is accomplished by actively monitoring critical control points and critical limits, and by identifying and facilitating corrective actions that ensure safe food. The way in which the principles are presented in Star Point 4 put into action and determine the success of the facility in serving and selling safe food and avoiding foodborne illness.

If your facility is asked to complete an RCP, it is critical that you perform verification of your prerequisite programs, standard operating procedures, and your HACCP plan. This verification leads to the next Star Point.

Star Point 4 Check for Understanding

(Circle one.)

1. The critical limit for chicken soup is ______________.

- **a.** cooking
- **b.** cooking to 165°F (73.8°C)
- **c.** washing your hands before you start cooking
- **d.** making sure to get your chicken from an approved source

2. Critical limits are ______________________________.

- **a.** based on science and must be measurable
- **b.** how fast you need to accomplish your daily tasks
- **c.** the act of observing or taking measurements to see if you CCPs are met
- **d.** none of the above

3. Times and temperatures should be checked for holding ______________________________.

- **a.** monthly
- **b.** daily
- **c.** weekly
- **d.** every 12 hours
- **e.** every 2 – 4 hours

4. Corrective actions are ________________________.

- **a.** actions taken immediately when CCPs are not met
- **b.** telling the manager that something went wrong
- **c.** always throwing away foods that did not meet the critical limits
- **d.** actions that can wait until the next shift to correct

5. When monitoring CCPs, employees must ____________________________________.

- **a.** decide which CCPs to monitor that day
- **b.** have equipment and tools needed to monitor the CCP
- **c.** follow SOPs
- **d.** both b and c
- **e.** all of the above

6. A Risk Control Plan is ________________________.

- **a.** a written plan that the regulatory official gives you to control an out of control risk factor
- **b.** a written plan that industry writes with input from the regulatory official to control an out-of-control risk factor
- **c.** a checklist of areas in the operational flow that need monitoring
- **d.** HACCP Principle 5

7. HACCP Principle 4 is ______________________.

- **a.** Critical Control Point
- **b.** Monitoring
- **c.** Critical Limits
- **d.** Corrective Action

8. HACCP Principal 5 is ______________________.

- **a.** Critical Control Point
- **b.** Monitoring
- **c.** Critical Limits
- **d.** Corrective Action

9. Which task is not necessary when corrective actions are needed?

- **a.** Establish the exact cause of the deficiency
- **b.** Determine who is to correct the problem
- **c.** Correct the problem
- **d.** Always throw away the food of concern
- **e.** Record the corrective actions that were taken

10. Critical limits may consist of __________________.

- **a.** physical dimensions of the food
- **b.** tasting the food
- **c.** time and temperature
- **d.** quality of the product
- **e.** both a and c

HACCP Star Point 5: HACCP Principles 6 & 7 – Confirm by Verification, Record Keeping, and Documentation

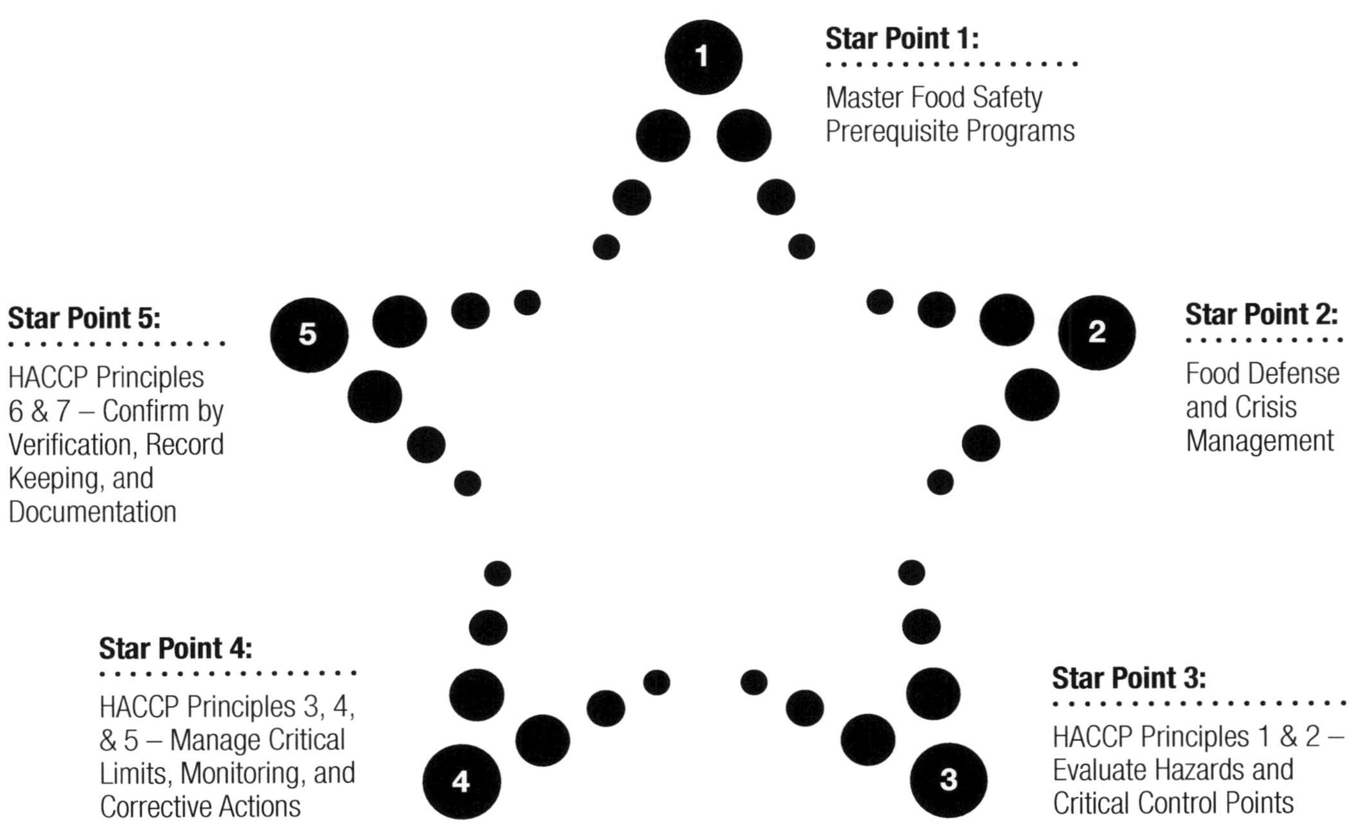

Star Point 5 Myth or Fact (Check one.)

1. Validation focuses on collecting and evaluating scientific and technical information.
___**Myth** ___**Fact**

2. Record keeping will verify your HACCP plan is working.
___**Myth** ___**Fact**

3. Verification of a HACCP plan is done by all employees.
___**Myth** ___**Fact**

4. You can verify a HACCP plan by observing employees performing tasks and reviewing the CCP monitoring records.
___**Myth** ___**Fact**

5. Verification is typically conducted yearly, whereas validation is an on-going process.
___**Myth** ___**Fact**

Star Point 5 Goals: You will learn to

- Confirm/verify that your system works (HACCP Principle 6).
- Maintain records and documentation (HACCP Principle 7).
- Understand Verification vs. Validation.

In this final Star Point, we discuss the checks and balances system of your HACCP plan. This consists of HACCP Principles 6 (Verification) and 7 (Record Keeping). Verification enables you to confirm that everything is working properly and actions are taken to modify your HACCP plan to conform to the appropriate standards. Record keeping, or documentation, is written proof that your HACCP system is functioning properly and that you are controlling and mitigating safety hazards. If a foodborne illness or outbreak were to occur, your HACCP records will show that your operation used all reasonable care. It will also give your operation and its attorneys a defense for any unfounded allegations. Records will show that the facility is using SOPs properly to control foodborne illness and that those SOPs are documented, monitored, and verified. No facility is perfect; therefore records will also verify corrective actions were taken when necessary.

HACCP Principle 6: Verify That the HACCP System Works

Verification, Principle 6, is a check or a **confirmation** that ensures the steps of the plan are adequately working. Verification ensures that your operation is maintaining an effective food safety management system (following the plan), and it provides a chance to update the plan as needed. Verification activities are always completed by the supervisor, director, or sometimes an outside firm.

Before the verification process takes place the following questions must be answered:

- **Who will perform the verification?**

  It is critical to remember that the person responsible for performing the verification process should reinforce management's commitment to HACCP; as well as, the prerequisite programs and achieve active managerial control. The leadership impact of verification is very powerful; therefore, it is important that a qualified professional be selected. This person should be responsible, credible, and have a strong commitment to food safety, your organization, and your brand. This person confirms, without a doubt, that the HACCP plan in place is working to prevent death or injury to you, your employees, and your customers.

- **What needs to be performed?**

Verification requires continuous review of logs, records, and corrective actions which are prepared in the Documentation Principle to understand whether the HACCP plan is working. The verification process requires a procedure be developed with specific objectives and steps to effectively determine that all Principles of the HACCP plan are working properly. Verification assessment is done by reviewing the logs, charts, and records that are prepared by others during the documentation phase. This assessment validates that employees were trained to maintain SOPs and prerequisite programs. Verification is based on the actual performance of management once a HACCP plan is in operation. For this reason, it is necessary to implement a HACCP plan, in a food service or retail operation confirming all of the processes and the required behavior is part of the normal routine and duties, rather than something out of the ordinary. If this is new to your facility, the HACCP team and leadership in your organization will develop audits, checklists, and systems to verify that the HACCP plan, including prerequisite programs and CCPs, are correct. If the HACCP plan is in place, then these audits and checklists should have been created and in use.

The following list of verification activity examples, from the National Advisory Committee On Microbiological Criteria For Foods, Hazard Analysis and Critical Control Point Principles and Application Guidelines, will provide practical guidance for how you may need to plan for verification activities in your facility.

A. Verification procedures may include:

1. Establishment of appropriate verification schedules;
2. Review of the HACCP plan for completeness;
3. Confirmation of the accuracy of the flow diagram;
4. Review of the HACCP system to determine if the facility is operating according to the HACCP plan;
5. Review of CCP monitoring records;
6. Review of records for deviations and corrective actions;
7. Validation of critical limits to confirm that they are adequate in order to control significant hazards;
8. Validation of HACCP plan, including on-site review;
9. Review of modifications of the HACCP plan; and
10. Sampling and testing to verify CCPs.

B. Verification should be conducted:

1. Routinely or on an unannounced basis, to assure CCPs are under control;
2. When there are emerging concerns about the safety of a product;
3. When foods have been implicated as a vehicle for foodborne disease;
4. To confirm that changes have been implemented correctly after a HACCP plan has been modified; and
5. To assess whether a HACCP plan should be modified, due to a change in the process, equipment, ingredients, etc.

C. Verification reports may include information on the presence and adequacy of:

1. The HACCP plan and the person(s) responsible for administering and updating the HACCP plan;
2. The records associated with CCP monitoring;
3. Direct recording of monitoring data of the CCP while in operation;
4. Certification that monitoring equipment is properly calibrated and in working order;
5. Corrective actions for deviations;
6. Sampling and testing methods used to verify that CCPs are under control;
7. Modifications to the HACCP plan;
8. Training and knowledge of individuals responsible for monitoring CCPs; and
9. Validation activities.

- **Where will this be performed?** Verification procedures can be performed either on-site or off-site. On-site procedures can include self inspections. Using observations and checklists, the verification team can review the HACCP plan, observe whether prerequisite programs are being followed, review deviations, and recommend corrective actions. Further, the team can take random samples for analysis, review CCP records and critical limits to verify that they are adequate to control hazards, and make any modifications to the HACCP plan, as necessary. Some off-site validation activities would be microbiological testing and analysis of data from the records, logs, and charts by scientists and highly skilled professionals.

- **When will verification be performed?** Verification must be routine, but unannounced, to ensure that the verification is of the actual processes and not of a staged event. Each operation is different, and a HACCP plan developed for each food facility will determine the correct frequency, based on the monitoring procedures. Prerequisite programs, including all SOPs, need to be reviewed on an annual basis. Verification must be performed on an ongoing basis when, new equipment is added to the kitchen, new items have been added to the menu, and after any personnel changes have occurred. In addition, HACCP verification is required when a foodborne illness has been reported or a foodborne illness is alleged to be associated with a food that your organization produces or serves. Finally, verification is needed when changes are made to the FDA Model Food Code and other regulations are modified, to ensure that you are in compliance with current codes.

- **Why?** Verification confirms that the HACCP plan is working on a continuous basis at your food service or retail establishment. This process ensures that you are serving and selling safe food, as well as, protecting your customers!

- **How will verification be performed?** Verification is performed by using a Verification Inspection Checklist, HACCP Plan Verification Worksheet, HACCP Plan Verification Summary, or some other systematic process that ensures potential problems are identified and corrective actions were taken. This is accomplished by reviewing records, logs, charts, calibrating equipment and tools, and by observing or interviewing personnel as they do their work. These recommended tools (Verification Inspection Checklist, HACCP Plan Verification Worksheet, and HACCP Plan Verification Summary) can be modified as required. Examples of these tools are located at the end of Principle 6 and in the Appendix of this book. The verification person or team can also take a random sample and compare their results with previously written records to ensure accuracy. Microbiological testing by laboratories can validate that the critical limits are preventing, reducing, or eliminating any hazards. Third-party audits can assist in the verification process by: analyzing food samples, checking the signature and date on records, logs, and charts, and by actually confirming all equipment is properly calibrated, maintained, and operating.

The **Verification Inspection Checklist**, **HACCP Plan Verification Worksheet**, and **HACCP Plan Verification Summary** are commonly used by regulatory authorities in checking all steps in the HACCP plan for accuracy and effectiveness. These are outstanding tools for food service and retail facility HACCP teams to use when evaluating their own HACCP plan, because they are logical and systematic. These worksheets and forms can be found in Appendix 3 of this book.

As a food service or retail manager, realize that a new menu or a concept change will require verification and modifications to your HACCP plan. Verification is important because it reviews every Star Point and confirms that your HACCP plan is working. Here is a quick review of verification activities:

- Review hazard analysis and CCPs;
- Check critical control point records;
- Validate critical limits;
- Understand why foods haven't reached their critical limits;
- Review monitoring records and frequency of activity;
- Observe employees performing tasks, especially monitoring CCPs;
- Check equipment temperatures;
- Confirm all equipment is working properly;
- Determine causes for equipment failure and procedure failure; and
- Ensure third-party or in-house validation is complete.

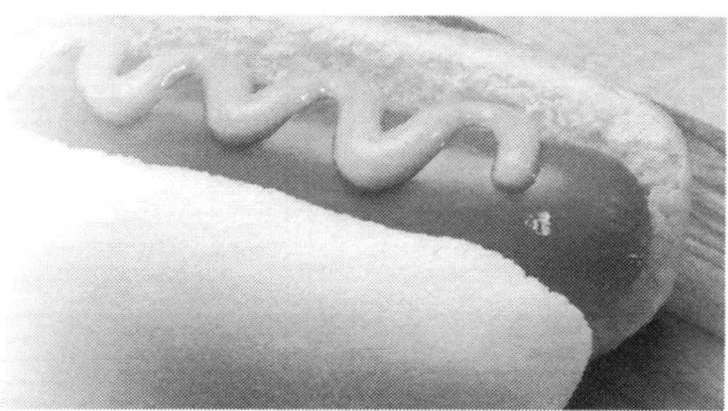

Star Knowledge Exercise:

Verification Scenarios

You are the person-in-charge of your facility. How would you handle the following situations? In the space provided, complete the scenario using your company procedures or best leadership practices to achieve successful verification. Then justify and explain why you took that course of action.

Situation	What Do You Do? Why?
1. As a manager performing verification, you notice that the cold-holding chart is perfect with every cold food product exactly documented at 41°F (5°C).	
2. During verification, you realize that the critical control point is not being met for cooking hamburgers.	
3. A memo has been posted on the bulletin board: "Attention all Employees: HACCP Verification/ Audit/Inspection is from the 10th to the 13th and everyone is expected to perform their very best, no matter what!" You're the person that arrives on the 10th to do the HACCP verification.	

Situation	What Do You Do? Why?
4. After reviewing the first three pages of records, you notice that the same employee completed the records with the same pen for all 4 days, and then you look at the employee schedule and realize that employee was on vacation during the week the records were completed.	
5. Using the ice-point method of calibration, you check the thermometers used for monitoring and find that there are five thermometers being used and the temperatures at ice point are as follows: a. 33°F (0.6°C) b. 31°F (–0.6°C) c. 29°F (–1.7°C) d. 35°F (1.7°C) e. 35°F (1.7°C)	
6. You are observing an employee preparing and cooking frozen chicken wings according to the standard operating procedure for fresh chicken wings.	
7. During verification, you observe an employee reheating meatballs for the third time in 3 hours.	
8. During your verification visit, a customer returns a chicken breast that is bloody in the center.	
9. A different customer brings back another bloody chicken sandwich and hands it to an employee. Then that same employee looks at you for direction.	
10. The microbiological testing results have come back positive for E. coli in the ground beef and you were just notified that the equipment used to cook the ground beef is not working properly.	

HACCP Principle 7: Record Keeping and Documentation

To achieve the final HACCP principle, you must keep all of the documents created while establishing and maintaining your HACCP plan. HACCP Principle 7 involves maintaining all the paperwork, including documents and logs used to achieve active managerial control and to protect the flow of food and the food safety management system. It is critical when documenting HACCP to gather and maintain sufficient information, to ensure your plan is effective. All records must be accurate and legible. As the manager or supervisor, it is your responsibility to set the example and ensure correct and accurate record keeping. Records must be legible. It is useless if others cannot read them. Never scribble or use initials or words that could be misunderstood. Never use correction tape or liquid as it may look to the outside observer that there is a cover up. Be sure employees are not dry labbing or falsifying records. The employees on your team will follow your example. For instance, never scribble or use correction tape or liquid because it may look like a cover-up. For errors, always draw a line through the mistake and initial it.

To be effective, your record keeping plans should include the following:

Prerequisite Records:

Note: Sample forms can be found in Appendix 3 of this book.

- Company Organization Chart
- Employee Health Records
  (FDA Forms: 1-A, 1-B, 1-C, Health Practitioner's Reference 1-D)
- Employee Training Log
- Food Defense Employee Training Form
- Schedules
- Standardized Recipe
- Equipment Monitoring Logs
- Equipment Maintenance Log
- Allergen Management
- List of Approved Chemicals
- Master Cleaning Checklist
- Sanitizer Checklist
- Pest Control Documentation
- Food Establishment Inspection Report
- SOPs* (Refer to Appendix 2)

Purchasing Records:

- Supplier Certification Records
- Processor Audit Record
- Invoices
- Shellstock Tags—mandatory records that must be filed in chronological order for at least 90 days

Receiving Records:

- Receiving Log
- Receiving Reject Form

Storing Records:

- Storage Temperature Logs
- Freezer Log
- Refrigeration/Cooler Log

Preparing Records:

- Preparation Log
- Grinding Log (Lot #'s)

Cooking Records:

- Cooking Log
- Time-Temperature Graphs

Holding Records:

- Time-Temperature Logs
- Cold Holding Food Logs
- Hot Holding Food Logs
- Cold Holding Equipment
- Hot Holding Equipment

Cooling Records:

- Cooling Logs

Reheating Records:

- Reheating Logs

Serving Records:

- Serving Line Temperature Log
- Cold-Serving Equipment
- Hot-Serving Equipment

HACCP:

HACCP Plan Form

Principle 1: Conduct a Hazard Analysis

Hazard Analysis Work Sheet

Flowcharts

Specifications of the Food Products

Principle 2: Determine Critical Control Points

Process 1—Food Preparation with Simple/No-Cook Step Chart

Process 2—Preparation for Same-Day Service

Process 3—Complex Food Preparation

Principle 3: Establish Critical Limits

Critical Limit Chart

Shelf Life Chart

Principle 4: Establish Monitoring Procedures

Calibrated Thermometers

Monitoring Procedures

Monitoring Report

Principle 5: Identify Corrective Actions

Corrective Actions Records

Discard Log (Waste Chart/Shrink Log)

Principle 6: Verify that the HACCP System Works

Verification Records

Principle 7: Record Keeping and Documentation

Foodborne Illness Investigation

Food Safety Checklist

This is a big list and at first glance. It is very daunting. But with the proper forms and training, the use of such documentation will become second nature to you and your employees. If you don't include such documentation in your HACCP plan, it will most likely fail. Keep all documentation for three years plus the current year.

Did You Know. . .Dry labbing is filling out forms or logs without taking any actual measurements. These are falsified documents and you could get in trouble if caught.

Record keeping provides a history that ensures your food service or retail industry is following standard operating procedures. By documenting these steps, you prove that your company is consistently preparing, serving, and selling safe food. The additional benefit for documenting these steps is a more efficient operation, better control of costs, and the security of knowing you have done everything possible to serve food safely.

Standardized Recipes

The following is a standardized USDA recipe checklist:

- ❑ Name of recipe
- ❑ Ingredients list
- ❑ Weight and measure
- ❑ Preparation directions
- ❑ Serving directions
- ❑ Yield
- ❑ Portion size information
- ❑ Variations
- ❑ Nutrients per serving
- ❑ Pan size, if appropriate

Pop Quiz:

Verification and Evaluation of HACCP Plan

Name three situations when verification should be done to evaluate the HACCP plan. Why?

1. ______________________________

____

2. ______________________________

____

3. ______________________________

____

Name the top five CDC foodborne illness risk factors known to cause 80% of foodborne illness outbreaks.

1. ______________________________

____

2. ______________________________

____

3. ______________________________

____

4. ______________________________

____

5. ______________________________

____

Validation

Conduct Periodic Validation of your HACCP System.

Validation, should be executed by a food safety professional if HACCP is required. Federal or state regulatory officials, qualified food safety consultants, or members of academia could complete this review. If a food service or retail facility executes a food safety management system voluntarily, is committed to active managerial control, then voluntary validation can be performed in house.

Once your HACCP system is established, you should periodically review it to determine whether the food safety hazards are controlled and the system is implemented properly. This review is known as validation.

Validation is not the same as Verification in HACCP Principal 6. Whereas verification is a check or a confirmation that ensures the steps of the plan are adequately working. **Validation focuses on collecting and evaluating scientific and technical information to determine if the HACCP system, when properly implemented, will effectively control the hazards.**

Validation assists you to:

- Improve the system and HACCP plan by identifying weaknesses;
- Eliminate unnecessary or ineffective controls; and
- Determine if the HACCP plan needs to be modified or updated.

Validation is conducted less frequently, typically **yearly**, whereas verification is an **on-going** process. It is a review or audit of the entire HACCP System to determine if:

- Any new product/processes/menu items have been added to the menu;
- Suppliers, customers, equipment, or facilities have changed;
- Prerequisite programs are current and implemented;
- Worksheets are still current;
- CCPs are still valid, or if new CCPs are needed;
- Critical limits are realistically set and are adequate to control the hazard (e.g., the time needed to cook a turkey to meet the Food Code internal temperature requirement); and
- Monitoring equipment has been calibrated as planned.

You can use the Validation Worksheet in the Appendix to assist with the validation process.

Changes in suppliers, products, or preparation procedures may prompt a **re-validation** of your food safety management system sooner than expected. A small change could result in a drastically different outcome from what you expect. You may benefit from both internal (quality assurance) and external validations that may involve assistance from the regulatory authority or other consultants. All records associated with a validation should be kept as part of your HACCP documentation.

Now, it is time to apply what you have learned. In the following exercises you will be required to complete the appropriate forms related to a Roasted Chicken Club being prepared and served under three different circumstances: Simple/No-Cook recipe, Same Day recipe, and Complex recipe.

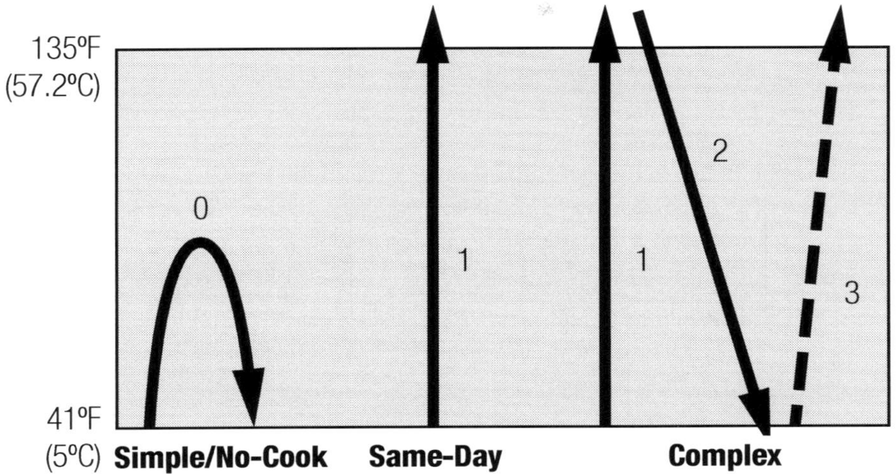

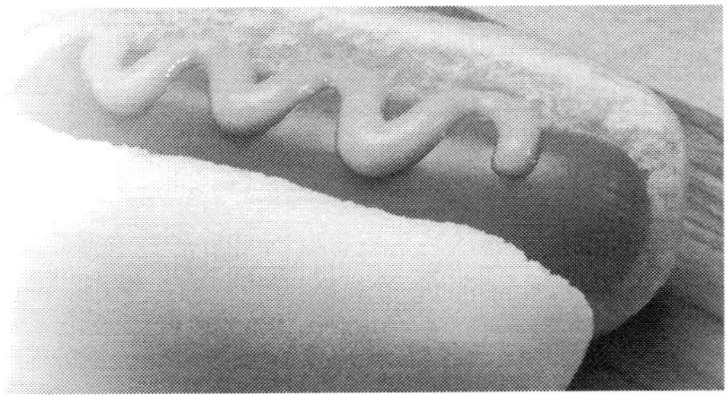

Star Knowledge Exercise:

Completing the HACCP Process

Use the Hazard Analysis Worksheets and HACCP Plan Forms on pages 287-296. The ingredients for Pre-made Roasted Chicken Club can be found on page 138 - 139.

A. Simple/No-Cook Recipe

Complete the A. Hazard Analysis Worksheet and the A. HACCP Plan Form for sale of a pre-made Roasted Chicken Club that follows a "Simple/No-Cook Recipe" process. Assume the bacon came to the facility fully cooked.

B. Same-Day Recipe

Complete the B. Hazard Analysis Worksheet and the B. HACCP Plan Form for sale of a Roasted Chicken Club that is prepared and served following a "Same-Day Recipe" process.

C. Complex Recipe

Complete the C. Hazard Analysis Worksheet and the C. HACCP Plan Form for sale of a Roasted Chicken Club that is prepared and served following a "Complex Recipe" process. Assume the chicken breast comes to the facility raw and you need to cook it.

Star Point 5 Conclusion

In Star Point 5, we have discussed two important Principles; **Principle 6 Verification** and **Principle 7 Record Keeping.** These are the checks and balances system of your HACCP plan. Record Keeping permits your employees to constantly monitor the food flow and provides proof that the HACCP plan is working properly. Verification confirms your plan is working properly. Together, Record Keeping and Verification confirms that that you're achieving active managerial control of foodborne risk factors. This is the final step in becoming a HACCP All-Star.

Now that you have learned all 5 points of the HACCP Star you can understand the benefits of all these points. First, with a carefully planned and implemented HACCP plan your facility provides for the health and safety of your customers and employees. Second, you now understand that a HACCP plan that is implemented provides for an overall improvement of your food service or retail operation, including food safety SOPs, food quality, cleanliness, sanitation, food defense SOPs, and a team better equipped to handle food. Finally, you know that by following the HACCP Star you can successfully proceed through the process of analyzing and controlling hazards. With your plan in place you can now manage a food service or retail operation that is proactive versus reactive. You will do your part with confidence to ensure the overall safety of our food supply from farm to table.

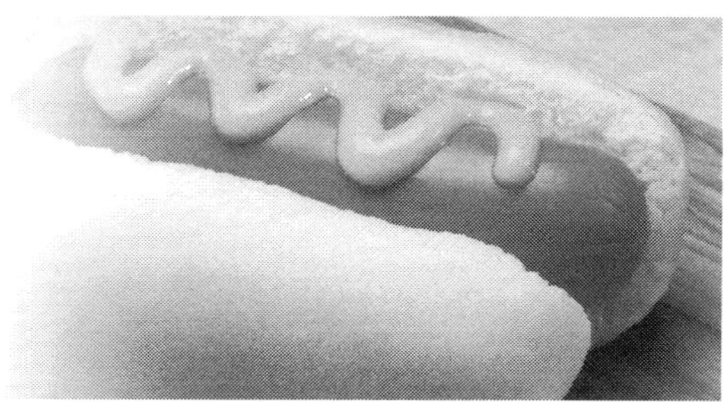

Star Knowledge Exercise:

HACCP Principles Match Game

Match the HACCP principles with the corresponding description.

HACCP Principle 1: _____	**a.** Establish Record Keeping and Documentation Procedures
HACCP Principle 2: _____	**b.** Establish Corrective Actions
HACCP Principle 3: _____	**c.** Conduct a Hazard Analysis
HACCP Principle 4: _____	**d.** Establish Critical Limits
HACCP Principle 5: _____	**e.** Determine Critical Control Points
HACCP Principle 6: _____	**f.** Establish Verification Procedures
HACCP Principle 7: _____	**g.** Establish Monitoring Procedures

7 HACCP Principles Match Game Results

How many points did you earn? _______

If you scored 7 points — Congratulations! You are a HACCP Principles All-Star!

If you scored 5–6 points — Good job! You have a basic understanding of HACCP principles.

If you scored 3–4 points — The time to review is now! What a great opportunity to fine-tune your HACCP principles skills.

If you scored 0–2 points — You should discuss with your trainer ways to better understand the HACCP principles so that you may apply them at your establishment to serve and sell safe food.

Star Point 5 Check for Understanding

(Circle one.)

1. Verification includes ________________________.

a. who will perform the task of verifying
b. what needs to be performed
c. when verification will be performed
d. how verification will be documented
e. all of the above

2. Verification is ________________________.

a. a check or confirmation that the HACCP plan is working
b. verification that employees come to work on time
c. proof that you have a successful business
d. both a and c

3. Record keeping involves ________________________.

a. having a phone number so you can call off work
b. all paperwork, documents, and logs that have been maintained as the flow of food is monitored
c. filling in random numbers on the log sheets when you are running behind schedule
d. getting rid of documents at the end of the week

4. When you keep records you should ______________.

a. never scribble on forms or log sheets
b. never dry lab
c. always neatly cross out mistakes
d. all of the above

5. HACCP principles 6 and 7 are ________________.

a. CCP and CP
b. Hazard Analysis and Monitoring
c. Verification and Record Keeping
d. Time and Temperature

6. Verification should be conducted when?

a. Routinely, and on an unannounced basis, to assure CCPs are under control
b. When foods have been implicated as a vehicle of foodborne disease
c. To confirm that changes have been implemented correctly after a HACCP plan has been modified
d. all of the above

7. What form(s) can be used for Verification of a HACCP plan?

a. A Verification Inspection Checklist
b. A log sheet of cooling times
c. HACCP Plan Verification Worksheet
d. both a and c
e. all of the above

8. What might prompt a HACCP plan to need re-validated sooner than expected?

a. When a new employee is hired
b. When a supplier is changed
c. Never
d. When a preparation procedure is changed
e. Both b and d

9. Verification should be conducted by ______________.

a. a Supervisor or Director
b. an outside firm
c. only the owner of the facility
d. both a and b
e. all of the above

10. Should a foodborne illness or outbreak occur, HACCP records will provide ________________________.

a. a reasonable care defense for your operation
b. a shield to hide behind
c. a pattern of bad behavior
d. proof that employees have neat handwriting

Are You a HACCP "All-Star"?

The goal of this manual is to help you to better understand the five points in the HACCP Star, to provide information to help you develop a HACCP program for your food service or retail facility, and to demonstrate how understanding these star points save lives! Each point of the HACCP Star helps you to create and use an effective HACCP plan. Now that you have a better understanding of a HACCP plan, it is up to you to be a valued HACCP team member by applying the standard operating procedures and HACCP principles learned in this book to your food service or retail operation and by leading your team members to make these steps a part of their daily routines. Your leadership will help to ensure that you're serving and selling safe food!

It is time to take your HACCP examination to test your understanding of this program. Upon successful completion of the examination, you will receive your HACCP All-Star Certificate. The HACCP certification is valid for four years and is recognized as advanced HACCP comprehension for managers. Please complete the evaluation on your trainer and prepare to take your HACCP examination.

Appendix 1: Technical Information

Time/Temperature Control for Safety of Food (TCS)

In this section, use Tables A and B to determine if a food requires time and temperature control for its safety. Table A is used for foods that are heat-treated and packaged. Table B is used for foods that are not heat-treated or heat-treated but not packaged. Additional information that you may need can be found on the following: Tables 1, 2, 3, 4 or at www.cfsan.fda.gov.

- Table 1 gives approximate water activity for pathogens.
- Table 2 provides approximate water activity for selected food categories.
- Table 3 gives approximate pH values permitting the growth of selected pathogens in food.
- Table 4 provides approximate pH values of common foods.

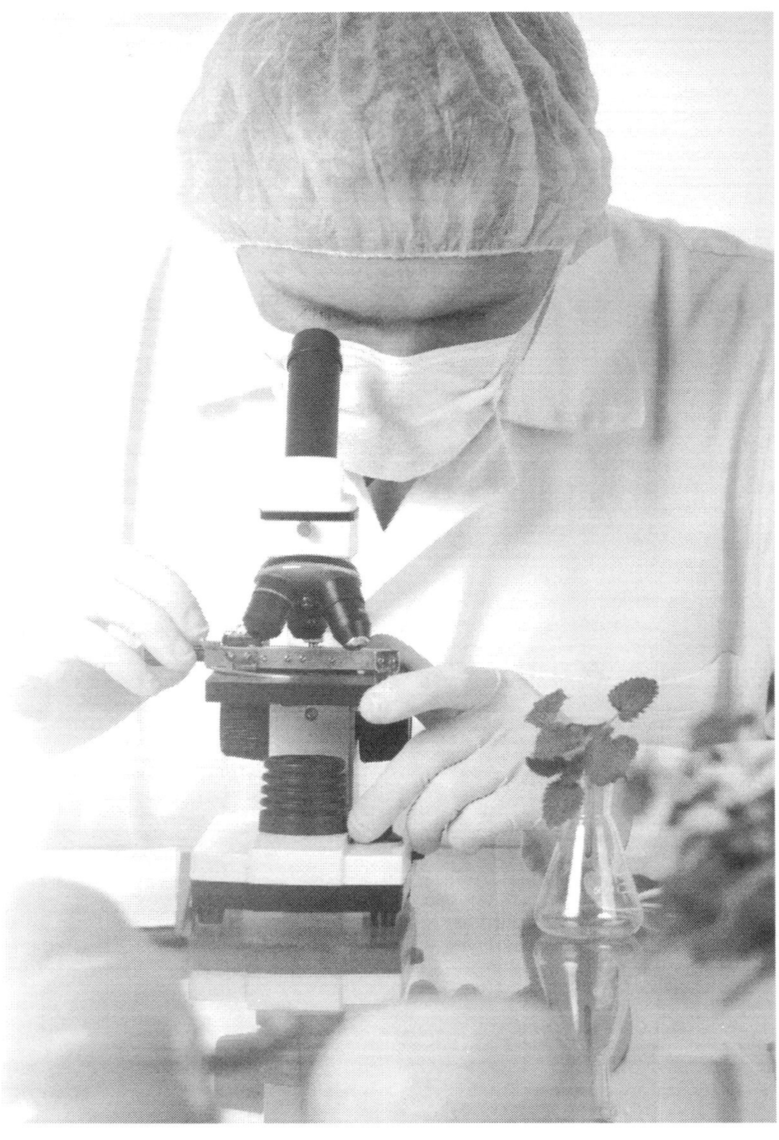

TCS Matrix

Table A. Interaction of pH and a_w for control of spores in food heat-treated to destroy vegetative cells and subsequently packaged

a_w values	pH values		
	4.6 or less	**> 4.6 - 5.6**	**> 5.6**
≤ 0.92	non-TCS food **	non-TCS food	non-TCS food
> 0.92 - .95	non-TCS food	non-TCS food	PA***
> 0.95	non-TCS food	PA	PA

** **TCS** Food means **T**ime/**T**emperature **C**ontrol for **S**afety Food
*** **PA** means **P**roduct **A**ssessment required

Table B. Interaction of pH and a_w for control of vegetative cells and spores in food not heat-treated or heat-treated but not packaged

a_w values	pH values			
	< 4.2	**4.2 - 4.6**	**> 4.6 - 5.0**	**> 5.0**
< 0.88	non-TCS food **	non-TCS food	non-TCS food	non-TCS food
0.88 - 0.90	non-TCS food	non-TCS food	PA***	PA***
> 0.90 - 0.92	non-TCS food	non-TCS food	PA	PA
> 0.92	non-TCS food	PA	PA	PA

** **TCS** Food means **T**ime/**T**emperature **C**ontrol for **S**afety Food
*** **PA** means **P**roduct **A**ssessment required

Table 1. Approximate a_w Values for Growth of Selected Pathogens in Food

Organism	Minimum	Optimum	Maximum
Campylobacter spp.	0.98	0.99	
Clostridium botulinum type E	0.97		
Clostridium botulinum types A and B	0.93		
Shigella spp.	0.97		
Yersinia enterocolitica	0.97		
Enterohemorrhagic *Escherichia coli*	0.95	0.99	
Vibrio vulnificus	0.96	0.98	0.99
Salmonella spp.	0.94	0.99	>0.99
Vibrio parahaemolyticus	0.94	0.98	0.99
Bacillus cereus	0.93		
Clostridium partfingens	0.943	0.95-0.96	0.97
Listeria monocytogenes	0.92		
Staphylococcus aureus growth	0.83	0.98	0.99
Staphylococcus aureus toxin	0.88	0.98	0.99

Table 2. Approximate Water Activity of Selected Food Categories

Animal Products	a_w
Fresh meat, poultry, fish	0.99-1.00
Natural cheeses	0.95-1.00
Pudding	0.97-0.99
Eggs	0.97
Cured meat	0.87-0.95
Condensed milk	0.83
Parmesan cheese	0.68-0.76
Honey	0.75
Dried whole egg	0.40
Dried whole milk	0.20
Plant Products	**a_w**
Fresh fruits, vegetables	0.97-1.00
Bread	~0.96
Bread, white	0.94-0.97
Bread, crust	0.30
Baked cake	0.90-0.94
Maple syrup	0.85
Jam	0.75-0.80
Jellies	0.82-0.94

Plant Products (continued)	a_w
Uncooked rice	0.80-0.87
Fruit juice concentrates	0.79-0.84
Fruit cake	0.73-0.83
Cake icing	0.76-0.84
Flour	0.67-0.87
Dried fruit	0.55-0.80
Cereal	0.10-0.20
Sugar	0.19
Crackers	0.10

Table 3. Approximate pH Values Permitting the Growth of Selected Pathogens in Food

Microorganism	Minimum	Optimum	Maximum
Campylobacter spp.	4.9	6.5-7.5	9.0
Clostridium botulinum toxin type E	4.6		8.5
Clostridium botulinum growth types A and B	4.6		8.5
Shigella spp.	4.9		9.3
Yersinia enterocolitica	4.2	7.2	9.6
Enterohemorrhagic *Escherichia coli*	4.4	6.0-7.0	9.0
Vibrio vulnificus	5.0	7.8	10.2
Salmonella spp.	4.2	7.0-7.5	9.5
Vibrio parahaemolyticus	4.8	7.8-8.6	11.0
Bacillus cereus	4.9	6.0-7.0	8.8
Clostridium perfringens	5.5-5.8	7.2	8.0-9.0
Listeria monocytogenes	4.39	7	9.4
Staphylococcus aureus growth	4.0	6.0-7.0	10.0
Staphylococcus aureus toxin	4.5	7.0-8.0	9.6

Table 4. Approximate pH Values of Selected Food Categories

Item	Approximate pH
Abalone	6.10-6.50
Abalone Mushroom	5.00
Anchovies	6.5
Anchovies, stuffed w/ capers, in olive oil	5.58-6.50
Antipasto	5.60
Apple, baked with sugar	3.20-3.55
Apple, eating	3.30-4.00
Apples	
Delicious	3.90
Golden Delicious	3.60
Jonathan	3.33
McIntosh	3.34
Juice	3.35-4.00
Sauce	3.10-3.60
Winesap	3.47
Apricots	3.30-4.80
Canned	3.40-3.78
Dried, stewed	3.30-3.51
Nectar	3.78
Pureed	3.42-3.83
Strained	3.72-3.95
Arrowroot crackers	6.63-6.80
Arrowroot cruel	6.37-6.87
Artichokes	5.50-6.00
Artichokes, canned, acidified	4.30-4.60
Artichokes, French, cooked	5.60-6.00
Artichokes, Jerusalem, cooked	5.93-6.00
Asparagus	6.00-6.70
Buds	6.70
Stalks	6.10
Asparagus, cooked	6.03-6.16
Asparagus, canned	5.00-6.00
Asparagus, frozen, cooked	6.35-6.48
Asparagus, green, canned	5.20-5.32
Asparagus, strained	4.80-5.09
Avocados	6.27-6.58
Baby corn	5.20

Item	Approximate pH
Baby food soup, unstrained	5.95-6.05
Bamboo shoots +	5.10-6.20
Bamboo Shoots, preserved	3.50-4.60
Bananas	4.50-5.20
Bananas, red	4.58-4.75
Bananas, yellow	5.00-5.29
Barley, cooked	5.19-5.32
Basil pesto	4.90
Bass, sea, broiled	6.58-6.78
Bass, striped, broiled	6.50-6.70
Beans	5.60-6.50
Black	5.78-6.02
Boston style	5.05-5.42
Kidney	5.40-6.00
Lima	6.50
Soy	6.00-6.60
String	5.60
Wax	5.30-5.70
Beans, pork and tomato sauce, canned	5.10-5.80
Beans, refried	5.90
Beans, vegetarian, tomato sauce, canned	5.32
Beets	5.30-6.60
Beets, cooked	5.23-6.50
Beets, canned, acidified	4.30-4.60
Beets, canned	4.90-5.80
Beets, chopped	5.32-5.56
Beets, strained	5.32.5.56
Blackberries, Washington	3.85-4.50
Blueberries, Maine	3.12-3.33
Blueberries, frozen	3.11-3.22
Bluefish, Boston, filet, broiled	6.09-6.50
Bran	
Flakes	5.45-5.67
All-Bran	5.59-6.19
Bread, white	5.00-6.20
Bread, Boston, brown	6.53
Bread, cracked wheat	5.43-5.50
Bread, pumpernickel	5.40

Item	Approximate pH
Bread, rye	5.20-5.90
Bread, whole wheat	5.47-5.85
Breadfruit, cooked	5.33
Broccoli, cooked	6.30-6.52
Broccoli, frozen, cooked	6.30-6.85
Broccoli, canned	5.20-6.00
Brussels sprout	6.00-6.30
Buttermilk	4.41-4.83
Cabbage	5.20-6.80
Green	5.50-6.75
Red	5.60-6.00
Savoy	6.30
White	6.20
Cactus	4.70
Calamari (squid)	5.80
Cantaloupe	6.13-6.58
Capers	6.00
Carp	6.00
Carrots	5.88-6.40
Carrots, canned	5.18-5.22
Carrots, chopped	5.30-5.56
Carrots, cooked	5.58-6.03
Carrots, pureed	4.55-5.80
Carrots, strained	5.10
Cauliflower	5.60
Cauliflower, cooked	6.45-6.80
Caviar, American	5.70-6.00
Celery	5.70-6.00
Celery, cooked	5.37-5.92
Celery, knob, cooked	5.71-5.85
Cereal, strained	6.44-6.45
Cheese, American, mild	4.98
Cheese, Camembert	7.44
Cheese, cheddar	5.90
Cheese, cottage	4.75-5.02
Cheese, cream	4.10-4.79
Cheese dip	5.80
Cheese, Edam	5.40

Item	Approximate pH
Cheese, Old English	6.15
Cheese, Roquefort	5.10-5.98
Cheese, parmesan	5.20-5.30
Cheese, snippy	5.18-5.21
Cheese, Stilton	5.70
Cheese, Swiss Gruyere	5.68-6.62
Cherries, California	4.01-4.54
Cherries, frozen	3.32-3.37
Cherries, black, canned	3.82-3.93
Cherries, maraschino	3.47-3.52
Cherries, red, water-pack	3.25-3.82
Cherries, Royal Ann	3.80-3.83
Chicory	5.90-6.05
Chili sauce, acidified	2.77-3.70
Chives	5.20-6.31
Clams	6.00-7.10
Clam chowder, New England	6.40
Coconut, fresh	5.50-7.80
Coconut milk	6.10-7.00
Coconut preserves	3.80-7.00
Codfish, boiled	5.30-6.10
Cod liver	6.20
Conch	7.52-8.40
Corn	5.90-7.30
Corn, canned	5.90-6.50
Cornflakes	4.90-5.38
Corn, frozen, cooked	7.33-7.68
Corn, Golden Bantam, cooked on cob	6.22-7.04
Crabmeat	6.50-7.00
Crabapple jelly, corn	2.93-3.02
Cranberry juice, canned	2.30-2.52
Crabmeat, cooked	6.62-6.98
Cream, 20 per cent	6.50-6.68
Cream, 40 per cent	6.44-6.80
Cream of asparagus	6.10
Cream of coconut, canned	5.51-5.87
Cream of potato soup	6.00
Cream of Wheat, cooked	6.06-6.16

Item	Approximate pH
Chrysanthemum drink	6.50
Cucumbers	5.12-5.78
Cucumbers, dill pickles	3.20-3.70
Cucumbers, pickled	4.20-4.60
Curry sauce	6.00
Curry paste, acidified	4.60-4.80
Cuttlefish	6.30
Dates, canned	6.20-6.40
Dates, dromedary	4.14-4.88
Eggplant	5.50-6.50
Eggs, new-laid, whole	6.58
White	7.96
Yolk	6.10
Eel	6.20
Escarole	5.70-6.00
Enchilada sauce	4.40-4.70
Fennel (anise)	5.48-5.88
Fennel, cooked	5.80-6.02
Figs, calamyrna	5.05-5.98
Figs, canned	4.92-5.00
Flounder, boiled	6.10-6.90
Flounder, filet, broiled	6.39-6.89
Four bean salad	5.60
Fruit cocktail	3.60-4.00
Garlic	5.80
Gelatin dessert	2.60
Gelatin, plain	6.08
Ginger	5.60-5.90
Ginseng, Korean drink	6.00-6.50
Gooseberries	2.80-3.10
Graham crackers	7.10-7.92
Grapes, canned	3.50-4.50
Grapes, Concord	2.80-3.00
Grapes, Lady Finger	3.51-3.58
Grapes, Malaga	3.71-3.78
Grapes, Niagara	2.80-3.27
Grapes, Ribier	3.70-3.80
Grapes, seedless	2.90-3.82

Item	Approximate pH
Grapes, Tokyo	3.50-3.84
Grapefruit	3.00-3.75
Grapefruit, canned	3.08-3.32
Grapefruit juice, canned	2.90-3.25
Grass jelly	5.80-7.20
Greens, mixed, chopped	5.05-5.22
Greens, mixed, strained	5.22-5.30
Grenadine syrup	2.31
Guava nectar	5.50
Guava, canned	3.37-4.10
Guava jelly	3.73
Haddock, filet, broiled	6.17-6.82
Hearts of palm	5.70
Herring	6.10
Hominy, cooked	6.00-7.50
Honey	3.70-4.20
Honey aloe	4.70
Horseradish, freshly ground	5.35
Huckleberries, cooked with sugar	3.38-3.43
Jackfruit	4.80-6.80
Jam, fruit	3.50-4.50
Jellies, fruit	3.00-3.50
Jujube	5.20
Junket-type dessert:	
Raspberry	6.27
Vanilla	6.49
Kale, cooked	6.36-6.80
Ketchup	3.89-3.92
Kippered, herring, Marshall	5.75-6.20
Herring, pickled	4.50-5.00
Kelp	6.30
Kumquat, Florida	3.64-4.25
Leeks	5.50-6.17
Leeks, cooked	5.49-6.10
Lemon Juice	2.00-2.60
Lentils, cooked	6.30-6.83
Lentil soup	5.80
Lettuce	5.80-6.15

Item	Approximate pH
Lettuce, Boston	5.89-6.05
Lettuce, iceberg	5.70-6.13
Lime juice	2.00-2.35
Lime	2.00-2.80
Lobster bisque	6.90
Lobster soup	5.70
Lobster, cooked	7.10-7.43
Loganberries	2.70-3.50
Loquat (may be acidified to pH 3.8)	5.10
Lotus root	6.90
Lychee	4.70-5.01
Macaroni, cooked	5.10-6.41
Mackerel, king, broiled	6.26-6.50
Mackerel, Spanish, broiled	6.07-6.36
Mackerel, canned	5.90-6.40
Mangoes, ripe	3.40-4.80
Mangoes, green	5.80-6.00
Maple syrup	5.15
Maple syrup, light (acidified)	4.60
Matzos	5.70
Mayhaw (a variety of strawberry)	3.27-3.86
Melba toast	5.08-5.30
Melon, casaba	5.78-6.00
Melons, honeydew	6.00-6.67
Melons, Persian	5.90-6.38
Milk, cow	6.40-6.80
Milk, acidophilus	4.09-4.25
Milk, condensed	6.33
Milk, evaporated	5.90-6.30
Milk, goat's	6.48
Milk, peptonized	7.10
Milk, sour, fine curd	4.70-5.65
Milkfish	5.30
Mint jelly	3.01
Molasses	4.90-5.40
Muscadine (a variety of grape)	3.20-3.40
Mushrooms	6.00-6.70
Mushrooms, cooked	6.00-6.22

Item	Approximate pH
Mushroom soup, cream of, canned	5.95-6.40
Mussels	6.00-6.85
Mustard	3.55-6.00
Nata de coco	5.00
Nectarines	3.92-4.18
Noodles, boiled	6.08-6.50
Oatmeal, cooked	6.20-6.60
Octopus	6.00-6.50
Okra, cooked	5.50-6.60
Olives, black	6.00-7.00
Olives, green, fermented	3.60-4.60
Olives, ripe	6.00-7.50
Onions, pickled	3.70-4.60
Onions, red	5.30-5.80
Onions, white	5.37-5.85
Onions, yellow	5.32-5.60
Oranges, Florida	3.69-4.34
Oranges, Florida "color added"	3.60-3.90
Oranges juice, California	3.30-4.19
Oranges juice, Florida	3.30-4.15
Orange marmalade	3.00-3.33
Oysters	5.68-6.17
Oyster, smoked	6.00
Oyster mushrooms	5.00-6.00
Palm, heart of	6.70
Papaya	5.20-6.00
Papaya marmalade	3.53-4.00
Parsley	5.70-6.00
Parsnip	5.30-5.70
Parsnips, cooked	5.45-5.65
Pate	5.90
Peaches	3.30-4.05
Peaches, canned	3.70-4.20
Peaches, cooked with sugar	3.55-3.72
Peaches, frozen	3.28-3.35
Peanut butter	6.28
Peanut soup	7.50
Pears, Bartlett	3.50-4.60

Item	Approximate pH
Pears, canned	4.00-4.07
Pears, sickle cooked w/sugar	4.04-4.21
Pear nectar	4.03
Peas, canned	5.70-6.00
Peas, chick, garbanzo	6.48-6.80
Peas, cooked	6.22-6.88
Peas, dried (split green), cooked	6.45-6.80
Peas, dried (split yellow), cooked	6.43-6.62
Peas, frozen, cooked	6.40-6.70
Peas, pureed	4.90-5.85
Pea soup, cream of, canned	5.70
Peas, strained	5.91-6.12
Peppers	4.65-5.45
Peppers, green	5.20-5.93
Persimmons	4.42-4.70
Pickles, fresh pack	5.10-5.40
Pimento	4.40-4.90
Pimento, canned, acidified	4.40-4.60
Pineapple	3.20-4.00
Pineapple, canned	3.35-4.10
Pineapple juice, canned	3.30-3.60
Plum Nectar	3.45
Plums, blue	2.80-3.40
Plums, Damson	2.90-3.10
Plums, frozen	3.22-3.42
Plums, Green Gage	3.60-4.30
Plums, Green Gage, canned	3.22-3.32
Plums, red	3.60-4.30
Plums, spiced	3.64
Plums, yellow	3.90-4.45
Pollock, filet, broiled	6.72-6.82
Pomegranate	2.93-3.20
Porgy, broiled	6.40-6.49
Pork and beans	5.70
Potatoes	5.40-5.90
Mashed	5.10
Sweet	5.30-5.60
Tubers	5.70

Item	Approximate pH
Potato Soup	5.90
Prunes, dried, stewed	3.63-3.92
Prune juice	3.95-3.97
Prune, pureed	3.60-4.30
Prune, strained	3.58-3.83
Puffed rice	6.27-6.40
Puffed wheat	5.26-5.77
Pumpkin	4.90-5.50
Quince, fresh, stewed	3.12-3.40
Quince jelly	3.70
Radishes, red	5.85-6.05
Radishes, white	5.52-5.69
Radishes, seedless	3.80-4.10
Rambutan (Thailand)	4.90
Raspberries	3.22-3.95
Raspberries, frozen	3.18-3.26
Raspberries, New Jersey	3.50-3.82
Raspberry jam	2.87-3.17
Razor clams	6.20
Razor shell (sea asparagus)	6.00
Rattan, Thailand	5.20
Red ginseng	5.50
Red pepper relish	3.10-3.62
Rhubarb, California, stewed	3.20-3.34
Rhubarb	3.10-3.40
Canned	3.40
Rice (all cooked)	
Brown	6.20-6.80
Krispies	5.40-5.73
White	6.00-6.70
Wild	6.00-6.50
Rolls, white	5.46-5.52
Romaine	5.78-6.06
Salmon, fresh, boiled	5.85-6.50
Salmon, fresh, broiled	5.36-6.40
Salmon, Red Alaska, canned	6.07-6.16
Sardines	5.70-6.60
Sardine, Portuguese, in olive oil	5.42-5.93

Item	Approximate pH
Satay sauce	5.00
Sauce, enchilada	5.50
Sauce, fish	4.93-5.02
Sauce, Shrimp	7.01-7.27
Sauerkraut	3.30-3.60
Scallion	6.20
Scallop	6.00
Scotch broth	5.92
Sea snail (top shell)	6.00
Shad roe, sautéed	5.70-5.90
Shallots, cooked	5.30-5.70
Sherbet, raspberry	3.69
Sherry-wine	3.37
Shredded Ralston	5.32-5.60
Shredded Wheat	6.05-6.49
Shrimp	6.50-7.00
Shrimp paste	5.00-6.77
Smelts, sautéed	6.67-6.90
Soda crackers	5.65-7.32
Soup	
Broccoli cheese soup, condensed	5.60
Chicken broth, RTS	5.80
Corn soup, condensed	6.80
Cream of celery soup, condensed	6.20
Cream of mushroom, condensed	6.00-6.20
Cream-style corn, condensed	5.70-5.80
Cream of potato soup, condensed	5.80
Cream of shrimp soup, condensed	5.80
Minestrone soup, condensed	5.40
Oyster stew, condensed	6.30
Tomato rice soup, condensed	5.50
Soy infant formula	6.60-7.00
Soy sauce	4.40-5.40
Soy bean curd (tofu)	7.20
Soybean milk	7.00
Spaghetti, cooked	5.97-6.40
Spinach	5.50-6.80
Spinach, chopped	5.38-5.52

Item	Approximate pH
Spinach, cooked	6.60-7.18
Spinach, frozen, cooked	6.30-6.52
Spinach, pureed	5.50-6.22
Spinach, strained	5.63-5.79
Squash, acorn, cooked	5.18-6.49
Squash, hubbard, cooked	6.00-6.20
Squash, white, cooked	5.52-5.80
Squash, yellow, cooked	5.79-6.00
Squid	6.00-6.50
Sturgeon	6.20
Strawberries	3.00-3.90
Strawberries, California	3.32-3.50
Strawberries, frozen	3.21-3.32
Strawberry jam	3.00-3.40
Straw mushroom	4.90
Sweet potatoes	5.30-5.60
Swiss chard, cooked	6.17-6.78
Tamarind	3.00
Tangerine	3.32-4.48
Taro syrup	4.50
Tea	7.20
Three-bean salad	5.40
Tofu (soybean curd)	7.20
Tomatoes	4.30-4.90
Tomatoes, canned	3.50-4.70
Tomatoes, juice	4.10-4.60
Tomatoes, paste	3.50-4.70
Tomatoes, puree	4.30-4.47
Tomatoes, strained	4.32-4.58
Tomatoes, wine-ripened	4.42-4.65
Tomato soup, cream of, canned	4.62
Trout, Sea, sauteed	6.20-6.33
Truffle	5.30-6.50
Tuna fish, canned	5.90-6.20
Turnips	5.29-5.90
Turnip, greens, cooked	5.40-6.20
Turnip, white, cooked	5.76-5.85
Turnip, yellow, cooked	5.57-5.82

Item	Approximate pH
Vegetable juice	3.90-4.30
Vegetable soup, canned	5.16
Vegetable soup, chopped	4.98-5.02
Vegetable soup, strained	4.99-5.00
Vermicelli, cooked	5.80-6.50
Vinegar	2.40-3.40
Vinegar, cider	3.10
Walnuts, English	5.42
Wax gourd drink	7.20
Water chestnut	6.00-6.20
Watercress	5.88-6.18
Watermelon	5.18-5.60
Wheaties	5.00-5.12
Worcestershire sauce	3.63-4.00
Yams, cooked	5.50-6.81
Yeast	5.65
Youngberries, frozen	3.00-3.70
Zucchini, cooked	5.69-6.10
Zwieback	4.84-4.94

APPENDIX 2: SAMPLE SOPs

Summary of Food Safety Standard Operating Procedures (SOPs) Samples

- Purchasing
- Receiving Deliveries
- Storage - Storing Food Properly
- Washing Hands
- Personal Hygiene
- Using Suitable Utensils When Handling Foods
- Washing Fruits and Vegetables
- Time-/Date-Marking Food
- Cooking TCS Foods
- Hot and Cold Holding of TCS Foods
- Cooling
- Reheating
- Cleaning and Sanitizing
- Serving Food
- Food Safety for Self-Service Areas

Sample Purchasing SOP

Purpose: To prevent contamination of food, foodborne illness, and to ensure safe foods are served and sold to customers by purchasing food products from approved suppliers.

Scope: This procedure applies to food service and retail managers who purchase foods from approved suppliers.

Key Words: Approved suppliers, regulatory services

Warning: Suppliers must be approved by appropriate regulatory services.

Instructions:

Contact regulatory services to ensure you are purchasing foods from approved suppliers. To find out if a supplier is approved, call:

- CDC—404-639-2213 or visit www.cdc.gov
- EPA—202-272-0167 or visit www.epa.gov
- FSIS—888-674-6854 or visit www.fsis.usda.gov
- FDA—888-463-6332 or visit www.cfsan.fda.gov

1. Domestic / imported food (including produce, bottled water, and other foods) but not meat and poultry	• Evidence of regulatory oversight: copy of suppliers' local enforcement agency permit, state or federal registration or license, or a copy of the last inspection report • Third-party audit results [many vendors now provide third-party guarantees, including NSF International or American Institute of Baking (AIB)] • Microbiological or chemical analysis/testing results. • Person-in-the-plant verification (i.e., chain food facilities may have their own inspector monitor food they buy) • Self-certification (guarantee) by a wholesale processor based on HACCP • For raw agricultural commodities such as produce, certification of Good Agricultural Practices or membership in a trade association such as the United Fresh Fruit and Vegetable Association • A copy of a wholesale distributor or processor's agreement with its suppliers of food safety compliance
2. Domestic / imported meat, poultry, and related products such as meat- or poultry-containing stews, frozen foods, and pizzas	• USDA mark on meat or poultry products • Registration of importers with USDA
3. Fish and Fish Products	• Evidence of regulatory oversight: copy of suppliers' local enforcement agency permit, state or federal registration or license, or a copy of the last inspection report • Third-party audit results • Person-in-the-plant verification

3. Fish and Fish Products	• Self-certification (guarantee) by a wholesale processor based on HACCP • A copy of a wholesale distributor or processor's agreement with its suppliers of HACCP compliance. • U.S. Department of Commerce (USDC) approved list of fish establishments and products located at seafood.nmfs.noaa.gov
4. Shellfish	• Shellfish tags • Listing in current Interstate *Certified Shellfish Shippers publication* • Gulf oyster treatment process verification if sold between April 1 and October 31 (November 1 to March 31 certification may be used in lieu of warning signs) • USDC-approved list of fish establishments and products located at seafood.nmfs.noaa.gov
5. Drinking water (non-bottled water)	• A recent certified laboratory report demonstrating compliance with drinking water standards • A copy of the latest inspection report
6. Alcoholic beverages	• Third-party audit results • Self-certification (guarantee) by a wholesale processor based on HACCP • Person-in-the-plant verification • Evidence of regulatory oversight: copy of suppliers' local enforcement agency permit, state or federal registration or license, or a copy of the last inspection report • A copy of a wholesale distributor or processor's agreement with its suppliers of food safety compliance

Monitoring:

1. Inspect invoices or other documents to determine approval by a regulatory agency.
2. Food service and retail managers are encouraged to make frequent inspections of the suppliers' on-site facilities, manufacturing facilities, and processing plants/farms. Inspections determine cleanliness standards and ensure that HACCP plans are in place and followed.

Corrective Action:

Food service and retail purchasing managers must find a new supplier if the supplier is not approved by the above regulatory services.

Verification and Record Keeping:

The food service and retail purchasing manager must maintain all documentation from food suppliers. Documentation must be maintained for three years plus the current year.

Date Implemented: ____________________ By: ______________________________

Date Reviewed: ______________________ By: ______________________________

Date Revised: _______________________ By: ______________________________

Sample Receiving Deliveries SOP

Purpose: To ensure that all food is received fresh and safe when it enters the food service or retail operation, and to transfer food to proper storage as quickly as possible.

Scope: This procedure applies to food service and retail employees who receive food.

Key Words: Cross contamination, temperatures, receiving, holding, frozen goods, delivery

Instructions:

1. Train food service and retail employees, who accept deliveries, on proper receiving procedures.
2. Schedule deliveries to arrive at designated times during operational hours.
3. Post the delivery schedule, including the names of vendors, days and times of deliveries, and drivers' names.
4. Establish a rejection policy to ensure accurate, timely, consistent, and effective refusal and return of rejected goods.
5. Organize freezer and refrigeration space, loading docks, and storerooms before receiving deliveries.
6. Before deliveries, gather product specification lists and purchase orders, temperature logs, calibrated thermometers, pens, flashlights, and be sure to use clean loading carts.
7. Keep receiving area clean and well lighted.
8. Do not touch ready-to-eat foods with bare hands.
9. Determine whether foods will be marked with the date of arrival or the "use-by" date, and mark accordingly upon receipt.
10. Compare delivery invoice against products ordered and products delivered.
11. Transfer foods to their appropriate locations as quickly as possible.

Monitoring:

1. Confirm vendor name, day and time of delivery, as well as driver's identification before accepting delivery. If the driver's name is different than what is indicated on the delivery schedule, contact the vendor immediately.
2. Inspect the delivery truck upon arrival to ensure that it is clean, free of putrid odors, and organized to prevent cross contamination. Be sure refrigerated foods are delivered on a refrigerated truck.
3. Check the interior temperature of refrigerated trucks.
4. Check the cleanliness of crates and other shipping containers before accepting products. Reject foods that are shipped in dirty crates.
5. Check the integrity of food packaging.

6. Check the temperature of refrigerated foods.
    - For fresh meat, fish, dairy, and poultry products, insert a calibrated, cleaned, and sanitized thermometer into the center of the product to ensure a temperature of 41°F (5°C) or below.
    - For packaged products, insert a food thermometer between two packages, being careful not to puncture the wrapper. If the temperature exceeds 41°F (5°C), it may be necessary to take the internal temperature before accepting the product.
    - For eggs, the interior temperature of the truck should be 45°F (7.2°C) or below.
7. Check dates of milk, eggs, and other perishable goods to ensure safety and quality.
8. Check frozen foods to ensure that they are all frozen solid and show no signs of thawing and refreezing, such as the presence of large ice crystals or liquids on the bottom of cartons.

Corrective Action:

Reject the following:

- Frozen foods with signs of previous thawing
- Cans that have signs of deterioration—swollen sides or ends, flawed seals or seams, dents, or rust
- Punctured packages
- Expired foods
- Foods that are out of the safe temperature zone or deemed unacceptable by the established rejection policy

Verification and Record Keeping:

The designated team member must maintain accurate complete records including, recording temperatures and any corrective actions taken on either the delivery invoice or on the receiving log. The team member receiving and rejecting product must report anything out of the normal practice to his or her supervisor. The food service and retail manager must verify that food service and retail employees are receiving products using the proper procedure by visually monitoring receiving practices and reviewing the receiving log at the close of each day. Receiving and corrective action logs are kept on file for a minimum of 1 year.

Date Implemented: ____________________ By: ________________________________

Date Reviewed: ______________________ By: ________________________________

Date Revised: ________________________ By: ________________________________

Sample Storage - Storing Food Properly SOP

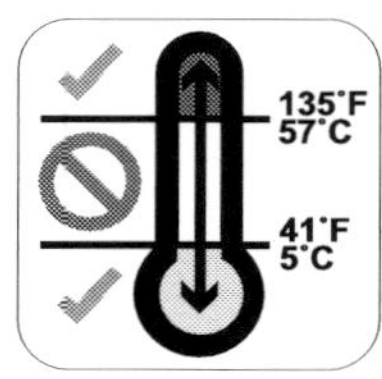

Purpose: To ensure that food is stored safely and put away as quickly as possible after it enters the food service and retail operation.

Scope: This procedure applies to food service and retail employees, who store, handle, prepare, or serve and sell food.

Key Words: Cross contamination, temperatures, storing, dry storage, refrigeration, freezer

Instructions:

1. Maintain freezer temperature at –10°F to 0°F (–23.3°C to –17.8°C).
2. Maintain refrigerator temperatures at between 36°F and 39°F (2.2°C to 3.9°C).
3. Maintain dry storage temperatures at between 50°F and 70°F (10°C and 21.1°C). Humidity is between 50 percent and 60 percent.
4. Record freezer and refrigerator temperatures on the appropriate log at the specific times.
5. Use a calibrated, cleaned, and sanitized thermometer (+/–2°F) or (+/– 1°C).
6. Utilize the FIFO (first-in, first-out) method to rotate all food products. Ensure that all items are dated upon delivery.
7. Ensure that all food stored in the freezer, refrigerator, and dry storage are covered, dated, labeled, and stored 6 inches off the floor.
8. All TCSs must be stored no more than 7 days at 41°F (5ºC) from the date of preparation.
9. All cooked and ready-to-eat foods must be stored above raw foods. Store other foods based on minimum internal cooking temperature.
10. Always store food in its original container as long as it is clean, dry, and intact. If not, notify your manager, director, or person-in-charge and make sure that any food not stored in its original container is properly marked.
11. Never put any food in a container that is not approved for food storage. Never put food in an empty chemical container. Never put chemicals in an empty food container.
12. Pesticides and chemicals must be stored in a secure and locked area away from food handling and storage areas. Never store pesticide and chemicals in the food preparation and storage areas.

Monitoring:

1. Check the cleanliness of the dry storage room, refrigeration units, and freezer units.
2. Check the integrity of food packaging.
3. Check the temperature of refrigerated foods.
    a. For fresh meat, fish, dairy, and poultry products, insert a calibrated, cleaned, and sanitized thermometer into the center of the product to ensure a temperature of 41ºF (5ºC) or below.

b. For packaged products, insert a food thermometer between two packages, being careful not to puncture the wrapper. If the temperature exceeds 41°F (5°C), it may be necessary to take the internal temperature.
c. For eggs, the ambient temperature should be 45°F (7.2°C) or below.

4. Check dates of milk, eggs, and other perishable goods to ensure safety and quality.
5. Check frozen foods to ensure that they are all frozen solid and show no signs of thawing and refreezing, such as the presence of large ice crystals or liquids on the bottom of cartons.

Corrective Action:

1. Discard the following:
   a. Frozen foods with signs of previous thawing
   b. Cans that have signs of deterioration—swollen sides or ends, flawed seals or seams, dents, or rust
   c. Punctured packages
   d. Expired foods
   e. Foods that have exceeded the safe temperature zone policy or deemed unacceptable by the established rejection policy

Verification and Record Keeping:

Record temperature and any corrective action must be taken on the appropriate storage log or chart. The food service and retail manager must verify that food service and retail employees are storing products using the proper procedure by visually monitoring storing practices during the shift and reviewing the storage log at the close of each day. Storage and corrective action logs are kept on file for a minimum of 1 year.

Date Implemented: ____________________ By: ________________________________

Date Reviewed: ______________________ By: ________________________________

Date Revised: ________________________ By: ________________________________

Sample Washing Hands SOP

Purpose: To prevent foodborne illness by contaminated hands from food service or retail employees.

Scope: This procedure applies to **ALL** employees including those who do not handle, prepare, and serve or sell food.

Keywords: Hand washing, cross contamination

Instructions:

1. Train all employees, including any individual that prepares or serves food, on proper hand washing. Training may include showing a hand washing video and demonstrating proper hand washing procedure.
2. Post hand washing signs or posters in a language understood by all food service and retail staff near all hand washing sinks, in food preparation areas, and in restrooms.
3. Use designated hand washing sinks for hand washing only. Do not use food preparation, utility, and dish washing sinks for hand washing. Do not use hand-washing sinks for food preparation, utility, or dish washing.
4. Provide warm running water, soap, and a means to dry hands. Provide a waste container at each hand washing sink or near the door in restrooms.
5. Make hand washing sinks accessible in any area where employees are working.
6. Hands must be washed:
    - Before starting work
    - During food preparation
    - When moving from one food preparation area to another
    - Before putting on or changing gloves
    - After using the toilet
    - After sneezing, coughing, or using a handkerchief or tissue
    - After touching hair, face, or body
    - After smoking, eating, drinking, or chewing gum or tobacco
    - After handling raw meats, poultry, or fish
    - After any cleanup activity such as sweeping, mopping, or wiping counters
    - After touching dirty dishes, equipment, or utensils
    - After handling trash
    - After handling money
    - After any time the hands may become contaminated
7. Use paper towel to open the door when exiting the restroom.

8. Follow proper hand washing procedures as indicated below:

   - Wet hands and forearms with warm, running water (at least 100ºF / 37.8°C) and apply soap.
   - Scrub lathered hands and forearms, under fingernails, and between fingers for at least 10 to 15 seconds. Rinse thoroughly under warm running water for 5 to 10 seconds.
   - Dry hands, and forearms thoroughly with single-use paper towels.
   - Dry hands, for at least 30 seconds, if using a warm-air hand dryer.
   - Turn off water by using paper towels.

9. Follow FDA recommendations when using hand antiseptics. These recommendations are as follows:

   - Use hand antiseptics only after hands have been properly washed and dried;
   - Use only hand antiseptics that comply with the **FDA Food Code**. Confirm with the manufacturers that the hand antiseptics used meet these requirements; and
   - Use hand antiseptics in the manner specified by the manufacturer.

Monitoring:

A designated manager will visually observe the hand washing practices of the food service or retail staff during all hours of operation. In addition, the designated manager will visually observe that hand washing sinks are properly supplied during all hours of operation.

Corrective Action:

Employees that are observed not washing their hands at the appropriate times or using the proper procedure must be instructed to re-wash their hands immediately. Employees must be retrained to ensure that the proper hand washing procedure is being followed.

Verification and Record Keeping:

The food service and retail manager will complete the Food Safety Checklist daily, to indicate that monitoring is being conducted as specified. Maintain Food Safety Checklist for a minimum of 1 year.

Date Implemented: ____________________ By: ________________________________

Date Reviewed: ______________________ By: ________________________________

Date Revised: ________________________ By: ________________________________

Sample Personal Hygiene SOP

Purpose: To prevent foodborne illness due to contamination of food by food service or retail employees.

Scope: This procedure applies to **ALL** employees including those who do not handle, prepare, and serve or sell food.

Key Words: Personal hygiene, cross contamination, contamination

Instructions:

1. Train food service and retail employees on the employee health policy (develop a SOP for implementing an employee health policy) and on practicing good personal hygiene.
2. Follow the employee health policy. Do not work if ill.
3. Report to work in good health, clean, and dressed in proper attire.
4. Change apron when it becomes soiled.
5. Wash hands properly, frequently, and at all appropriate times.
6. Keep fingernails trimmed, filed, and maintained so that the edges are cleanable and not rough.
7. Avoid wearing artificial fingernails and fingernail polish.
8. Wear single-use gloves if artificial fingernails or fingernail polish is worn.
9. Do not wear any jewelry except for a plain ring, such as a wedding band.
10. Treat and bandage wounds and sores immediately. When hands are bandaged, single-use gloves must be worn.
11. Cover a lesion containing pus with a bandage. If the lesion is on a finger, hand, or wrist, cover with a bandage and finger cot and a single-use glove, or a bandage and a single-use glove.
12. Eat, drink, use tobacco, or chew gum only in designated break areas where food or food-contact surfaces may not become contaminated.
13. Taste food the correct way, by using the following procedure:
    - **a.** Place a small amount of food into a separate container.
    - **b.** Step away from exposed food and food-contact surfaces.
    - **c.** Use a teaspoon to taste the food. Remove the used teaspoon and container to the dish room. Never reuse a spoon that has already been used for tasting.
    - **d.** Wash hands immediately.
14. Wear suitable and effective hair restraints while in the kitchen.
15. Follow state and local public health requirements.

Monitoring:

A designated food service or retail manager must inspect employees when they report to work to be sure that each employee is following this SOP. The designated food service and retail employee will ensure that all food service and retail employees are adhering to the personal hygiene policy during all hours of operation.

Corrective Action:

Any food service and retail employee not following this procedure must be stopped and retrained at the time of the incident. Affected food must be discarded.

Verification and Record Keeping:

The food service and retail manager must verify that food service and retail employees are following this policy by visually observing the employees during all hours of operation. The food service and retail manager must complete the Food Safety Checklist daily. Food service and retail employees must record any discarded food on the Damaged or Discarded Product Log, which will be kept on file for a minimum of 1 year.

Date Implemented: ____________________ By: ________________________________

Date Reviewed: ______________________ By: ________________________________

Date Revised: ________________________ By: ________________________________

Sample Using Suitable Utensils When Handling Foods SOP

Purpose: To prevent foodborne illness due to hand-to-food cross contamination by food service or retail employees.

Scope: This procedure applies to food service and retail employees who handle, prepare, and serve food.

Key Words: Ready-to-eat food, cross contamination

Instructions:

1. Use proper hand washing procedures to wash hands and exposed arms prior to preparing or handling food or at any time when the hands may have become contaminated.
2. Do not use bare hands to handle ready-to-eat foods at any time with the exception of washing fruits and vegetables.
3. Use suitable utensils when working with ready-to-eat food. Suitable utensils may include the following:
   - Single-use gloves
   - Deli tissue
   - Foil wrap
   - Tongs, spoodles, spoons, and spatulas
4. Wash hands and change gloves:
   - Before beginning food preparation
   - Before beginning a new task
   - After touching equipment, such as refrigerator doors or utensils that are not cleaned and sanitized
   - After contacting chemicals
   - When interruptions in food preparation occur, such as when answering the telephone or checking in a delivery
   - When handling money
   - Anytime a glove is torn, damaged, or soiled
   - Anytime contamination of a glove might have occurred
5. Follow state and local public health requirements.

Monitoring:

A designated food service or retail manager must visually observe that gloves or suitable utensils are used and changed at the appropriate times, during all hours of operation.

Corrective Action:

Employees observed touching ready-to-eat food with bare hands must be stopped immediately and retrained at the time of the incident. Ready-to-eat food, touched with bare hands, must be discarded.

Verification and Record Keeping:

The food service and retail manager must verify that food service and retail workers are using suitable utensils by visually monitoring food service and retail employees during all hours of operation. The food service and retail manager must complete the Food Safety Checklist daily. The designated food service or retail manager responsible for monitoring must record any discarded food on the Damaged and Discarded Product Log. This log will be maintained for a minimum of 1 year.

Date Implemented: ____________________ By: ________________________________

Date Reviewed: _______________________ By: ________________________________

Date Revised: ________________________ By: ________________________________

Sample Washing Fruits and Vegetables SOP

Purpose: To reduce the risk of foodborne illness or injury by contaminated fruits and vegetables and to prevent cross contamination by food service or retail employees.

Scope: This procedure applies to food service and retail employees who handle, prepare, and serve food.

Key Words: Fruits, vegetables, cross contamination, washing

Instructions:

1. Train food service and retail employees who prepare or serve food on how to properly wash and store fresh fruits and vegetables.
2. Wash hands using the proper procedure.
3. Wash, rinse, sanitize, and air-dry all food-contact surfaces, equipment, and utensils that will be in contact with produce, such as cutting boards, knives, and sinks.
4. Follow manufacturer's instructions for proper use of chemicals used in the washing of fruits and vegetables.
5. Wash all raw fruits and vegetables thoroughly before combining with other ingredients, including:
    - Unpeeled fresh fruit and vegetables that are served whole or cut into pieces; and
    - Fruits and vegetables that are peeled and cut to use in cooking or served ready-to-eat.
6. Wash fresh produce vigorously under cold running water or by using chemicals approved for washing fruits and vegetables that comply with the *Food Code*. Packaged fruits and vegetables labeled as being previously washed and ready-to-eat do not require re-washing.
7. Scrub the surface of firm fruits or vegetables such as apples or potatoes, using a clean and sanitized brush designated for this purpose.
8. Remove any damaged or bruised areas.
9. Label, date, and refrigerate fresh-cut items.
10. Serve cut melons within 7 days if held at 41ºF (5ºC) or below (see SOP for Date-Marking Ready-to-Eat, TCS Food).
11. Do not serve raw seed sprouts to highly susceptible populations, such as people taking medication, pregnant women, elderly people, immune compromised persons, persons with certain diseases, or children.
12. Follow state and local public health requirements.

Monitoring:

The food service and retail manager must visually monitor that fruits and vegetables are being properly washed, labeled, and dated during all hours of operation. In addition, food service and retail employees must check daily the quality of fruits and vegetables in cold storage.

Corrective Action:

Unwashed fruits and vegetables will be removed from service and washed immediately before being served. Unlabeled fresh-cut items will be labeled and dated. Discard cut melons held at 41°F (5°C) or below after 7 days.

Verification and Record Keeping:

The food service and retail manager must complete the Food Safety Checklist daily to indicate that monitoring is being conducted as specified in this procedure.

Date Implemented: ____________________ By: ________________________________

Date Reviewed: ______________________ By: ________________________________

Date Revised: _______________________ By: ________________________________

Sample Time-/Date-Marking Food SOP

Purpose: To ensure appropriate rotation of ready-to-eat food to prevent or reduce foodborne illness, such as *Listeria* monocytogenes and prevent cross contamination by food service or retail employees.

Scope: This procedure applies to food service and retail employees, who store, handle, prepare, and serve food.

Key Words: Ready-to-eat food, TCS food, date marking, cross contamination

Instructions:

1. Establish a date-marking system and train employees accordingly. The best practice for a date-marking system is to include a label with the product name, the day or date, and time it is prepared or opened. Examples of how to indicate when the food is prepared or opened include:
   - Labeling food with a calendar date, such as "cut cantaloupe, 5/26, 8:00 a.m.";
   - Identifying the day of the week, such as "cut cantaloupe, Monday, 8:00 a.m.,"; or
   - Using color-coded marks or tags, such as "cut cantaloupe, blue dot, and 8:00 a.m." means "cut on Monday at 8:00 a.m."
2. Label ready-to-eat, TCS foods that are prepared on-site and held for more than 24 hours.
3. Label any processed, ready-to-eat, TCS foods when opened, if they are to be held for more than 24 hours.
4. Refrigerate all ready-to-eat, TCS foods at 41ºF (5ºC) or below.
5. Use, serve, or discard refrigerated, ready-to-eat, TCS foods within 7 days.
6. Indicate with a separate label the date prepared, the date frozen, and the date thawed, of any refrigerated, ready-to-eat, TCS foods.
7. Calculate the 7-day time period by counting only the days that the food is under refrigeration. For example:
   - On Thursday, 7/11, lasagna is cooked, properly cooled, and refrigerated with a label that reads, "Lasagna–Cooked–7/11."
   - On Friday, 7/12, the lasagna is frozen with a second label that reads, "Frozen–7/12." Two labels now appear on the lasagna. Since the lasagna was held under refrigeration from Thursday, 7/11 to Friday, 7/12, only 1 day is counted toward the 7-day time period.
   - On Tuesday, 7/23, the lasagna is pulled out of the freezer. A third label is placed on the lasagna that reads, "Thawed–7/23." All three labels now appear on the lasagna. The lasagna must be served or discarded within 6 days.
8. Follow state and local public health requirements.

Monitoring:

A designated employee must check refrigerators daily to verify that foods are date marked and that foods exceeding the 7-day time period are not being used or stored.

Corrective Action:

Any food service or retail employee found not following appropriate date marking and rotation of food will be retrained. Foods that are not date marked or that exceed the 7-day time period must be discarded.

Verification and Record Keeping:

The food service and retail manager must complete the Food Safety Checklist daily.

Date Implemented: ____________________ By: ________________________________

Date Reviewed: ______________________ By: ________________________________

Date Revised: ________________________ By: ________________________________

Sample Cooking TCS Foods SOP

Purpose: To prevent foodborne illness by ensuring that all foods are cooked to the appropriate internal temperature and prevent cross contamination by food service and retail employees.

Scope: This procedure applies to food service and retail employees who handle, prepare, and serve food.

Key Words: Cross contamination, temperatures, cooking

Instructions:

1. Train food service and retail employees who prepare or serve food on how to calibrate and use a food thermometer, and cook foods using this procedure.
2. If a recipe contains a combination of meat products, cook the product to the highest required temperature.
3. Follow state or local health department requirements regarding internal cooking temperatures.

   If state or local health department requirements are based on the 2017 FDA Food Code, cook products to the following temperatures:

   - 135°F (57.2°C)—Fresh, frozen, or canned fruits and vegetables that are going to be held on a steam table or in a hot box are to be held at 135°F (57.2°C).
   - 145°F (62.8°C) for 15 seconds—Seafood, beef, pork, and eggs cooked to order that are placed onto a plate and immediately served. (Roast 145°F/62.8°C for 4 minutes.)
   - 155°F (68.3°C) for 17 seconds—Ground products containing beef, pork, or fish, fish nuggets or sticks, eggs held on a steam table, cubed or Salisbury steaks
   - 165°F (73.9°C) for < 1 second—Poultry, stuffed fish, pork, or beef, pasta stuffed with eggs, fish, pork, or beef (such as lasagna or manicotti)

Monitoring:

1. Use a calibrated, cleaned, and sanitized probe thermometer (preferably a thermocouple).
2. Avoid inserting the thermometer into pockets of fat or near bones when taking internal cooking temperatures.
3. Take at least **two** internal temperatures from each batch of food by inserting the thermometer into the thickest part of the product (usually the center).
4. Take at least **two** internal temperatures of each large food item, such as a turkey, to ensure that all parts of the product reach the required cooking temperature.

Corrective Action:

Any food service or retail employee found not ensuring that all foods are cooked to the appropriate internal temperature of food will be retrained. Continue cooking food until the internal temperature reaches the required temperature for the specific amount of time.

Verification and Record Keeping:

Food service and retail employees must record product name, time, the two temperatures/times, and any corrective action taken on the Cooking–Reheating Temperature Log.

The food service and retail manager must verify that food service and retail employees have taken the required cooking temperatures by visually monitoring food service and retail employees and preparation procedures during the shift and reviewing, initialing, and dating the temperature log at the close of each day. The Cooking–Reheating Temperature Logs are kept on file for a minimum of 1 year.

Date Implemented: ____________________ By: ________________________________

Date Reviewed: ______________________ By: ________________________________

Date Revised: ________________________ By: ________________________________

Sample Hot and Cold Holding of TCS Foods SOP

Purpose: To prevent foodborne illness by ensuring that all foods are held under the proper temperature and prevent cross contamination by food service or retail employees.

Scope: This procedure applies to food service and retail employees who handle, prepare, and serve food.

Key Words: Cross contamination, temperatures, holding, hot holding, cold holding, storage

Instructions:

1. Train food service and retail employees who prepare or serve food about proper hot- and cold-holding procedures. Include, in the training, a discussion of the temperature danger zone (TDZ).
2. Follow state or local health department requirements regarding required hot holding and cold holding temperatures. If state or local health department requirements are based on the 2017 FDA Food Code:
    - Hold hot foods at 135ºF (57.2°C) or above.
    - Hold cold foods at 41ºF (5°C) or below.
3. Preheat steam tables and hot boxes.

Monitoring:

1. Use a calibrated, cleaned, and sanitized probe thermometer to measure the temperature of the food.
2. Take temperatures of foods by inserting the thermometer near the surface of the product, at the thickest part, and at other various locations.
3. Take temperatures of holding units by placing a calibrated thermometer in the coolest part of a hot-holding unit or warmest part of a cold-holding unit.
4. For hot foods held for service:

    a. Verify that the air/water temperature of any unit is at 135ºF (57.2°C) or above before use.

    b. Reheat foods in accordance with the Reheating for Hot Holding SOP.

    c. All hot TCS foods should be 135ºF (57.2°C) or above before the food is placed for display or service.

    d. Take the internal temperature of food before placing it on a steam table or in a hot-holding unit and at least every 2 hours thereafter.

5. For cold foods held for service:

    a. Verify that the air/water temperature of any unit is at 41ºF (5°C) or below before use.

    b. Chill foods, if applicable, in accordance with the Cooling (TCS) SOP.

    c. All cold TCS foods should be 41ºF (5°C) or below before placing the food out for display or service.

    d. Take the internal temperature of the food before placing it onto any salad bar, display cooler, or cold serving line and at least every 2 hours thereafter.

6. For cold foods in storage:

   a. Take the internal temperature of the food before placing it into any walk-in cooler or reach-in cold holding unit.

   b. Chill food in accordance with the Cooling TCS Foods SOP if the food is not 41ºF (5°C) or below.

   c. Verify that the air temperature of any cold holding unit is at 41ºF or below before use and at least every 4 hours thereafter during all hours of operation.

Corrective Action:

For hot foods:

1. Reheat the food to 165ºF (73.9°C) for 15 seconds if the temperature is found to be below 135ºF (57.2°C) and the last temperature measurement was 135ºF (57.2°C) or higher and taken within the last 2 hours. Repair or reset holding equipment before returning the food to the unit, if applicable or;

2. Discard the food if it cannot be determined how long the food temperature was below 135ºF (57.2°C).

For cold foods:

1. Rapidly chill the food using an appropriate cooling method, if the temperature is found to be above 41ºF (5°C) and the last temperature measurement was 41ºF (5°C) or below and taken within the last 2 hours.

2. To rapidly chill the food, place the food in shallow containers (no more than 4 inches deep), cover loosely, and put on the top shelf in the back of the walk-in or reach-in cooler:

   - Use a quick-chill unit like a blast chiller;
   - Stir the food in a container placed in an ice-water bath;
   - Add ice as an ingredient;
   - Separate food into smaller or thinner portions; or
   - Use a combination of these methods to cool the food as quickly as possible.

3. Repair or reset holding equipment before returning the food to the unit, if applicable.

4. Discard the food if it cannot be determined how long the food temperature was above 41ºF (5°C).

Verification and Record Keeping:

Food service and retail employees must record temperatures of food items and document corrective actions taken on the Hot Holding and Cold Holding Temperature Log. A designated food service and retail employee must record air temperatures of coolers and cold holding units on the Refrigeration Logs.

The food service and retail manager must verify that food service and retail employees have taken the required holding temperatures by visually monitoring food service and retail employees during the shift, and reviewing the temperature logs at the close of each day. Maintain the temperature logs for a minimum of 1 year.

Date Implemented: ____________________ By: ______________________________

Date Reviewed: ______________________ By: ______________________________

Date Revised: ________________________ By: ______________________________

Sample Cooling SOP

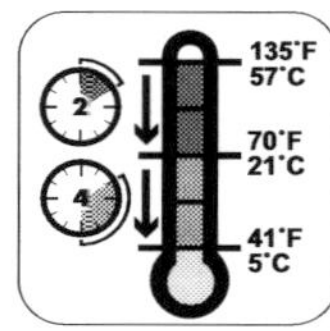

Purpose: To prevent foodborne illness by ensuring that all foods are properly cooled and prevent contamination of food by food service or retail employees.

Scope: This procedure applies to food service and retail employees who handle, prepare, and serve food.

Key Words: Cooling method, quick-chill

Instructions:

1. TCS foods must be cooled to 70°F (21.1°C) within 2 hours and to 41°F (5°C) within an additional 4 hours, for a total of 6 hours.
2. Rapidly chill the food using an appropriate cooling method if the temperature is found to be above 41°F (5°C) and the last temperature measurement was 41°F (5°C) or below and taken within the last 2 hours.
3. To rapidly chill the food, place the food in shallow containers (no more than 4 inches deep), cover loosely, and put on the top shelf in the back of the walk-in or reach-in cooler or:
    - Use a quick-chill unit like a blast chiller;
    - Stir the food in a container placed in an ice-water bath;
    - Add ice as an ingredient;
    - Separate food into smaller or thinner portions; or
    - Use a combination of these methods to cool the food as quickly as possible.
4. Repair or reset holding equipment before returning the food to the unit, if applicable.
5. Discard the food if it cannot be determined how long the food temperature was above 41°F (5°C).

Monitoring:

A designated food service and retail manager must inspect employees and storage areas to be sure that each employee is following this SOP. The designated food service and retail manager must monitor all food service and retail employees to ensure that they adhere to the storage policy during all hours of operation.

Corrective Action:

Any food service or retail employee found not following this procedure must be stopped and retrained at the time of the incident. Disregarded food must be discarded and the Corrective Action Log must be completed.

Verification and Record Keeping:

The food service and retail manager must verify that food service and retail employees are following this policy by visually observing the employees during all hours of operation. The food service and retail manager must complete the Food Safety Checklist daily.

Date Implemented: ____________________ By: ______________________________

Date Reviewed: ______________________ By: ______________________________

Date Revised: ________________________ By: ______________________________

Sample Reheating SOP

Purpose: To prevent foodborne illness by ensuring that all foods are properly reheated and prevent contamination of food by food service or retail employees.

Scope: This procedure applies to food service and retail employees who handle, prepare, or serve food.

Key Words: (TCS), Ready-to-eat food (RTE), preparation

Instructions:

1. A calibrated, cleaned, and sanitized thermometer (+/– 2ºF) (+/– 1ºC) must be used to take the temperatures of TCS foods.
2. Discard foods if:
    - They are held in the temperature danger zone (41ºF – 135ºF or 5ºC – 57.2ºC) for more than 4 hours;
    - It cannot be determined how long the food temperature was below 135ºF (57.2ºC);
    - They have been cooled too slowly; and
    - They are not reheated to 165ºF (73.8ºC) (in the thickest part) within 2 hours.
3. TCS foods must be cooled to 70ºF (21.1ºC) within 2 hours and to 41ºF (5ºC) within an additional 4 hours, for a total of 6 hours.
4. Reheat food to 165ºF (73.8ºC) or higher for at least 15 seconds within 2 hours if the food will not cool to 70ºF (21.1ºC) within 2 hours. Serve the food immediately or begin the cooling process. Use practical means to speedily cool.
5. If reheated in a microwave, foods must be reheated to an internal temperature of 165ºF (73.8ºC) and should stand for 2 minutes (this allows the heat to spread evenly throughout the food). Food should be stirred or rotated when possible.
6. Foods are to be labeled with the date and time of preparation before storing.
7. Refrigerated, TCS, ready-to-eat foods that are held for more than 24 hours after preparation must be used within 7 days or less, if the food is held at 41ºF (5ºC) or lower.
8. To reduce temperatures, TCS foods are cooled with an ice paddle, in an ice bath, or in shallow pans.

Monitoring:

A designated food service and retail manager will observe employees following this SOP. The designated food service and retail manager must monitor that all food service and retail employees are adhering to the proper reheating practices during all hours of operation. The Reheating Log must be completed and reviewed.

Corrective Action:

Any food service and retail employee found not following this procedure must be stopped and retrained at the time of the incident. Affected food will be discarded and the Corrective Action Log must be completed.

Verification and Record Keeping:

The food service and retail manager must verify that food service and retail employees are following this policy by visually observing the employees during all hours of operation. The food service and retail manager must complete the Food Safety Checklist daily and review the Reheating and Corrective Action Logs.

Date Implemented: ____________________ By: ______________________________

Date Reviewed: ______________________ By: ______________________________

Date Revised: ________________________ By: ______________________________

Sample Cleaning and Sanitizing SOP

Purpose: To prevent foodborne illness by ensuring that all equipment, utensils, and food contact surfaces are properly cleaned and sanitized by food service or retail employees.

Scope: This procedure applies to food service and retail employees who handle, prepare, or serve food.

Key Words: Kitchenware, fixed equipment, sanitizing, contamination

Instructions:

1. Train food service and retail employees on how to:
    a. Properly wash, rinse, and sanitize kitchenware after each use; and
    b. Clean equipment that comes in contact with TCS foods at least every 4 hours.
2. Ensure that the third sink of the three-compartment sink is used for sanitizing, and that you sanitize items by immersing them in either:
    a. Hot water temperatures that vary based on regulatory requirements from 171°F to 180°F (77.2°C to 82.2°C) for 30 seconds; or
    b. A properly mixed and approved chemical sanitizing solution for the recommended time.
3. If using a machine with hot-water sanitizing, the wash water temperatures 150°F to 165°F (65.5°C to 73.9°C) and the sanitizing water 165°F to 194°F (73.9°C to 90°C) temperatures are checked, recorded, and maintained daily. (Temperatures vary depending on type of equipment.)
4. For fixed equipment, removable parts are removed, washed, rinsed, and sanitized by immersion after each use, and non-removable food-contact surfaces are washed, rinsed, and sanitized with a cloth.
5. Sanitizing solution for worktables is kept in a labeled container and changed at least every 2 hours, frequently depending on use.

Monitoring:

A designated food service and retail employee must inspect employees as they work to be sure that each employee is following this SOP. The designated food service and retail employee must monitor that all employees are adhering to the cleaning and sanitizing policy during all hours of operation.

Corrective Action:

Any food service and retail employee found not following this procedure must be stopped and retrained at the time of the incident. Affected food will be discarded, and affected equipment must be cleaned and the Corrective Action log must be completed.

Verification and Record Keeping:

The food service and retail manager must verify that food service and retail employees are following this policy by visually observing the employees during all hours of operation. The food service and retail manager must complete the Food Safety Checklist daily.

Date Implemented: ____________________ By: ________________________________

Date Reviewed: ______________________ By: ________________________________

Date Revised: ________________________ By: ________________________________

Sample Serving Food SOP

Purpose: To prevent contamination of food during service either by customers or food service or retail employees.

Scope: This procedure applies to food service and retail employees who handle, prepare, or serve food.

Key Words: Hand washing, cross contamination, sanitize

Instructions:

1. Hand washing must be monitored and enforced before the food handler is permitted to prepare or serve food.
2. Food handlers must be made aware of poor personal habits, such as touching the mouth, face, hair, dirty apron, or dirty cloth because they may be sources of cross contamination.

Employees must be trained:

1. Not to touch plates, utensils, drinking glasses or cups where the customer's food or mouth will come in contact with that surface;
2. When dishing a customer plate, to wipe drips with a clean cloth or fresh paper towel. The counter cloth should not be used in order to prevent cross contamination;
3. To use sanitized utensils to handle food, not their bare hands;
4. To use proper serving utensils with long handles so as to prevent handles from coming in contact with food;
5. When scoop and ladles are not in use, to store them in the food with the handle out. Tongs must be stored on a dry, clean surface or in a separate pan;
6. To use gloves for some operations involving handling ready-to-eat foods and for which utensils are not practical, such as sandwich making. Gloves must be changed under the same conditions as hand washing; and
7. To be aware of related duties which require hand washing before continuing with service, such as:
    a. Picking up an item from the floor;
    b. Handling soiled dishes and linens;
    c. Answering the telephone; and
    d. Handling cash.

At self-service stations:

1. Use sneeze guards to protect food;
2. Provide sufficient long-handled utensils so that the handles do not come in contact with the food;
3. Do not overfill containers so that food comes in contact with utensil handles;
4. Require that customers use a fresh plate with each return to the self-service station;
5. Do not allow eating or picking with hands at the station; and
6. Constantly monitor the customers while they are at the station to prevent cross contamination of food.

Monitoring:

A designated food service and retail employee must inspect employees while they are serving to be sure that each employee is following this SOP. The designated food service and retail employee must monitor that all food service and retail employees are adhering to the service policy during all hours of operation.

Corrective Action:

Any food service and retail employee found not following this procedure must be stopped and retrained at the time of the incident. Affected food will be discarded and the Corrective Action log must be completed.

Verification and Record Keeping:

The food service and retail manager must verify that food service and retail employees are following this policy by visually observing the employees during all hours of operation. The food service and retail manager must complete the Food Safety Checklist daily.

Date Implemented: ____________________ By: ______________________________

Date Reviewed: ______________________ By: ______________________________

Date Revised: _______________________ By: ______________________________

Sample Food Safety for Self-Service Areas SOP

Purpose: To prevent contamination of food by either customers or food service or retail employees.

Scope: This procedure applies to food service and retail employees who handle, prepare, or serve food.

Key Words: TCS, ice bath, blast chiller

Instructions:

1. Separate raw meat, fish, and poultry from cooked and ready-to-eat food. If raw products are provided for individual servings, ensure they are separated from RTE food items.
2. Monitor customers for unsanitary hygiene practices, such as the following:
    - Tasting items;
    - Handling multiple breads with their bare hands;
    - Putting fingers directly into the food; and
    - Reusing plates and utensils; instead, hand out fresh plates to customers.
3. Label all food items.
4. Maintain proper temperatures.
    - TCS must be cooled to 70ºF (21.1°C) within 2 hours and to 41ºF (5°C) within an additional 4 hours, for a total of 6 hours.
    - Rapidly chill the food using an appropriate cooling method if the temperature is found to be above 41ºF (5°C) and the last temperature measurement was 41ºF (5°C) or below and taken within the last 2 hours.
    - Place food in shallow containers (no more than 4 inches deep) and *uncovered* on the top shelf in the back of the walk-in or reach-in cooler.
    - Use a quick-chill unit such as a blast chiller.
    - Stir the food in a container placed in an ice-water bath.
    - Add ice as an ingredient.
    - Repair or reset holding equipment before returning the food to the unit, if applicable.
    - Discard the food if it cannot be determined how long the food temperature was above 41ºF (5°C).
    - Separate food into smaller or thinner portions.
    - When refilling items, never mix old food with new food.

Monitoring:

A designated food service and retail employee must inspect employees to be sure that each employee is following this SOP. The designated food service and retail employee must monitor all self-service areas during all hours of operation.

Corrective Action:

Any food service and retail employee found not following this procedure must be stopped and retrained at the time of the incident. Affected food will be discarded and the Corrective Action log must be completed.

Verification and Record Keeping:

The food service and retail manager must verify that food service and retail employees are following this policy by visually observing the employees during all hours of operation. The food service and retail manager must complete the Food Safety Checklist daily.

Date Implemented: ____________________ By: ________________________________

Date Reviewed: ______________________ By: ________________________________

Date Revised: ________________________ By: ________________________________

APPENDIX 3: Sample Forms

- Food Defense Self-Inspection Checklist
- Foodborne Illness Complaint Form
- Sample Food Recall SOP
- Form FDA 3177 - Recall Notification Report and Sample Recall Notices
- First Responder Emergency Contact Information
- Verification Inspection Checklist
- HACCP Plan Verification Worksheet
- HACCP Plan Verification Summary
- Form 1 - A Conditional Employee and Food Employee Interview
- Form 1 - B Conditional Employee or Food Employee Reporting Agreement
- Form 1 - C Conditional Employee or Food Employee Medical Referral
- Paraphrased form the FDA Food Code for Health Practitioner's Reference
- Equipment Monitoring Chart
- Sanitizer Checklist
- Food Establishment Inspection Report
- Receiving Temperature Form
- Receiving Log
- Receiving Reject Form
- Refrigerator/Cooler Log
- Cooking Log
- Time Temperature Log
- Cooling Log Part 1
- Cooling - Corrective Action Log Part 2
- Hazard Analysis Worksheet
- HACCP Plan Form
- Process 1 - Food Preparation for Simple/No-Cook Recipes
- Process 2 - Food Preparation for Same Day Recipes
- Process 3 - Food Preparation for Complex Recipes
- Thermometer Calibration
- Waste/Shrink/Discard Chart
- Reheating Log
- Preliminarily Foodborne Illness Investigation
- Food Safety Checklist

Food Defense Self-Inspection Checklist

Instructions: Use this checklist to conduct a food defense assessment of your food service or retail establishment.

Management	Yes	No	Action Taken
A food defense plan has been implemented at the facility.	❑	❑	
Food defense inspections of the facility are conducted.	❑	❑	
Appropriate management personnel have received training in food defense.	❑	❑	
The firm has an established food defense management team and/or food defense professional.	❑	❑	
Responsible personnel know who to contact in the event of an emergency (both internally and externally).	❑	❑	
Security management program reviewed, verified, and revised, at least annually, if necessary.	❑	❑	
Personnel	**Yes**	**No**	**Action Taken**
Background checks, as allowed by law, are done on prospective employees.	❑	❑	
Employment applications are required.	❑	❑	
Employment references are checked.	❑	❑	
Personnel receive food defense training when they are hired.	❑	❑	
Only authorized personnel are allowed access to restricted parts of the facility.	❑	❑	
The facility has a system of positive identification and recognition for all personnel, e.g., issuing photo ID.	❑	❑	
Customers are restricted to public areas.	❑	❑	
There are restrictions on personal items brought into the facility.	❑	❑	
Contractors are restricted to their work required areas.	❑	❑	
Contractors and vendors are monitored while they are at the food service or retail facility.	❑	❑	
Employee sick leave policy encourages individuals to report illnesses and not work when they have gastrointestinal symptoms or a communicable disease.	❑	❑	

Property	Yes	No	Action Taken
A closed circuit television system is used to monitor high risk areas inside the facility.	❑	❑	
Security cameras are used to monitor the loading docks and exits.	❑	❑	
Hazardous chemical storage areas are secured.	❑	❑	
Doors opening onto the loading dock are kept locked when not in use.	❑	❑	
All truck shipments (incoming and outgoing) are monitored by food service and retail employees.	❑	❑	
Products are inspected upon delivery.	❑	❑	
There is good lighting for all high-risk areas at the facility.	❑	❑	
High-risk areas are marked "employees only" and access is limited to employees who work in the area.	❑	❑	
There is a key control system for store keys.	❑	❑	
Products	**Yes**	**No**	**Action Taken**
Products are purchased from reputable established sources.	❑	❑	
Purchase records are maintained for product trace back and recalls.	❑	❑	
Products arrive at the food or retail facility in clean and secure transport vehicles.	❑	❑	
Products are never left unsupervised on the loading dock.	❑	❑	
Products are inspected for tampering prior to preparation or service.	❑	❑	
The facility has guidelines for handling product tampering incidents.	❑	❑	
Food items are prepared by personnel trained in food safety and food defense procedures.	❑	❑	
Potable water is used for rinsing and preparing food items.	❑	❑	
Salad bars and self-serve carts are closely monitored by staff to prevent contamination and product tampering.	❑	❑	

Foodborne Illness Complaint Form

Date: ______________________ Time: ______________________

Information received by (complete name): ______________________

____

Person-in-charge notified (complete name / date / time): ______________________

____

Complainant information (complete name): ______________________

Phone: H (   )   -   Cell (   )   -   W (   )   -

E-mail address: ______________________

Fax: ______________________

Mailing address: ______________________

____

Who: (Name(s) and contact information of people with illness) ______________________

____

____

What: (Alleged complaint) ______________________

____

____

Where: (Location) ______________________

____

When: (Date/time food was eaten) ______________________

Date/time of illness: ______________________

Why: (Ask the symptoms that they are experiencing / do not assist / just LISTEN) ______________________

____

How: Suspect food ______________________

____

Local regulatory authorities notified (yes/no): ______________________

____

Comments: ______________________

____

____

SOP: Food Recall (Sample)

Purpose: To identify the procedures and personnel responsible in the event of a food recall and to document the procedure to be followed

Scope: This procedure applies to the food service or retail manager. (Listing by title ensures that the procedure does not have to be revised and approved every time there is a personnel change.)

General: (Definitions and general statements)

- Recall—An action by a manufacturer or distributor to remove a food product from the market because it may cause health problems or possible death.
- Hold—A time period used for investigation after a USDA commodity food has been identified as potentially unsafe. The hold process is unique to USDA commodity foods.
- Release—When the product on hold has been found safe and can be used.
- Physical segregation—Product is removed to a separate area of storage from other foods.

Personnel Responsible: *(List by title for each responsibility below.)*

Distributor contact: ______________________________

Documentation of training: ______________________________

Food safety coordinator: ______________________________

Public communications contact person: ______________________________

Training on recall procedures: ______________________________

____

Procedures: (Responsibilities When a Food Recall Notice Is Received)
Personnel responsible must complete the assigned tasks described in the attached Food Recall Action Checklist. (Add job titles to Food Recall Action Checklist under Person Responsible and attach the checklist to the standard operating procedure.)

Communication:

Communication will be handled as follows: (Example - Initial communication when a Food Recall Notice is received will be phoned directly to the contact person responsible at the site. A log will be maintained to document contacts by date and time. Any printed materials needed at the sites such as recall notices will be faxed to each site.)

Contacts for Public Communications:

Contact person will handle all public communications. (Include the contact person or other personnel responsible for public communications. Attach a copy of the policy and procedure for public communications.)

Product Segregation:

The recalled food product must be physically separated by: (Describe the procedure to segregate the recalled product. The procedure may be product-type-specific. For example, frozen product placed on hold will be placed in a plastic bag, securely taped, and placed on a separate shelf.)

Requirements for On-Site Destruction of Recalled Product:
(Describe specific state or local requirements for disposal of food products. Some state public health departments require notification of all food products to be destroyed before any action is taken).

(Procedures need to be approved by at least two persons.)

Approved: ______________________ Date: ______________________

Approved: ______________________ Date: ______________________

FORM FDA 3177

Sample Food Recall Notification Report from the USDA Food Safety and Inspection Service
October 13, 2002

Recall Notification Report

U.S. DEPARTMENT OF AGRICULTURE
FOOD SAFETY AND INSPECTION SERVICE

*****EXPANDED*****

Product(s) Recalled:

Turkey and Chicken Products
On October 03, 2002, and October 04, 2002, FSIS collected samples from structural and equipment surfaces at the establishment as part of an ongoing food safety investigation. Several of the samples were reported positive for Listeria monocytogenes by the FSIS Midwestern Laboratory. The results strongly suggest that the general processing environment at the establishment may be the source of widespread product contamination. Based on this and following a scientific and technical review of plant practices and company records by FSIS, the firm has voluntarily expanded the recall 090-2002 to include turkey and chicken products produced between May 01, 2002, through October 11, 2002, because these products may be contaminated with Listeria monocytogenes. In addition, the establishment has voluntarily suspended operations.

Production Dates / Identifying Codes: The following turkey and chicken products are subject to the expanded recall that were produced between May 01, 2002 and October 11, 2002: This list has been modified and does not include the complete listing of products recalled.

- Various sized boxes of "WAMPLER FOODS OVEN ROASTED TURKEY BREAST WITH BROTH BONELESS, 10003." Packed in each box are 9-pound package of "WAMPLER FOODS TURKEY BREAST WITH BROTH WHITE MEAT ADDED • BONELESS OVEN ROASTED 95% FAT FREE." The products subject to recall bear a sell-by date of "7/22/02 to 1/2/03."
- Various sized boxes of "WAMPLER FOODS OVEN ROASTED TURKEY BREAST WITH BROTH BONELESS, 10004." Packed in each box are 9-pound packages of "WAMPLER FOODS TURKEY BREAST WITH BROTH BONELESS OVEN ROASTED 97% FAT FREE." The products subject to recall bear a sell-by date of "7/22/02 to 1/2/03."
- Various sized boxes of "WAMPLER FOODS OVEN ROASTED TURKEY BREAST WITH BROTH BONELESS, 10005." Packed in each box are 9-pound packages of "WAMPLER FOODS TURKEY BREAST WITH BROTH BONELESS • OVEN ROASTED 98% FAT FREE." The products subject to recall bear a sell-by date of "7/22/02 to 1/2/03."
- Various sized boxes containing 9-pound packages of "FULLY COOKED DELI STYLE SMOKED TURKEY BREAST SMOKE FLAVOR ADDED, 10006." The products subject to recall bear a code "MFG 4/30/02 to 10/10/02."
- Various sized boxes containing 9-pound packages of "FULLY COOKED, DELI STYLE, TURKEY BREAST, 10007." The products subject to recall bear a code "MFG 4/30/02 to 10/10/02."

All of the products bear the establishment number "P-1351" inside the USDA mark of inspection unless otherwise noted.

Problem/Reason for Recall: The products may be contaminated with *Listeria monocytogenes*.

How/When Discovered: In response to a food safety investigation, FSIS collected a microbiological investigative sample on October 02, 2002, that returned positive results for *Listeria monocytogenes* on October 08, 2002. On October 03, 2002, and October 04, 2002, FSIS collected samples from structural and equipment surfaces at the establishment as part of an ongoing food safety investigation. Several of the samples were reported positive for *Listeria monocytogenes* by the FSIS Midwestern Laboratory. The results strongly suggest that the general processing environment at the establishment may be the source of widespread product contamination. Based on this and following a scientific and technical review of plant practices and company records by FSIS, the firm has voluntarily expanded the recall 090-2002 to include turkey and chicken products produced between May 01, 2002, and October 11, 2002. In addition, the establishment has voluntarily suspended operations.

Federal Establishment:	01351 P Pilgrim's Pride Corporation Doing business as: Wampler Foods, Inc. 471 Harleysville Pike Franconia, PA 18924
Consumer Contact:	Consumer Information Recall Hotline, 877-260-7110
Media Contact:	Ray Atkinson, Public Relations Manager, 540-896-0406
Quantity Recalled:	Approximately **28 million pounds** (This includes the 295,000 pounds of the October 09, 2002, Recall).

Distribution:	Nationwide
Recall Classification:	Class I
Recall Notification Level: **Press Release:**	Consumer and User (food service) Yes
Direct Notification Means:	The firm has notified its customers orally and will follow up in writing.
FSIS Follow-up Activities:	Effectiveness checks by the FSIS.
Other Agencies Involved:	FSIS is working with the Centers for Disease Control and Prevention (CDC) and various northeastern state health officials.
FSIS Contacts:	• Compliance/Recall Coordinator: 202-418-8874 • Recall Management Division: 202-690-6389 • Media Inquiries: 202-720-9113 • Congressional Inquiries: 202-720-3897 • Consumer Inquiries: 1-800-535-4555 • Web Site: www.fsis.usda.gov

Date of Recall Meeting:	October 09, 2002, **expanded on October 12, 2002**
Recall Case Number:	090-2002
For Further Information, Contact:	
• **Consumers:**	Meat and Poultry Hotline, 1-800-535-4555 or (202) 720-3333 (voice); 1-800-256-7072 (TTY)
• **Media:**	(202) 720-3897

Source: USDA Food Safety and Inspection Service

E. coli 0157:H7 Model Press Release

FOR IMMEDIATE RELEASE **DATE**

COMPANY CONTACT AND PHONE NUMBER

FOOD CO. RECALLS **PRODUCT** BECAUSE OF POSSIBLE HEALTH RISK

Company Name of **City, State** is recalling **Quantity and/or Type of Product** because it may be contaminated with Escherichia coli 0157:H7 bacteria (E. Coli 0157:H7). E. coli 0157:H7 causes a diarrheal illness often with bloody stools. Although most healthy adults can recover completely within a week, some people can develop a form of kidney failure called Hemolytic Uremic Syndrome (HUS). HUS is most likely to occur in young children and the elderly. The condition can lead to serious kidney damage and even death.

Product was distributed by ______________. Listing of states and areas where the product was distributed and how it reached consumers (e.g., through retail stores, mail order, direct delivery).

Specific information on how the product can be identified (e.g., type of container [plastic/metal/glass], size or appearance of product, product brand name, flavor, codes, expiration dates, etc.).

Status of the number of and types of related illnesses that have been CONFIRMED to date (e.g., "No illnesses have been reported to date.")

Provide a brief explanation about what is known about the problem, such as how it was revealed, and what is known about its source. An example of such a description: "The recall was initiated after it was discovered that product was contaminated with E. coli 0157:H7. Subsequent investigation indicates the problem was caused by a temporary breakdown in the company's production and packaging processes."

Information on what consumers should do with the product and where they can get additional information (e.g., "Consumers who have purchased Brand X are urged to return it to the place of purchase for a full refund. Consumers with questions may contact the company at 1-800-XXX-XXXX").

(SAMPLE PRESS RELEASE)

XYZ Inc.
123 Smith Lane
Anywhere, MS

FOR IMMEDIATE RELEASE **DATE**
Sam Smith /555-555-5555

XYZ RECALLS "SNACKIES" BECAUSE OF POSSIBLE HEALTH RISK

XYZ Inc. of Anywhere, MS, is recalling its 5-ounce packages of "Snackies" food treats because they have the potential to be contaminated with Escherichia coli 0157:H7. E. coli 0157:H7 causes a diarrheal illness, often with bloody stools. Although most healthy adults can recover completely within a week, some people can develop a form of kidney failure called Hemolytic Uremic Syndrome (HUS). HUS is most likely to occur in young children and the elderly; the condition can lead to serious kidney damage and even death.

The recalled "Snackies" were distributed nationwide in retail stores and through mail orders.

The product comes in a 5-ounce, clear-plastic package marked with lot # 7777777 on the top and with an expiration date of 03/17/06 stamped on the side.

No illnesses have been reported to date in connection with this problem.

The potential for contamination was noted after routine testing by the company detected the presence of E. coli 0157:H7.

Production of the product has been suspended while FDA and the company continue their investigation as to the cause of the problem.

Consumers who have purchased 5-ounce packages of "Snackies" are urged to return them to the place of purchase for a full refund. Consumers with questions may contact the company at 1-800-XXX-XXXX.

First Responder Emergency Contact Information

Date compiled/updated: ______________________

Poison Control

Contact name: ______________________

Phone number: ______________________

Fax number: ______________________

Email: ______________________

Address: ______________________

Call if: ______________________

Attorney/Legal Representative

Contact name: ______________________

Phone number: ______________________

Fax number: ______________________

Email: ______________________

Address: ______________________

Call if: ______________________

Media Spokesperson

Contact name: ______________________

Phone number: ______________________

Fax number: ______________________

Email: ______________________

Address: ______________________

Call if: ______________________

Consultant

Contact name: ______________________

Phone number: ______________________

Fax number: ______________________

Email: ______________________

Address: ______________________

Call if: ______________________

Owner/Director/Person-in-Charge

Contact name: ______________________

Phone number: ______________________

Fax number: ______________________

Email: ______________________

Address: ______________________

Call if: ______________________

Manager

Contact name: ______________________

Phone number: ______________________

Fax number: ______________________

Email: ______________________

Address: ______________________

Call if: ______________________

Manager

Contact name: ______________________

Phone number: ______________________

Fax number: ______________________

Email: ______________________

Address: ______________________

Call if: ______________________

Manager

Contact name: ______________________

Phone number: ______________________

Fax number: ______________________

Email: ______________________

Address: ______________________

Call if: ______________________

Form

Verification Inspection Checklist

Date: ________ Time: ___________ Scheduled (S)/Unscheduled (U): ____________________

Establishment Name: ____

Establishment Address: ____

Person-in-Charge: ______________________________ Health Inspector: __________________

1. Documents provided for review:

Type of Document	Reviewed (Yes or No)	Comments/Strengths/ Weaknesses Noted
Prerequisite Programs (list them below)		
Menu or Food List or Food Preparation Process		
Flow Diagrams (Food Preparation)		
Equipment Layout		
Training Protocols		
Hazard Analysis		
Written Plan for Food Safety Management System		
Other		

2. List critical control points (CCPs) and critical limits (CLs) identified by the establishment's HACCP plan.

Food Item or Process	Critical Control Point (CCP)	Critical Limits (CL)	Comments/Problems Noted

Form (continued)

3. What monitoring records are required by the plan?

Type of Record	Monitoring Frequency and Procedure	Record Location

4. Describe the strengths or weaknesses with the current monitoring or record keeping regimen.

Comments: ____

5. Who is responsible for verification that the required records are being completed and being properly maintained?

Comments: ____

6. Describe the training that has been provided to support the system.

Comments: ____

7. Describe examples of any documentation that the above training was accomplished.

Comments: ____

Form (continued)

Record Review and On-site Inspection

(Choose at random one week from the previous four)

8. Are monitoring actions performed according to the plan?

a. Full Compliance b. Partial Compliance c. Non-Compliance

Comments: ______________________

____

____

9. When critical limits established by the plan are not met, are immediate corrective actions taken and recorded?

☐ Yes ☐ No

Comments: ______________________

____

____

10. Do the corrective actions taken reflect the same actions described in the establishment's plan?

☐ Yes ☐ No

Comments: ______________________

____

____

11. Are routine calibrations required and performed according to the plan?

☐ Yes ☐ No

Comments: ______________________

____

____

Form (continued)

(Examine the current day's records, if possible)

12. Are the records for the present day accurate for the observed situation in the facility?

☐ Yes ☐ No

Comments: ____________________

____

____

13. Do managers and employees demonstrate knowledge of the system?

Managers: ☐ Yes ☐ No

Employees: ☐ Yes ☐ No

Comments: ____________________

____

____

14. Have there been any changes to the menu or recipes since the last verification visit?

☐ Yes ☐ No

Comments: ____________________

____

____

15. Additional comments or recommendations:

____

____

____

____

____

____

____

Form

HACCP Plan Verification Worksheet

Establishment Name:				Type of Facility:	
Physical Address:				Person-in-Charge:	
City:		State:		Zip:	County:
Inspection Time In:	Inspection Time Out:		Date:	Candidate's Name:	
Agency:		Standard's Name:		Indicate Person Filling Out Form: (circle one) Candidate's Form / Standard's Form	

Cold Holding Requirement For Jurisdiction: [41°F (5°C)__] or [45°F (7°C)__] or [41°F (5°C) and 45°F (7°C) combination:__]

1. Have there been any changes to the food establishment menu?

☐ Yes ☐ No

Describe: ______________________________

____

____

2. Was there a need to change the food establishment HACCP plan because of these menu changes?

☐ Yes ☐ No

Describe: ______________________________

____

____

3. List critical control points (CCPs) and critical limits (CLs) identified by the establishment HACCP plan.

CCPs	CLs
______________	______________
______________	______________
______________	______________

Form (continued)

4. What monitoring records for CCPs are required by the plan?

Type of Record	Monitoring Frequency	Record Location
______	______	______
______	______	______
______	______	______
______	______	______

5. Record compliance under 4G of the FDA Standardization Inspection Report (ANNEX 2 Section 1). Are monitoring actions performed according to the plan?

☐ Yes ☐ No Describe under 4G of the FDA Standardization Inspection Report.

Describe: ______________________________

____

____

6. Is immediate corrective action taken and recorded when CLs established by the plan are not met?

☐ Yes ☐ No

Describe: ______________________________

____

____

7. Are the corrective actions the same as described in the plan?

☐ Yes ☐ No

Describe: ______________________________

____

____

8. Who is responsible for verification that the required records are being properly maintained?

Describe: ______________________________

____

____

Form (continued)

9. Did employees and managers demonstrate knowledge of the HACCP plan?

☐ Yes ☐ No

Describe: ____________________

____

____

10. What training has been provided to support the HACCP plan?

Describe: ____________________

____

____

11. Describe examples of any documentation that the above training was accomplished.

Describe: ____________________

____

____

12. Are calibrations of equipment/thermometers performed as required by the plan?

☐ Yes ☐ No

Describe: ____________________

____

____

Additional Comments:

____

____

____

____

____

Person Interviewed: ____________________

Form

HACCP Plan Verification Summary

Establishment Name:			Type of Facility:	
Physical Address:			Person-in-Charge:	
City:	State:		Zip:	County:
Inspection Time In:	Inspection Time Out:		Date:	Candidate's Name:
Agency:	Standard's Name:		Indicate Person Filling Out Form: (circle one) Candidate's Form / Standard's Form	

Cold Holding Requirement For Jurisdiction: [41°F (5°C)__] or [45°F (7°C)__] or [41°F (5°C) and 45°F (7°C) combination:__]

Chart 2: HACCP Plan Verification Summary

HACCP Plan Verification Summary (circle YES or NO)

	Record #1	**Record #2**	**Record #3**
	Today's Date:	**2nd Selected Date:**	**3rd Selected Date:**
Required Monitoring Recorded[1]	YES / NO	YES / NO	YES / NO
Accurate and Consistent[2]	YES / NO	YES / NO	YES / NO
Corrective Action Documented[3]	YES / NO	YES / NO	YES / NO

Total # of record answers that are in Disagreement with the Standard = _________ (This box for Completion by Standard only.)

The use of a HACCP plan by a food establishment can be verified through a review of food establishment records and investigating the following information:

1. Does the food establishment's HACCP documentation indicates that the required monitoring procedures were followed (frequency, initials, dated, etc.) on the 3 selected dates? A "YES" answer would indicate that all required monitoring was documented. If any required monitoring was not documented, a "NO" answer would be circled in this section.

2. Does the food establishment's HACCP documentation for the selected dates appear accurate and consistent with other observations? A "YES" answer would indicate that the record appears accurate and consistent. A "NO" answer would indicate that there is inaccurate or inconsistent HACCP documentation.

3. Was corrective action documented in accordance with the HACCP plan when CLs were not met on each of the 3 selected dates? A "YES" answer would indicate that corrective action was documented for each CL not met for each of the 3 selected dates. A "Yes" can also mean that no corrective action was needed. A "NO" answer would indicate any missing or inaccurate documentation of corrective action.

Form 1-A **Conditional Employee and Food Employee Interview**

Preventing Transmission of Diseases through Food by Infected Food Employees or Conditional Employees with Emphasis on Illness due to Norovirus, Salmonella Typhi (S. Typhi), Shigella spp., ShigaToxin-producing Escherichia coli (STEC), nontyphoidal Salmonella or Hepatitis A Virus

The purpose of this interview is to inform conditional employees and food employees to advise the person in charge of past and current conditions described so that the person in charge can take appropriate steps to preclude the transmission of foodborne illness.

Conditional employee name (print):______________________

Food employee name (print):______________________

Address: ______________________

Telephone Daytime: ______________________ Evening: ______________________

Date: ______________________

Are you suffering from any of the following symptoms? (Circle one)

		If YES, Date of Onset
Diarrhea?	YES /NO	____________
Vomiting?	YES /NO	____________
Jaundice?	YES /NO	____________
Sore throat with fever?	YES /NO	____________
Or		

Infected cut or wound that is open and draining, or lesions containing pus on the hand, wrist, an exposed body part, or other body part and the cut, wound, or lesion not properly covered? YES /NO

(Examples: boils and infected wounds, however small)

In the Past:

Have you ever been diagnosed as being ill with typhoid fever (Salmonella Typhi) YES /NO

If you have, what was the date of the diagnosis? ______________________

If within the past 3 months, did you take antibiotics for S. Typhi? YES /NO

If so, how many days did you take the antibiotics?______________________

If you took antibiotics, did you finish the prescription?______________________ YES /NO

History of Exposure:

1. Have you been suspected of causing or have been exposed to a confirmed foodborne disease outbreak recently? YES /NO

   If YES, date of outbreak: ______________________

   a. If YES, what was the cause of the illness and did it meet the following criteria?

   Cause: ______________________

   i. Norovirus (last exposure within the past 48 hours) Date of illness outbreak: ____________
   ii. E.coli 0157:H7 infection (last exposure with the past 3 days) Date of illness outbreak: ____________
   iii. Hepatitis A virus (last exposure within the past 30 days) Date of illness outbreak: ____________
   iv. Salmonella Non-Typhiodal (last exposed within the past 3 days) Date of illness outbreak: ____________
   v. Typhoid fever (last exposure within the past 14 days) Date of illness outbreak: ____________
   vi. Shigellosis (last exposure within the past 3 days) Date of illness outbreak: ____________

Form 1-A (continued)

b. If YES, did you:

i. Consume food implicated in the outbreak? ______________________________

ii. Work in a food establishment that was the source of the outbreak? ______________________________

iii. Consume food at an event that was prepared by person who was ill? ______________________________

2. Did you attend an event or work in a setting, that recently had a confirmed disease outbreak? YES /NO

If so, what was the cause of the confirmed disease outbreak? ______________________________

If the cause was one of the following five pathogens, did exposure to the pathogen meet the following criteria?

a. Norovirus (last exposure within the past 48 hours) YES /NO

b. E. coli 0157:H7 (or other EHEC/STEC (last exposure within the past 3 days) YES /NO

c. Shigella spp. (last exposure within the past 3 days) YES /NO

d. S. Typhi (last exposure within the past 14 days) YES /NO

e. hepatitis A virus (last exposure within the past 30 days) YES /NO

Do you live in the same household as a person diagnosed with Norovirus, Shigellosis, typhoid fever, hepatitis A, or illness due to E.coli 0157:H7 or other STEC?

YES /NO Date of onset of illness ______________

3. Do you have a household member attending or working in a setting where there is a confirmed disease outbreak of Norovirus, typhoid fever, Shigellosis, STEC infection, or hepatitis A?

YES /NO Date of onset of illness ______________

Name, Address, and Telephone Number of your Healthcare Practitioner or doctor:

Name: ______________________________

Address: ______________________________

Telephone – Daytime: ______________________________ Evening: ______________________________

Signature of Conditional Employee: ______________________________ Date: ______________

Signature of Food Employee: ______________________________ Date: ______________

Signature of Permit Holder or Representative: ______________________________ Date: ______________

Form 1-B

Conditional Employee or Food Employee Reporting Agreement

Preventing Transmission of Diseases through Food by Infected Conditional Employees or Food Employees with Emphasis on Illness due to Norovirus, Salmonella Typhi, Shigella spp., or Shiga toxin-producing Escherichia coli (STEC), nontyphoidal Salmonella or Hepatitis A Virus

The purpose of this agreement is to inform conditional employees or food employees of their responsibility to notify the person-in-charge when they experience any of the conditions listed so that the person-in-charge can take appropriate steps to preclude the transmission of foodborne illness.

I AGREE TO REPORT TO THE PERSON-IN-CHARGE:

Any Onset of the Following Symptoms, Either While at Work or Outside of Work, Including the Date of Onset:

1. Diarrhea
2. Vomiting
3. Jaundice
4. Sore throat with fever
5. Infected cuts or wounds, or lesions containing pus on the hand, wrist, an exposed body part, or other body part and the cuts, wounds, or lesions are not properly covered (such as boils and infected wounds, however small)

Future Medical Diagnosis:

Whenever diagnosed as being ill with Norovirus, typhoid fever (Salmonella Typhi), Salmonella Non-Typhoidal, shigellosis (Shigella spp.infection), Escherichia coli O157:H7 or other STEC infection, or hepatitis A (hepatitis A virus infection)

Future Exposure to Foodborne Pathogens:

1. Exposure to or suspicion of causing any confirmed disease outbreak of Norovirus, typhoid fever, (Salmonella Typhi), shigellosis, (Shigella spp. infection), Escherichia coli O157:H7 or other STEC infection, nontyphoidal Salmonella or hepatitis A (hepatitis A virus infection)
2. A household member diagnosed with Norovirus, typhoid fever, shigellosis, illness due to STEC, or hepatitis A.
3. A household member attending or working in a setting experiencing a confirmed disease outbreak of Norovirus, typhoid fever, shigellosis, E.coli O157:H7 or other STEC infection, or hepatitis A.

I have read (or had explained to me) and understand the requirements concerning my responsibilities under the Food Code and this agreement to comply with:

1. Reporting requirements specified above involving symptoms, diagnoses, and exposure specified;
2. Work restrictions or exclusions that are imposed upon me; and
3. Good hygienic practices.

I understand that failure to comply with the terms of this agreement could lead to action by the food establishment or the food regulatory authority that may jeopardize my employment and may involve legal action against me.

Conditional Employee Name (please print): ______________________________

Signature of Conditional Employee: ______________________________ Date: __________

Food Employee Name (please print): ______________________________

Signature of Food Employee: ______________________________ Date: __________

Signature of Permit Holder or Respresentative: ______________________________ Date: __________

Form 1-C

Conditional Employee or Food Employee Medical Referral

Preventing Transmission of Diseases through Food by Infected Food Employees with Emphasis on illness due to **Norovirus, Typhoid fever *(Salmonella Typhi), Salmonella Non-Typhiodal, Shigellosis (Shigella spp.***), ***Escherichia coli*** 0157:H7 or other Enterohemorrhagic (EHEC) or Shiga toxin-producing ***Escherichia coli*** (STEC), and **Hepatitis A Virus**

The **Food Code** specifies, under **Part 2-2 Employee Health Subpart 2-201 Disease or Medical Condition**, That Conditional Employees and Food Employees obtain medical clearance from a health practitioner licensed to practice medicine, unless the Food Employees have complied with the provisions specified as an alternative to providing medical documentation, whenever the individual:

1. Is chronically suffering from a symptom such **as diarrhea**; or
2. **Has a current illness** involving Norovirus, typhoid fever (**Salmonella Typhi**, Salmonella Non-Typhoidal, shigellosis (**Shigella spp.**) **E.coli 0157:H7** infection (or other STEC), or hepatitis A virus (hepatitis A); or
3. Reports **past illness** involving typhoid fever (**S.Typhi**) within the past three months (while salmonellosis is fairly common in U.S., typhoid fever, caused by infection with **S.Typhi**, is rare).

Conditional employee being referred: (Name, please print) ____________________

Food Employee being referred: (Name, please print) ____________________

4. Is the employee assigned to a food establishment that serves a population that meets the Food Code definition of a highly susceptible population such as a day care center with preschool age children, a hospital kitchen with immunocompromised persons, or an assisted living facility or nursing home with older adults?

YES ☐ NO ☐

Reason for Medical Referral: The reason for this referral is checked below:

- ☐ Is chronically suffering from vomiting or diarrhea; or (specify) ____________________
- ☐ Diagnosed or suspected Norovirus, typhoid fever, shigellosis, E.coli 0157:H7 (or other STEC) infection, nontyphoidal *Salmonella* or hepatitis A.(Specify) ____________________
- ☐ Reported past illness from typhoid fever within the past 3 months. (Date of illness): ____________________
- ☐ Other medical condition of concern per the following description: ____________________

Health Practitioner's Conclusion: (Circle the appropriate one; refer to reverse side of form)

- ☐ Food employee is free of Norovirus infection, typhoid fever (S.Typhi infection), Shigella spp. infection, E.coli 0157:H7 (or other STEC infection), nontyphoidal *Salmonella* infection or hepatitis A virus infection, and may work as a food employee without restrictions.
- ☐ Food employee is an asymptomatic shedder of E.coli 0157:H7 (or other STEC), Shigella spp., or Norovirus, and is restricted from working with exposed food; clean equipment, utensils, and linens; and unwrapped single-service and single-use articles in food establishments that do not serve highly susceptible populations.
- ☐ Food employee is not ill but continues as an asymptomatic of E.coli 0157:H7 (or other STEC), Shigella spp. and should be excluded from food establishments that serve highly susceptible populations such as those who are preschool age, immunocompromised, or older adults and in a facility that provides preschool custodial care, health care, or assisted living.
- ☐ Food employee is an asymptomatic shedder of hepatitis A virus and should be excluded from working in a food establishment until medically cleared.
- ☐ Food employee is an asymptomatic shedder of Norovirus and should be excluded from working in a food establishment until medically cleared, or for at least 24 hours from the date of the diagnosis.

Form 1-C (Continued)

☐ Food employee is suffering from Norovirus, typhoid fever, shigellosis, E.coli 0157:H7 (or other STEC infection), or hepatitis A and should be excluded from working in a food establishment.

COMMENTS: (In accordance with Title I of the Americans with Disabilities Act (ADA) and to provide only the information necessary to assist the food establishment operator in preventing foodborne disease transmission, please confine comments to explaining your conclusion and estimating when the employee may be reinstated.)

____

____

____

____

____

____

Signature of Health Practitioner: ____________________________ Date: ________________

Paraphrased from the FDA Food Code for Health Practitioner's Reference

From Subparagraph 2-201.11(A)(2) **Organisms of Concern:**

Any foodborne pathogen, with special emphasis on these 5 organisms:
1. **Norovirus** 2. **S. Typhi** 3. **Shigella** spp. 4. **E.coli** 0157:H7 (or other STEC) 5. **Hepatitis A** virus 6. **Salmonella Non-Typhiodal**

From Subparagraph 2-201.11(A)(1) **Symptoms:**

Have any of the following symptoms:

Diarrhea **Vomiting** **Jaundice** **Sore throat with fever**

From Subparagraph 2-201.11(A)(4)-(5) **Conditions of Exposure of Concern:**

(1) Suspected of causing a foodborne outbreak or being exposed to an outbreak caused by 1 of the 6 organisms above, at an event such as a family meal, church supper, or festival because the person:

Prepared or consumed an implicated food; or

Consumed food prepared by a person who is infected or ill with the organism that caused the outbreak or who is suspected of being a carrier;

(2) Lives with, and has knowledge about, a person who is diagnosed with illness caused by 1 of the 6 organisms; or

(3) Lives with, and has knowledge about, a person who works where there is an outbreak caused by 1 of the 6 organisms.

From Subparagraph 2-201.12 **Exclusion and Restriction:**

Decisions to exclude or restrict a food employee are made considering the available evidence about the person's role in actual potential foodborne illness transmission. Evidence includes:

Symptoms **Diagnosis** **Past illnesses** **Stool/blood tests**

In facilities serving highly susceptible populations such as day care centers and health care facilities, a person for whom there is evidence of foodborne illness is almost always excluded from the food establishment.

In other establishments such as restaurants and retail food stores, that offer food to typically healthy consumers, a person might only be restricted from certain duties, based on the evidence of foodborne illness.

Exclusion from any food establishment is required when the person is:

- Exhibiting or reporting diarrhea or vomiting;
- Diagnosed with illness caused by S. Typhi; or
- Jaundiced within the last 7 days.

For **Shigella** spp. or **Escherichia coli** 0157:H7 or other **STEC** infections, the person's stools must be negative for 2 consecutive cultures taken no earlier than 48 hours after antibiotics are discontinued, and at least 24 hours apart or the infected individual must have resolution of symptoms for more than 7 days or at least 7 days have passed since the employee was diagnosed.

Equipment Monitoring Chart

Week Ending:

Menu Items:	Saturday		Sunday		Monday		Tuesday		Wednesday		Thursday		Friday	
	a.m.	p.m.	a.m.	p.m.	a.m.	p.m.	a.m.	p.m.	a.m.	p.m.	a.m.	p.m.	a.m.	p.m.
Freezer # 1														
# 2														
Freezer # 1														
# 2														
Products														
# 1														
# 2														
# 3														
Deliveries														
# 1														
# 2														
# 3														
Sanitizer (ppm)														
# 1														
# 2														
# 3														
# 4														

Sanitizer Checklist

Date:	Taken by:	Comments:
Sanitizer in Use	☐ Yes ☐ No	
Proper concentration of sanitizer	☐ Yes ☐ No	
Test Strips used to verify concentration	☐ Yes ☐ No	
Equipment Sanitized		
Cutting boards	☐ Yes ☐ No	
Knives	☐ Yes ☐ No	
Slicers	☐ Yes ☐ No	
Work surfaces	☐ Yes ☐ No	
Prep sinks	☐ Yes ☐ No	
Pocket thermometers	☐ Yes ☐ No	
Thermometers sanitized each use	☐ Yes ☐ No	

Form 3-A	**Food Establishment Inspection Report**	
As governed by State Code Section	No. of Risk Factor / Intervention Violations No. of Risk Factor / Intervention Violations Score (Optional)	Date______ Time in______ Time out______

Establishment License / Permit #	Address	City/State	Zip	Phone
	Permit Holder	Purpose of Inspection	Est. Type	Risk Category

FOODBORNE ILLNESS RISK FACTORS AND PUBLIC HEALTH INTERVENTIONS

Circle designated compliance status (IN, OUT, N/O, N/A) for each number item: **IN** = in compliance, **OUT** = not in compliance, **N/O** = not observed, **N/A** = not applicable
Mark "**X**" in appropriate box for COS and R: **COS** = corrected on site during inspection, **R** = repeat violation

Compliance Status			Cos	R
Supervision				
1	IN OUT	Person in charge present, demonstrates knowledge, and performs duties		
2	IN OUT	Certfied Food protection Manager		
Employee Health				
3	IN OUT	Management, food employee and conditional employee knowledge, responsibilities and reporting		
4	IN OUT	Proper use of reporting, restriction and exclusion		
5	IN OUT	Procedures for responding to vomiting and diarrheal events		
Good Hygienic Practices				
6	IN OUT N/O	Proper, eating, tasting, drinking, or tobacco use		
7	IN OUT N/O	No discharge from eyes, nose, and mouth		
Preventing Contamination by Hands				
8	IN OUT	Hands clean and properly washed		
9	IN OUT N/A N/O	No bare hand contact with ready-to-eat foods or approved alternate method properly followed		
10	IN OUT	Adequate handwashing facilities supplied and accessible		
Approved Source				
11	IN OUT	Food obtained from approved source		
12	IN OUT N/A N/O	Food received at proper temperature		
13	IN OUT	Food in good condition, safe, and unadulterated		
14	IN OUT N/A N/O	Required records available shellstock tags parasite destruction		
Protection from Contamination				
15	IN OUT N/A	Food separated and protected		
16	IN OUT N/A	Food-contact surfaces: cleaned and sanitized		
17	IN OUT	Proper disposition of returned, previously served, reconditioned, and unsafe food		
Time/Temperature Control for Safety				
18	IN OUT N/A N/O	Proper cooking time and temperatures		
19	IN OUT N/A N/O	Proper reheating procedures for hot holding		
20	IN OUT N/A N/O	Proper cooling time and temperatures		
21	IN OUT N/A N/O	Proper hot holding temperatures		
22	IN OUT N/A N/O	Proper cold holding temperatures		
23	IN OUT N/A N/O	Proper date marking and disposition		
24	IN OUT N/A N/O	Time as public health control proc. & record		
Consumer Advisory				
25	IN OUT N/A	Consumer advisory provided for raw or undercooked foods		
Highly Susceptible Populations				
26	IN OUT N/A	Pasteurized foods used: prohibited foods not offered		
Chemical				
27	IN OUT N/A	Food additives: approved and properly used		
28	IN OUT	Toxic substances properly identified, stored, used		
Conformance with Approved Procedures				
29	IN OUT N/A	Compliance with variance, specialized process and HACCP plan		

Risk factors are food preparation practices and employees behaviors most commonly reported to the Centers for Disease Control and Prevention as contributing factors in foodborne illness outbreaks. **Public Health interventions** are control measures to prevent foodborne illness or injury.

GOOD RETAIL PRACTICES

Good Retail Practices are preventive measures to control the introduction of pathogens, chemicals and physical object into foods.
Mark "X" in box if numbered item is not compliance Mark "x" in appropriate box for COS and/or R: **COS** = corrected on site during inspection **R** = repeat violation

			Cos	R
Safe Food and Water				
30		Pasteurized eggs used where required		
31		Water and ice from approved source		
32		Variance obtained for specialized processing methods		
Food Temperature Control				
33		Proper cooling method used adequate equipment for temperature control		
34		Plant food properly cooked for hot holding		
35		Approved thawing methods used		
36		Themometers provided and accurate		
Food Identification				
37		Food properly labeled: original container		
Prevention of Food Contamination				
38		Insects, rodents, and animals not present		
39		Contamination prevented during food preparation, storage & display		
40		Personal cleanliness		
41		Wiping cloths: properly used and stored		
42		Washing fruits and vegetables		
Proper Use of Utensils				
43		In-use utensils: properly stored		
44		Utensils, equipment, and linens: properly stored, dried, handled		
45		Single-use/single-service articles: properly stored, used		
46		Gloves used properly		
Proper Use of Utensils				
47		Food and non food-contact surfaces cleanable, properly designed, constructed, and used		
48		Warewashing facilities: installed, maintained, used, test strips		
49		Nonfood-contact surfaces clean		
Physical Facilities				
50		Hot and cold water available adequate pressure		
51		Plumbing installed proper backflow devices		
52		Sewage and waste water properly disposed		
53		Toilet facilities properly constructed supplied cleaned		
54		Garbage/refuse properly disposed facilities maintained		
55		Physical facilities installed maintained and clean		
564		Adequate ventilation and lighting designated areas use		

Person-in-Charge (Signature):______________________ Date:______________

Receiving Temperature Form

Date	Product	Temperature	Initials / Comments

Reviewed by: ______________________________ Date: ____________________

Receiving Log

Date	Time	Food Product Description	Product Code	Corrective Action Taken	Employee Initials	Manager Initials

Receiving Reject Form

Date	Product	Temperature	Initials /Comments

Reviewed by: ______________________________ Date: ____________________

Refrigeration/Cooler Log

	6:00 AM	10:00 AM	2:00 PM	6:00 PM	10:00 PM	
Date	Temp.	Temp.	Temp.	Temp.	Temp.	Initials / Comments

Cooking Log

Date:	Time:	Food Product	Internal Temperature ___°F/____°C	Corrective Action	Employee Initials	Manager Initials

Corrective Actions: ____

Time Temperature Log

Product:	Product Temperatures					Initials
Time:						
7:00 a.m.						
9:00 a.m.						
11:00 a.m.						
1:00 p.m.						
3:00 p.m.						
5:00 p.m.						
7:00 p.m.						
9:00 p.m.						
11:00 p.m.						
1:00 a.m.						
3:00 a.m.						
5:00 a.m.						

Reviewed by: ______________________________ Date: ____________________

Cooling Log Part 1:

Date	Food Product	Time *After 1 Hour*	°F/°C *After 1 Hour*	Time *After 2 Hour*	°F/°C ***Must*** *70°F (21.1°C)*	Time *After 3 Hours*	°F/°C *After 3 Hours*	Time *After 4 Hours*	°F/°C *After 4 Hours*	Time *After 5 Hours*	°F/°C *After 5 Hours*	Time *After 6 Hours*	°F/°C **Must** *41°F (5°C)*

Cooling—Corrective Action Log Part 2:

Date	Food Product	Time	Temperature ***Must:*** 70°F (21.1°C)—2 Hours ***Must:*** 41°F (5°C)—6 Hours	Corrective Action Taken • ***Must:*** Reheat • **Must:** Discard	Employee Initials	Manager Initials

Form

Hazard Analysis Worksheet

Firm Name: **Product Description:**

Firm Address: **Method of Distribution and Storage:**

Intended Use and Consumer:

(1)	(2)	(3)	(4)	(5)	(6)
Ingredient/ Processing Step	**Identify Potential Hazards Introduced, Controlled, or Enhanced at this Step(1)**	**Are any Potential Food Safety Hazards Significant? (Yes/No)**	**Justify your decision for Column 3**	**What Preventive Measure(s) can be Applied for the Significant Hazards?**	**Is this Step a Critical Control Point? (Yes/No)**
	Biological				
	Chemical				
	Physical				
	Biological				
	Chemical				
	Physical				
	Biological				
	Chemical				
	Physical				

HACCP Plan Form

Firm Name:____________________ **Product Description:**____________________

Firm Address:____________________ **Method of Distribution and Storage:**____________________

Intended Use and Consumer:

(1)	(2)	(3)	(4)	(5)	(6)	(7)	(8)	(9)	(10)
Significant Hazard(s)	Critical Control Point (CCP)	Critical Limits for each Preventive Measure	What	How	Frequency	Who	Corrective Action(s)	Verification	Records
			Monitoring						

Signature of Company Official:____________________ Date:__________

Process 1 — Food Preparation for Simple/No-Cook Recipes

Process #1 — Food Preparation Simple/No-Cook Recipes

Food/Menu Items: ____________________

Hazard(s)	Critical Control Points (List Only The Operational Steps That Are CCPs)	Critical Limits	Monitoring	Corrective Actions	Verification	Records
Prerequisite Programs						

Process #1 — Food Preparation for Simple/No-Cook Recipes

Food/Menu Items: ____________________

Process Step	Hazard(s)	CCP (Y/N)	Critical Limits	Monitoring	Corrective Actions	Verification	Records
Receive							
Store							
Prepare							
Hold							
Serve							
Prerequisite Programs							

Process 2 — Food Preparation for Same-Day Recipes

Process #2 — Food Preparation for Same-Day Recipes

Food/Menu Items: ____________________

Hazard(s)	Critical Control Points (List Only The Operational Steps That Are CCPs)	Critical Limits	Monitoring	Corrective Actions	Verification	Records
Prerequisite Programs						

Process #2 — Food Preparation for Same-Day Recipes

Food/Menu Items: ____________________

Process Step	Hazard(s)	CCP (Y/N)	Critical Limits	Monitoring	Corrective Actions	Verification	Records
Receive							
Store							
Prepare							
Cook							
Hold							
Serve							
Prerequisite Programs							

Process 3 — Food Preparation for Complex Recipes

Process #3 — Food Preparation for Complex Recipes

Food/Menu Items: ______________________________

Hazard(s)	Critical Control Points (List Only The Operational Steps That Are CCPs)	Critical Limits	Monitoring	Corrective Actions	Verification	Records
Prerequisite Programs						

Process #3 — Food Preparation for Complex Recipes

Food/Menu Items: ______________________________

Process Step	Hazard(s)	CCP (Y/N)	Critical Limits	Monitoring	Corrective Actions	Verification	Records
Receive							
Store							
Prepare							
Cook							
Cool							
Reheat							
Hold							
Serve							
Prerequisite Programs							

Thermometer Calibration

Thermometer Calibration Log

Date	Manager	Employee	AM Time	MID Time	PM Time	Date	Manager	Employee	AM Time	MID Time	PM Time

Waste/Shrink/Discard Chart

Discard Log

Date	Code	Food Product Description	• Hold • Discard • Return • Credit	Explain Action Taken Reason	Employee Initials	Manager Initials

Reheating Log

Date	Time	Food Product	Internal Temperature	Corrective Action Taken	Employee Initials	Manager Initials

Preliminary Foodborne Illness Investigation*

Food Service or Retail Name: ______________________________

Address: ______________________________

Suspected Food/Beverages (be specific): ______________________________

Date Meal Eaten: ____________ Time: ____________ Onset Date: ____________ Onset Time: ____________

Caller Name: ______________ Phone: ______________ Incub Time: ______________

Address: ______________________________

Person's Name Who Became Ill: Name / Age / Sex / Occupation

____

Doctor Seen: ❑ YES ❑ NO Diagnosis / Lab Results: ______________________________

Clinic Name / Doctor's Name: ______________________________

Address: ______________________________ Phone: ______________

❑ Stool ❑ Blood ❑ Other ______________ Results: ______________

Date Received: ______________ Call Received By: ______________

SYMPTOMS

❑ Vomiting	❑ Fever	❑ Nausea	❑ Burning Mouth
_______ No. of Days	❑ Chills	❑ Muscle Ache	❑ Itching
_______ No. of Times	❑ Cramps	❑ Excess Salivation	❑ Rash
❑ Diarrhea	❑ Headache	❑ Cough	❑ Dizziness
_______ No. of Days	❑ Perspiration	❑ Metallic Taste	❑ Numbness
_______ No. of Times			❑ Double Vision
❑ Bloody	❑ Other: ______________		
❑ Explosive	______________		
❑ Watery			

Preliminary Foodborne Illness Investigation* (continued) FOOD HISTORY		
1st 24 Hours/ Date Meal Consumed Dinner Lunch Breakfast	All Foods Consumed	Where
2nd 24 Hours (Previous Day) Dinner Lunch Breakfast		
3rd 24 Hours (2 Days Prior) Dinner Lunch Breakfast	All Foods Consumed at Food Service or Retail	
1. Was this a take-out order? 2. (If yes) Elapsed time between pickup to consumption__________HRS 3. Are there any other ill contacts (including pets)?________________________ 4. If yes to #4, please list symptoms:________________________ 5. Please note anything unusual noticed about meal? (temperature, taste, etc.)________________________ ________________________ ________________________ ________________________		

Food Safety Checklist

Date: ______________________________ **Observer:** ______________________________

Directions: Use this checklist daily to determine areas in your food service or retail operation that require corrective action. Record corrective actions taken and keep completed records in a notebook for future reference.

Personal Hygiene	**Yes**	**No**	**Corrective Action**
• Employees wear clean and proper uniform including shoes	❑	❑	__________
• Effective hair restraints are properly worn	❑	❑	__________
• Fingernails are short, unpolished, and clean (no artificial nails)	❑	❑	__________
• Jewelry is limited to a plain ring such as a wedding band	❑	❑	__________
• Hands are washed properly, frequently, and at appropriate times	❑	❑	__________
• Burns, wounds, sores or scabs, or splints and water-proof bandages on hands are bandaged and completely covered with a food service glove while handling food.	❑	❑	__________
• Eating, drinking, chewing gum, smoking, or using tobacco are allowed only in designated areas away from preparation, service storage, and ware-washing areas.	❑	❑	__________
• Employees appear in good health	❑	❑	__________
• Hand sinks are unobstructed, operational, and clean	❑	❑	__________
• Hand sinks are stocked with soap, disposable towels, and warm water	❑	❑	__________
• A handwashing reminder sign is posted	❑	❑	__________
• Employee restrooms are operational and clean	❑	❑	__________

Food Preparation	**Yes**	**No**	**Corrective Action**
• All food stored or prepared in facility is from approved sources	❑	❑	__________
• Food equipment utensils, and food contact surfaces are properly washed, rinsed, and sanitized before every use	❑	❑	__________
• Frozen food is thawed under refrigeration or in cold running water	❑	❑	__________
• Preparation is planned so ingredients are kept out of the temperature danger zone	❑	❑	__________
• Food is tasted using the proper procedure	❑	❑	__________
• Procedures are in place to prevent cross contamination	❑	❑	__________
• Food is handled with suitable utensils such as single use gloves or tongs	❑	❑	__________
• Food is prepared in small batches to limit the time it is in the temperature danger zone	❑	❑	__________

- Clean reusable towels are used only for sanitizing equipment, surfaces and not for drying hands, utensils or floors ❑ ❑ ______________
- Food is cooked to the required safe temperature for the appropriate time. The temperature is tested with a calibrated, cleaned, and sanitized food thermometer. ❑ ❑ ______________

Hot Holding	**Yes**	**No**	**Corrective Action**
• Hot holding unit is clean	❑	❑	______________
• Food is heated to the required safe internal temperature before placing in hot holding. Hot holding units are not used to reheat potentially hazardous foods.	❑	❑	______________
• Hot holding unit is preheated before hot food is placed in unit	❑	❑	______________
• Temperature of hot food being held is at or above 135°F (57.2°C)	❑	❑	______________
• Food is protected from contamination	❑	❑	______________

Cold Holding	**Yes**	**No**	**Corrective Action**
• Refrigerators are kept clean and organized	❑	❑	______________
• Temperature of cold food being held is at or below 41°F (5°C)	❑	❑	______________
• Food is protected from contamination	❑	❑	______________

Refrigerator, Freezer, and Milk Cooler	**Yes**	**No**	**Corrective Action**
• Thermometers are available and accurate	❑	❑	______________
• Temperature is appropriate for pieces of equipment	❑	❑	______________
• Food is stored 6 inches off the floor or in walk-in cooling equipment	❑	❑	______________
• Refrigerator and freezer units are clean and neat	❑	❑	______________
• Proper chilling procedures are used	❑	❑	______________
• All foods are properly wrapped, labeled, and dated	❑	❑	______________
• The FIFO (First In, First Out) method of inventory management is used	❑	❑	______________
• Ambient air temperature of all refrigerators and freezers is monitored and documented at the beginning and end of each shift	❑	❑	______________

Food Storage and Dry Storage	**Yes**	**No**	**Corrective Action**
• Temperature of dry storage area is between 50°F (10°C) and 70°F (21.1°C)	❑	❑	______________
• All food and paper supplies are stored 6 to 8 inches off the floor	❑	❑	______________
• All food is labeled with name and received date	❑	❑	______________
• Open bags of food are stored in containers with tight fitting lids and labeled with common name	❑	❑	______________

	Yes	No	Corrective Action
• The FIFO (First In, First Out) method of inventory management is used	❑	❑	____________
• There are no bulging or leaking canned goods	❑	❑	____________
• Food is protected from contamination	❑	❑	____________
• All food surfaces are clean	❑	❑	____________
• Chemicals are clearly labeled and stored away from food and food related supplies	❑	❑	____________
• There is regular cleaning schedule for all food surfaces	❑	❑	____________

Cleaning and Sanitizing	**Yes**	**No**	**Corrective Action**
• Three compartment sink is properly set up for ware washing	❑	❑	____________
• Dishmachine is working properly (i.e. gauges and chemicals are at recommended levels)	❑	❑	____________
• Water is clean and free of grease and food particles	❑	❑	____________
• Water temperatures are correct for wash and rinse	❑	❑	____________
• If heat sanitizing, the utensils are allowed to remain immersed in 171°F (77.2°C) water for 30 seconds	❑	❑	____________
• If using a chemical sanitizer, it is mixed correctly and sanitizer strip is used to test chemical concentration	❑	❑	____________
• Smallware and utensils are allowed to air dry	❑	❑	____________
• Wiping cloths are stored in sanitizing solution while in use	❑	❑	____________

Utensils and Equipment	**Yes**	**No**	**Corrective Action**
• All small equipment and utensils, including cutting boards and knives, are cleaned and sanitized between uses	❑	❑	____________
• Small equipment and utensils are washed, sanitized, and air-dried	❑	❑	____________
• Work surfaces and utensils are clean	❑	❑	____________
• Work surfaces are cleaned and sanitized between uses	❑	❑	____________
• Thermometers are calibrated on a routine basis	❑	❑	____________
• Thermometers are cleaned and sanitized after each use	❑	❑	____________
• Can opener is clean	❑	❑	____________
• Drawers and racks are clean	❑	❑	____________
• Clean utensils are handled in a manner to prevent contamination of areas that will be direct contact with food or a person's mouth	❑	❑	____________

Large Equipment	**Yes**	**No**	**Corrective Action**
• Food slicer is clean	❑	❑	____________
• Food slicer is broken down, cleaned and sanitized before and after every use	❑	❑	____________
• Boxes, containers, and recyclables are removed from site	❑	❑	____________
• Loading dock and area around dumpsters are clean and odor-free	❑	❑	____________
• Exhaust hood and filters are clean	❑	❑	____________

Garbage Storage and Disposal	**Yes**	**No**	**Corrective Action**
• Kitchen garbage cans are clean and kept covered	❑	❑	____________
• Garbage cans are emptied as necessary	❑	❑	____________
• Boxes and containers are removed from site	❑	❑	____________
• Loading dock and area around dumpster are clean	❑	❑	____________
• Dumpsters are clean	❑	❑	____________

Pest Control	**Yes**	**No**	**Corrective Action**
• Outside doors have screens, are well sealed, and are equipped with a self-closing device	❑	❑	____________
• No evidence of pests is present	❑	❑	____________
• There is a regular schedule of pest control by licensed pest control operator	❑	❑	____________

APPENDIX 4- HACCP Worksheets and Forms

- A. Hazard Analysis Worksheet - Simple
- A. HACCP Plan Form - Simple
- B. Hazard Analysis Worksheet - Same Day (two pages)
- B. HACCP Plan Form - Same Day
- C. Hazard Analysis Worksheet - Complex (two pages)
- C. HACCP Plan Form - Complex (two pages)

Form

A. Hazard Analysis Worksheet

Firm Name: *Company XYZ*

Product Description: *Roasted Chicken Club: Simple/No-Cook menu*

Firm Address: *Anywhere, USA*

Method of Distribution and Storage: *Retail Sale*

Intended Use and Consumer: *General Public - Immediate and take-out service*

(1)	(2)	(3)	(4)	(5)	(6)
Ingredient/ Processing Step	**Identify Potential Hazards Introduced, Controlled, or Enhanced at this Step(1)**	**Are any Potential Food Safety Hazards Significant? (Yes/No)**	**Justify your decision for Column 3**	**What Preventive Measure(s) can be Applied for the Significant Hazards?**	**Is this Step a Critical Control Point? (Yes/No)**
Receiving	*Biological*				
	Chemical				
	Physical				
Storage	*Biological*				
	Chemical				
	Physical				
Cold Holding for Sale and/or Service	*Biological*				
	Chemical				
	Physical				

Form

A. HACCP Plan Form

Firm Name: *Company XYZ* **Product Description:** *Roasted Chicken Club: Simple/No-Cook menu*

Firm Address: *Anywhere, USA* **Method of Distribution and Storage:** *Retail Sale*

Intended Use and Consumer: *General Public - Immediate and take-out service*

(1)	(2)	(3)	(4)	(5)	(6)	(7)	(8)	(9)	(10)
Critical Control Point (CCP)	Significant Haz-ard(s)	Critical Limits for each Preventive Measure	Monitoring				Corrective Action(s)	Records	Verification
			What	How	Frequency	Who			

Signature of Company Official: ______________________ Date: __________

Form

B. Hazard Analysis Worksheet

Firm Name: *Company XYZ*

Product Description: *Roasted Chicken Club: Same-Day Recipe*

Firm Address: *Anywhere, USA*

Method of Distribution and Storage: *Retail Sale*

Intended Use and Consumer: *General Public - Immediate and take-out service*

(1)	(2)	(3)	(4)	(5)	(6)
Ingredient/ Processing Step	**Identify Potential Hazards Introduced, Controlled, or Enhanced at this Step(1)**	**Are any Potential Food Safety Hazards Significant? (Yes/No)**	**Justify your decision for Column 3**	**What Preventive Measure(s) can be Applied for the Significant Hazards?**	**Is this Step a Critical Control Point? (Yes/No)**
Receiving	*Biological*				
	Chemical				
	Physical				
Storage	*Biological*				
	Chemical				
	Physical				
Preparation	*Biological*				
	Chemical				
	Physical				

Form (continued)

B. Hazard Analysis Worksheet

(1) Ingredient/ Processing Step	(2) Identify Potential Hazards Introduced, Controlled, or Enhanced at this Step(1)	(3) Are any Potential Food Safety Hazards Significant? (Yes/No)	(4) Justify your decision for Column 3	(5) What Preventive Measure(s) can be Applied for the Significant Hazards?	(6) Is this Step a Critical Control Point? (Yes/No)
Cooking	*Biological*				
	Chemical				
	Physical				
Hot Holding	*Biological*				
	Chemical				
	Physical				
Assembly for Service	*Biological*				
	Chemical				
	Physical				

Form

B. HACCP Plan Form

Firm Name: *Company XYZ* **Product Description:** *Roasted Chicken Club: Same-Day Recipe*

Firm Address: *Anywhere, USA* **Method of Distribution and Storage:** *Retail Sale*

Intended Use and Consumer: *General Public - Immediate and take-out service*

(1)	(2)	(3)	(4)	(5)	(6)	(7)	(8)	(9)	(10)
			Monitoring						
Critical Control Point (CCP)	Significant Haz-ard(s)	Critical Limits for each Preventive Measure	What	How	Frequency	Who	Corrective Action(s)	Records	Verification

Signature of Company Official: ______________________ Date: __________

Form

C. Hazard Analysis Worksheet

Firm Name: *Company XYZ* **Product Description:** *Roasted Chicken Club: Complex Recipe - using raw, not pre-cooked chicken.*

Firm Address: *Anywhere, USA* **Method of Distribution and Storage:** *Retail Sale*

Intended Use and Consumer: *General Public - Immediate and take-out service*

(1) Ingredient/ Processing Step	(2) Identify Potential Hazards Introduced, Controlled, or Enhanced at this Step(1)	(3) Are any Potential Food Safety Hazards Significant? (Yes/No)	(4) Justify your decision for Column 3	(5) What Preventive Measure(s) can be Applied for the Significant Hazards?	(6) Is this Step a Critical Control Point? (Yes/No)
Receiving	*Biological*				
	Chemical				
	Physical				
Storage	*Biological*				
	Chemical				
	Physical				
Preparation	*Biological*				
	Chemical				
	Physical				
Cooking	*Biological*				
	Chemical				
	Physical				

Form (continued)

C. Hazard Analysis Worksheet

(1) Ingredient/ Processing Step	(2) Identify Potential Hazards Introduced, Controlled, or Enhanced at this Step(1)	(3) Are any Potential Food Safety Hazards Significant? (Yes/No)	(4) Justify your decision for Column 3	(5) What Preventive Measure(s) can be Applied for the Significant Hazards?	(6) Is this Step a Critical Control Point? (Yes/No)
Cooling	*Biological*				
	Chemical				
	Physical				
Reheating	*Biological*				
	Chemical				
	Physical				
Hot Holding	*Biological*				
	Chemical				
	Physical				
Assembly for Service	*Biological*				
	Chemical				
	Physical				

Form

C. HACCP Plan Form

Firm Name: *Company XYZ*

Product Description: *Roasted Chicken Club: Complex Recipe - using raw not pre-cooked chicken.*

Firm Address: *Anywhere, USA*

Method of Distribution and Storage: *Retail Sale*

Intended Use and Consumer: *General Public - Immediate and take-out service*

(1)	(2)	(3)	(4)	(5)	(6)	(7)	(8)	(9)	(10)
Critical Control Point (CCP)	Significant Haz-ard(s)	Critical Limits for each Preventive Measure	Monitoring				Corrective Action(s)	Records	Verification
			What	How	Frequency	Who			

Signature of Company Official: ____________________ Date: __________

Form

C. HACCP Plan Form

Firm Name: *Company XYZ*

Product Description: *Roasted Chicken Club: Complex Recipe - using raw not pre-cooked chicken.*

Firm Address: *Anywhere, USA*

Method of Distribution and Storage: *Retail Sale*

Intended Use and Consumer: *General Public - Immediate and take-out service*

(1)	(2)	(3)	(4)	(5)	(6)	(7)	(8)	(9)	(10)
Critical Control Point (CCP)	Significant Haz-ard(s)	Critical Limits for each Preventive Measure	Monitoring				Corrective Action(s)	Records	Verification
			What	How	Frequency	Who			

Signature of Company Official: ______________________ Date: ____________

Glossary

A

Acceptable Level - The minimum point at which the risk of a biological, chemical, and/or physical hazard is reduced such that the likelihood of a foodborne illness or injury is considered by regulatory to be remote.

Acid - A substance with a pH of less than 7.0.

Active Managerial Control - The purposeful incorporation of specific actions or procedures by management in the operation of a business to attain control over the five foodborne illness risk factors identified by the CDC.

Adulterated - Food that contains a poisonous or deleterious substance that causes it to be hazardous or unfit for human consumption.

Aerobic - Able to reproduce and live only in the presence of free oxygen.

Alkali - A substance with a pH of more than 7.0.

Anaerobic - Able to reproduce and live in the absence of free oxygen.

Approved Source - A regulatory authority deemed acceptable supplier based on a determination of conformity with laws, statutes, regulations, principles, practices, and generally recognized standards of operation that protect public health and safety.

B

Bacteria - Single-cell microorganisms,usually classified as the simplest of plants.

Biological Hazard - Danger to food from disease-causing microorganisms known as pathogens, poisonous plants, mushrooms, and fish that carry harmful toxins.

Bioterrorism - Intentionally infecting people with the intent to cause illness and death by the spread of highly contagious diseases such as smallpox, anthrax, botulism, plague, and viral hemorrhagic fevers.

Boiling-Point - The temperature at which a liquid changes to a gas. The boiling point of water, is 212°F (100°C) at sea level.

C

CCP - See Critical Control Point.

CDC - Centers for Disease Control and Prevention.

CFR - See Code of Federal Regulations.

Chemical Hazard - Danger to food posed by chemical substances, especially toxic metals, pesticides, and food additives.

CIP - Clean in place. The process of washing, rinsing, and sanitizing equipment through a piping/mechanical system such as in frozen dessert machines.

Clean - Free of soil.

Code of Federal Regulations (CFR) - The application of codes to the general and permanent rules established by federal agencies and departments and published in the Federal Register.

Contamination - The presence in food of potentially harmful substances, including microorganisms (bacteria, virus, parasites), chemicals (pesticides, toxic metals), physical objects (hair, dirt, glass), or filth.

Control Measure - Any action or activity that can be used to prevent, eliminate, or reduce an identified biological, chemical, or physical hazard. Control measures, determined to be essential for food safety, are applied at critical control points in the flow of food.

Control Point (CP) - Any step in the flow of food when control can be applied to prevent, reduce, or eliminate a biological, chemical, or physical hazard. Loss of control, at this point, will not result in an unsafe or high-risk level of food.

Corrective Action - An act that is done by a person whenever a critical limit is not met or a deviation occurs.

CP - See Control Point.

Criterion - A requirement on which a judgment or decision can be based.

Critical Control Point (CCP) - An operational step, point, or procedure in a food preparation process at which control can be applied and is essential to prevent or eliminate a biological, chemical, or physical hazard or reduce it to acceptable levels. A loss of control at this point results in unsafe and high-risk levels in food.

Critical Limit (CL) - A criterion of one or more prescribed parameters that must be met to ensure that a CCP effectively controls a hazard within the flow of food.

Cross-Contact - Occurs when an allergen is inadvertently transferred from a food containing an allergen to a food that does not contain the allergen.

Cross Contamination - The transfer of harmful substances or diseases from one surface to another. Examples include: hands, food-contact surfaces, sponges, cloth towels, equipment, storage, and utensils.

D

Danger Zone - The temperature range between 41°F (5°C) and 135°F (57°C) that favors the growth of pathogenic microorganisms.

Date Marking - The practice of documenting the date or day by which all food should be consumed, sold, or discarded.

Decline/Death Phase - The phase of bacteria growth, following the stationary phase, in which the rate of death, within the colony, exceeds the rate of reproduction and the number of living cells, begins to decrease.

Deleterious Substance - A substance that is harmful or injurious.

Deviation - The failure to meet a required critical limit for a critical control point.

E

Escherichia Coli (E.coli) - Bacteria often associated with cattle that causes human illness when undercooked, contaminated ground beef is eaten. Infection can also occur after drinking raw milk or contact with sewage-contaminated water. Food service and retail employees with E.coli must report this infection to the proper health authorities.

Exclude - To prevent a person from working, as a food employee, or entering a food establishment except for those areas open to the general public.

F

FATTOM - An acronym for food, acidity, time, temperature, oxygen, and moisture. The letters in FATTOM stand for the conditions needed for microorganisms to grow.

FDA - United States Food and Drug Administration.

Fish - A fresh or saltwater finfish, crustaceans, and other forms of aquatic life (including alligator, frog, aquatic turtle, jellyfish, sea cucumber, and sea urchin) and all mollusks, if intended for human consumption.

Food - Raw, cooked, or processed edible substance, ice, beverage, chewing gum, or ingredient used or intended for use or for sale in whole or in part for human consumption.

Food Allergy - Condition caused by an immune response reaction to a naturally occurring protein in a food or a food ingredient. Major food allergens and the "Big 8" are the foods that account for 90 percent or more of all food allergies. They are shellfish (crab, lobster, or shrimp); fish (bass, flounder, or cod); peanuts; tree nuts (almonds, pecans, chestnuts, pistachios, Brazil nuts, etc.); milk; eggs; soy/tofu; and wheat.

Foodborne Illness Outbreak - The occurrence of two or more cases of illness resulting from the ingestion of a common food.

Food Defense - The protection of food products from intentional adulteration/contamination.

Food Establishment - An operation at the food service and retail level that serves or offers food directly to the consumer and that, includes a production, storage, or distributing operation that supplies the direct-to-consumer operation.

Food Poisoning - A general term often used for intoxication or infection caused by consumption of contaminated food.

Food Preparation Process - A series of operational steps conducted to produce a food ready to be consumed.

Food Safety - The protection of food products from unintentional or accidental contamination.

Food Security - Best defined by the World Health Organization (WHO); food security is "the implication that all people at all times have both physical and economic access to enough food for an active, healthy life." Internationally, food security is defined as a 2-year supply of food for a particular country.

G

Game Animal - In general, an animal such as bison, deer, elk, rabbit, raccoon, and squirrel. Game animals are not ratites or livestock.

H

HACCP - Hazard Analysis and Critical Control Point.

HACCP Plan - A written document that is based on the principles of HACCP and describes the procedures to be followed to ensure the control of a specific process or procedure.

HACCP System - The result of implementing the HACCP principles in an operation that has foundational comprehensive, prerequisite programs in place. A HACCP system includes all prerequisite programs and the HACCP plan, including all seven HACCP principles.

HACCP Team - A group of people who are responsible for developing and implementing a HACCP plan.

Hazard - A biological, physical, or chemical contaminant that may cause a food to be unsafe for human consumption.

Hazard Analysis and Critical Control Point (HACCP) - A prevention based food safety system that identifies and monitors specific food safety hazards (biological, chemical, physical) that can adversely affect the safety of food products.

Hepatitis A - A virus that can be transmitted through direct contact with an infected person, or ingestion of a contaminated food or water. A food service and retail employee diagnosed with this virus must report it to the proper health authorities.

Hermetically Sealed Container - A container that is designed to keep microorganisms from entering products such as low-acid canned foods.

Highly Susceptible Population (HSP) - Persons who are more likely than other populations to experience foodborne disease because they are either immunocompromised, preschool-age children (infants or toddlers), or older adults.

Hoax - A false accusation or fraudulent report. Common hoaxes include false claims of illness or an intentional contamination of food and then claiming damage.

Hygiene - Practices necessary for establishing and maintaining good health.

I

Ice Point - The temperature at which a liquid changes to a solid. The ice point of water is 32°F (0°C).

Incubation Period - The phase, in the course of an infection, between the invasion of the host by the pathogen and the appearance of the symptoms of illness.

Infection - Disease caused by invasion of living pathogenic organisms, which multiply within the body, causing illness.

Intoxication - Disease caused by consumption of poisons (toxins), which may be chemical, naturally occurring in food, or produced by pathogenic microorganisms.

J

Jaundice - A condition that causes the skin and eyes to yellow.

L

Lag Phase - The period of bacterial growth following transfer to a new environment, when adaptation to new conditions takes place and there is little or no increase in the number of cells in the colony.

Log Phase - The period of bacterial growth following the lag phase, when the multiplication rate is constant, rapid, and the number of cells in the colony increases exponentially.

M

Meat - The flesh of animals used as food, including the dressed flesh of cattle, swine, sheep, or goats and other edible animals, except fish, poultry, and wild-game animals.

Microbe - A general term for microscopic organisms, particularly pathogens.

Microorganisms - A form of life that can be seen only with a microscope, including bacteria, viruses, yeast, and single-celled animals.

Molluscan Shellfish - Any edible species of raw flesh or frozen oysters, clams, mussels, and scallops or edible portions thereof, except when the scallop product consists only of the shucked adductor muscle.

Monitoring - The act of observing and making measurements to help determine if critical limits are being met and maintained.

N

National Shellfish Sanitation Program (NSSP) - The voluntary system by which regulatory authorities for shellfish-harvesting waters and shellfish processing and transportation and the shellfish industry implement specified controls to ensure that raw and frozen shellfish are safe for human consumption.

Non-Continuous Cooking - The process of cooking food is stopped for a time, then started again to complete cooking.

Norovirus - A gastrointestinal virus that is commonly called the "Norwalk-like virus," "small round-structured virus," and "winter vomiting disease," resulting in nausea, diarrhea, vomiting, and stomach cramps. Because it is highly contagious, a Norovirus must be reported to the proper health authorities.

NSSP - National Shellfish Sanitation Program.

O

Operational Step - An activity or stage in the flow of food through a food establishment, such as purchasing, receiving, storage, preparation, cooking, holding, cooling, reheating, and serving.

Organism - An individual living thing.

P

Parasite - An organism that lives on or in another, usually larger, host organism in a way that harms or is of no advantage to the host.

Pathogen - A microorganism (bacteria, parasites, viruses, or fungi) that causes disease in humans.

Pathogenic - Disease-causing microorganisms.

PCO - Pest control operator (licensed).

Personal Hygiene - Individual cleanliness habits.

Person-In-Charge - The individual present at a food establishment who is responsible for the operation at the time of inspection.

pH - The measure of the acidity of a product. Key: pH 0 to 7 is acidic; pH of 7 is neutral; and pH 7 to 14 is alkaline.

Poultry - Any domesticated bird (chicken, turkey, duck, geese, guineas, ratites, squab) or game bird (pheasant, partridge, quail, grouse, pigeon).

Prerequisite Programs - Procedures, including standard operating procedures (SOPs) that address basic operational and sanitation conditions in an establishment.

Preventative Measure - Physical, chemical, or other factors that can be used to control an identified safety hazard.

Procedural Step - An individual activity in applying the HACCP Principles to a food service or retail establishment's operations.

Process Approach - A method of categorizing food operations into one of three categories:

- Simple/No-Cook: Food preparation with no-cook step wherein ready-to-eat food is received, stored, prepared, held, and served.
- Same-Day: Food preparation for same-day service wherein food is received, stored, prepared, cooked, held, and served.

- Complex: Complex food preparation wherein food is received, stored, prepared, cooked, cooled, reheated, hot-held, and served.

R

Ratite - A flightless bird like an ostrich, emu, and rhea.

Ready-To-Eat (RTE) Food - RTE foods include the following:

- Raw animal foods that have been properly cooked;
- Fish intended for raw consumption that has been frozen to destroy parasites;
- Raw fruits and vegetables that are washed;
- Fruits and vegetables that are cooked for hot holding;
- Plant food for which further washing, cooking, or other processing is not required for food safety, and from which rinds, peels, husks, or shells, if naturally present, are removed;
- Substances derived from plants such as spices, seasonings, and sugar; a bakery item such as bread, cakes, pies, fillings, or icing for which further cooking is not required for food safety;
- Dry, fermented sausages, such as dry salami or pepperoni;
- Salt-cured meat and poultry products, such as prosciutto ham, country-cured ham, Parma ham; and
- Dried meat and poultry products, such as jerky or beef sticks, and low-acid foods that have been thermally processed and packaged in hermetically sealed containers.

Record - A documentation of monitoring observations and verification activities.

Regulatory Authority - A federal, state, local, or tribal enforcement body or authorized representative having jurisdiction over the food establishment.

Restrict - To limit the activities of an employee so that there is no risk of transmitting a disease that is transmissible through food. Also the food employee may not work with exposed food, clean equipment, utensils, linens, and unwrapped single-service or single-use articles.

Risk Analysis - An estimate of the likely occurrence of a hazard.

Risk Control Plan (RCP) - A concisely written management plan developed by food service and retail operators with input from the health inspector that describes a management system for controlling specific out-of-control risk factors.

Risk Factor - One of the broad categories of contributing factors to foodborne illness outbreaks, as identified by the CDC, that directly relates to foodborne safety concerns within food service and retail establishments. The five factors are poor personal hygiene, inadequate cooking temperatures, improper holding temperatures, contaminated equipment, and food from unsafe sources.

S

Salmonella - A bacteria that can cause diarrhea, fever, and stomach pain in people who have eaten food or had contact with animals with the Salmonella bacteria. This could be highly contagious, so food service and retail employees with this disease should report it to the proper health authorities.

Sanitary - Free of disease-causing organisms and other harmful substances.

Sanitization - The reduction of the number of pathogenic microorganisms on a surface to levels accepted as safe by regulatory authorities.

Severity - The seriousness of the effect(s) due to a hazard.

Shigellosis - A bacterial infection causing severe diarrhea that can pass from person to person or from eating contaminated food. Food may become contaminated by infected food handlers who do not properly wash hands after using the restroom. Flies and sewage contaminated water are other sources. Any food handler with shigellosis must report it to the proper health authorities.

SOP - Standard operating procedure.

Spore - A very tough, dormant form of certain bacterial cells that is very resistant to dehydration, heat, and a variety of chemical and radiation treatments that are otherwise lethal to vegetative cells.

Spore Former - A bacterium capable of producing spores under adverse conditions. Spore formers in food include *Clostridium botulinum*, *Bacillus cereus*, and *Clostridium perfringens*.

Standard Operating Procedure (SOP) - A written method of controlling a practice in accordance with predetermined specifications to obtain a desired outcome.

Stationary Phase - The period of bacterial growth, following the log phase, in which the number of bacterial cells remains more or less constant, as cells compete for space and nourishment.

T

TC - Temperature control.

TCS (Time/Temperature Control For Safety of Food) - A food that requires time and temperature control to limit pathogenic microorganism growth or toxin formation.

Temperature Measuring Device - A thermometer, thermocouple, thermistor, or other device used for measuring the temperature of food, air, or water.

Toxigenic Microorganisms - Pathogenic bacteria that cause foodborne illness in humans due to the ingestion of poisonous toxins produced in food.

Toxin - A poisonous substance that may be found in food.

Traceability - Is the ability to trace the history, application, or location of an item or activity with the help of documentation.

U

USDA - United States Department of Agriculture.

V

Validation - That element of verification focused on collecting and evaluating scientific and technical information to determine if the HACCP plan, when properly implemented, will effectively control the hazards.

Variance - A written waiver or modification to requirements issued and authorized by a regulatory agency.

Vegetative Cell - A bacterial cell that is capable of actively growing.

Verification - Ensuring that monitoring and other functions of HACCP plan are being properly implemented.

Virus - The smallest of microorganisms that is dependent on a living host cell to survive and multiply and; therefore, cannot multiply in or on food.

W

Water Activity (a_w) - The amount of water available in the product to allow bacteria to live and grow. Scientifically, it is the quotient of the water vapor pressure of the substance, divided by the vapor pressure of pure water at the same temperature.

Z **Zoonotic Disease** - A disease that is communicable from animals to humans such as BSE (mad cow), avian flu, E. coli, Salmonella, rabies, and malaria.

Resources

We recommend that all food service and retail establishments should give this resource list, their employee contact list, and the completed first-responder emergency contact list to all management and the company's media spokesperson.

AFDO (Association of Food and Drug Officials) is an international nonprofit organization that has six regional affiliates that serve as resources for regulator, industry, and academia. www.afdo.org. These are the six regional affiliates:

- AFDOSS—Association of Food and Drug Officials of the Southern States
  www.afdoss.org
- CASA—Central Atlantic States Association of Food and Drug Officials
  www.casafdo.org
- MCAFDO—Mid-Continental Association of Food and Drug Officials
  www.mcafdo.org
- NCAFDO—North Central Association of Food and Drug Officials
  www.ncafdo.org
- NEFDOA—North East Food and Drug Officials Association
  www.nefdoa.org
- WAFDO—Western Association of Food and Drug Officials
  www.wafdo.org

American State Health Officials: 202-371-9090

- www.statepublichealth.org

Centers for Disease Control and Prevention: 800-CDC-INFO or 888-232-6348

- www.statepublichealth.org
- www.bt.cdc.gov/

Center for Safety and Applied Nutrition: 1-888-SAFEFOOD

- www.cfsan.fda.gov/~dms/foodcode.html
- www.cfsan.fda.gov/~dms/secgui11.html
- www.cfsan.fda.gov/~dms/secguid6.html

Department of Homeland Security: 202-324-0001

- www.ready.gov or http://www.dhs.gov

FBI / Federal Bureau of Investigations: 202-456-1111

- www.fbi.gov

FDA: 1-888-INFO-FDA/1-888-463-6332 or 301-443-1240

- www.fda.gov
- www.fda.gov/oc/bioterrorism/bioact.html
- www.fda.gov/oc/bioterrorism/report_adulteration.html
- www.fda.gov/ora/training/orau/FoodSecurity/default.htm

FSIS / Food Safety and Inspection Service: 1-800-333-1284

- www.fsis.usda.gov/ (FSIS Main Page)
- www.fsis.usda.gov/oa/topics/securityguide.htm
- www.fsis.usda.gov/oa/recalls/rec_intr.htm (Recall Information Center)
- www.fsis.usda.gov/oa/pubs/recallfocus.htm
- www.cfsan.fda.gov/-lrd/recall2.html

General Accounting Office: 202-512-4800

- www.gao.gov

International Association for Food Protection: 800-369-6337

- 6200 Aurora Avenue, Suite 200W
  Des Moines, IA 50322
- www.foodprotect.org

NEHA / National Environmental Health Association: 866-956-2258

- 720 S. Colorado Blvd.
  Suite 1000-N
  Denver, CO 80246
- www.neha.org

Regulatory Services for Approved Suppliers

- CDC Food Safety Office-404-639-2213 or www.cdc.gov
- EPA-202-272-0167 or www.epa.gov
- FSIS-888-674-6854 or www.fsis.usda.gov
- FDA-888-463-6332 or www.cfsan.fda.gov
- USDC (approved list of fish products) - www.seafood.nmfs.noaa.gov

U.S. Department of Agriculture: 202-720-3631 or 1-800-233-3935

- Office of the Director

  USDA FSIS PPID/HACCP

  Room 6912, Suite 6900E

  1099 14th Street, N.W.

  Washington, DC 20250-3700

  202-501-7319 Fax: 202-501-7639
- www.usda.gov/wps/portal/usda/usdahome

FDA Publications and Federal Regulations

FDA Food Code – available from the U.S. Department of Commerce, National Technical Information Service, via telephone: 703-487-4650 or electronically on the FDA Web site at: http://www.fda.gov/Food/FoodSafety/RetailFoodProtection/FoodCode/default.htm

Fish and Fishery Products - Code of Federal Regulations, Title 21, Part 123 Fish and Fishery Products. Electronically via the FDA Web site at: http://www.accessdata.fda.gov/scripts/cdrh/cfdocs/cfCFR/CFRSearch.cfm?CFRPart=123

Fish and Fishery Products Hazards and Controls Guide, Available via telephone: 240-402-2300 or electronically on the FDA Web site at: http://www.fda.gov/food/guidancecomplianceregulatoryinformation/guidancedocuments/seafood/fishandfisheriesproductshazardsandcontrolsguide/default.htm

National Shellfish Sanitation Program Model Ordinance for Molluscan Shellfish, Electronically via the FDA Web site at: http://www.fda.gov/Food/FoodSafety/Product-SpecificInformation/Seafood/FederalStatePrograms/NationalShellfishSanitationProgram/ucm046353.htm

Report of the FDA Retail Food Program Database of Foodborne Illness Risk Factors, Electronically via the FDA Web site at: http://www.fda.gov/Food/FoodSafety/RetailFoodProtection/FoodCode/FoodCode2001/ucm123544.htm

FDA Report on the Occurrence of Foodborne Illness Risk Factors in Selected Institutional Retail foodservice, Restaurant, and Retail Food Store Facility Types, Electronically via the FDA Web site at: http://www.fda.gov/Food/FoodSafety/RetailFoodProtection/FoodborneIllnessandRiskFactorReduction/RetailFoodRiskFactorStudies/ucm224321.htm

There are many resources available of information and training on the subject of food defense. Some examples are:

- **ALERT** - For food safety managers and regulators. This is a food defense awareness program intended to raise the awareness of state and local government agency and industry representatives regarding food defense issues and preparedness. http://www.fda.gov/Food/FoodDefense/ToolsResources/ucm296009.htm
- **Employees FIRST** - Employee are the First Line of Food Defense. This training kid is available on-line and contains handouts, presentations and videos for employee training. This program educates front-line food industry workers from farm to table about the risk of intentional food contamination and the actions they can take to identify and reduce these risks. http://www.fda.gov/Food/FoodDefense/ToolsResources/ucm295997.htm
- **CARVER plus SHOCK** - An offensive targeting prioritization tool that has been adapted for the food industry. It is a vulnerability assessment software program and mitigation strategies database. Available at http://www.fsis.usda.gov/PDF/Carver.pdf and www.fda.gov/fooddefense
- **FDA Industry Guidance** - these pamphlets include guidance for food processors, producers or transporter; importers and filers; the dairy industry; the cosmetic industry; retail food facilities; and consumers. http://www.fda.gov/Food/GuidanceComplianceRegulatoryInformation/GuidanceDocuments/FoodDefenseandEmergencyResponse/ucm082751.htm
- **FREE-B** - Food Related Emergency Exercise Bundle is a serious of scenarios based on intentional and unintentional food contamination events. http://www.fda.gov/Food/FoodDefense/ToolsResources/ucm295902.htm
- **See Something, Say Something™ Campaign** - Outreach documents targeted for Food Service and Retail Food Establishments. www.fda.gov/downloads/Food/FoodDefense/UCM245306.pdf
- **Vulnerability Assessment Software Tool** - to be used to assess vulnerabilities within a system or infrastructure of the food industry. http://www.fda.gov/Food/FoodDefense/ToolsResources/ucm295900.htm

- **Guidance for Industry: Retail Food Stores and Food Service Establishments: Food Security Preventive Measures Guidance** - http://www.fda.gov/Food/GuidanceComplianceRegulatoryInformation/GuidanceDocuments/FoodDefenseandEmergencyResponse/ucm082751.htm
- **Food Defense & Emergency Response Guidance Document** http://www.fsis.usda.gov/food_defense_&_emergency_response/Guidance_Materials/index.asp
- **FSIS Food Defense Guidelines for Slaughter and Processing Establishments*** http://www.fsis.usda.gov/PDF/Securityguide.pdf
- **FSIS Safety and Security Guidelines for the Transportation and Distribution of Meat, Poultry, and Egg Products*** http://www.fsis.usda.gov/oa/topics/transportguide.pdf
- **FSIS Guide to Developing a Food Defense Plan for Warehouses and Distribution Centers*** http://www.fsis.usda.gov/pdf/guidance_document_warehouses.pdf
- **Guidelines for the Disposal of Intentionally Adulterated Food Products and the Decontamination of Food Processing Facilities** http://www.fsis.usda.gov/pdf/Disposal_Decontamination_Guidelines.pdf
- **World Health Organization (WHO)-Terrorist Threats to Food-Guidelines for Establishing and Strengthening Prevention and Response Systems** http://www.who.int/foodsafety/publications/fs_management/terrorism/en/
- **U.S. Food and Drug Administration (FDA)-Food Defense & Terrorism** http://www.fda.gov/food/fooddefense/default.htm
- **USDA, Food and Nutrition Service (FNS) A Biosecurity Checklist for Food Service Programs, Developing a Biosecurity Management Plan** http://healthymeals.nal.usda.gov/hsmrs/biosecurity.pdf

Answer Key

HACCP Pre-Test
(pages 9 - 11)

1. b
2. d
3. c
4. a
5. c
6. b
7. c
8. a
9. b
10. d
11. c
12. b
13. a
14. d
15. c
16. c
17. d
18. a
19. d
20. c

Star Point 1 Myth or Fact Answers
(page 13)

1. Myth
2. Myth
3. Fact
4. Myth
5. Fact

Star Point 1 Check for Understanding Answers
(page 113)

1. d. Hazard Analysis and Critical Control Point
2. d. written methods of controlling a practice in accordance with predetermined specifications to obtain a desired outcome
3. d. Hepatitis B
4. c. 41°F – 135°F (5°C – 57.2°C)
5. c. are procedures, including standard operating procedures, that address basic operational and sanitation conditions in an establishment
6. c. Pickled beets
7. d. two or more people eat the same food and get the same illness
8. b. Chemical, Physical, Biological
9. c. pH
10. a. Hurdle Effect

Star Point 2 Myth or Fact Answers
(page 79)

1. Myth
2. Fact
3. Myth
4. Fact
5. Fact

Star Point 2 Check for Understanding Answers
(page 154)

1. e. all of the above
2. b. preventing intentional contamination of food
3. c. having a 2 year supply of food
4. e. both b and c
5. c. Employee health awareness
6. d. both a and b
7. e. all of the above
8. a. proactive rather than reactive
9. b. Public Health Security and Bioterrorism Preparedness and Response Act
10. d. all of the above

Star Point 3 Myth or Fact
(page 81)

1. Fact
2. Fact
3. Fact
4. Fact
5. Myth

Star Point 3 Check for Understanding (page 155)

1. c. control point
2. b. Hazard Analysis and Critical Control Point
3. d. Determine Critical Control Points
4. b. one of the last steps where you can prevent, eliminate, or reduce a food safety hazard
5. b. Raw broccoli
6. c. Purchase and Serve
7. d. Cook
8. b. Same-Day
9. a. Biological
10. a. Low

Star Point 4 Myth or Fact (page 112)

1. Myth
2. Myth
3. Fact
4. Myth
5. Fact

Star Point 4 Check for Understanding (page 177)

1. b. cooking to 165°F (73.8°C) for 15 seconds
2. a. based on science and must be measurable
3. e. every 2 - 4 hours
4. a. actions taken immediately when CCPs are not met
5. d. both b and c
6. b. a written plan that industry writes with input from the regulatory official to control an out-of-control risk factor
7. b. Monitoring
8. d. Corrective Action
9. d. Always throw away the food of concern
10. e. both a and c

Star Point 5 Myth or Fact Answers (page 193)

1. Fact
2. Myth
3. Myth
4. Fact
5. Myth

HACCP Principles Match Game (page 192)

1. c
2. e
3. d
4. g
5. b
6. f
7. a

Star Point 5 Check for Understanding (page 179)

1. e. all of the above
2. a. a check or confirmation that the HACCP plan is working
3. b. all paperwork, documents, and logs that have been maintained as the flow of food is monitored
4. d. all of the above
5. c. Verification and Record Keeping
6. d. all of the above
7. d. both a and c
8. e. both b and d
9. d. both a and b
10. a. a reasonable care defense for your operation

Index

D

E

F

G

H

I

J

K

L

M

N

O

P

Q

R

S

T

U